A
GAME
CHANGER'S
MEMOIR

A GAME CHANGER'S MEMOIR

EX-SEBI CHIEF RECOUNTS THE
DEFINING MOMENTS OF HIS TENURE

G.N. BAJPAI

**PORTFOLIO
PENGUIN**

An imprint of Penguin Random House

PORTFOLIO

USA | Canada | UK | Ireland | Australia
New Zealand | India | South Africa | China | Singapore

Portfolio is part of the Penguin Random House group of companies
whose addresses can be found at global.penguinrandomhouse.com

Published by Penguin Random House India Pvt. Ltd
4th Floor, Capital Tower 1, MG Road,
Gurugram 122 002, Haryana, India

Penguin
Random House
India

First published in Portfolio by Penguin Random House India 2018

The views and opinions expressed in this book are the author's own and the
facts are as reported by him which have been verified to the extent possible,
and the publishers are not in any way liable for the same.

ISBN 9780670090518

Typeset in Aldine401 BT by Manipal Digital Systems, Manipal

Printed at Replika Press Pvt. Ltd, India

www.penguin.co.in

This is a legitimate digitally printed version of the book and therefore might not
have certain extra finishing on the cover.

To Asha, my wife, who has been by my side in my successes and failures

CONTENTS

FOREWORD

Generally, people in positions write about their tenure in exalted assignments within a year or two of retirement. Hence, readers may wonder why I took more than a decade to write? Like others, I too was tempted to pen down my memoir immediately after the conclusion of my tenure. However, even at the peril of obsolescence of the stories, several factors prevented me from writing the book.

The purpose of writing the book is not to highlight my achievements but to present an objective account, which warranted elimination of emotions for which time is the best moderator. The reason to postpone was also to assess whether the framework to minimize structural, systematic and operational risks recreated during those years withstood the test of time. Since the full impact of regulatory changes is felt over a period of time, the readers can now assess the boons and banes of the changes brought about during my tenure in the years 2002–05.

When I was moved from Life Insurance Corporation of India (LIC) to Securities and Exchange Board of India (SEBI), the capital market was seething under severe pain of widespread market misconduct unleased by various persons/entities in the year 2000–01 including the infamous Ketan Parekh Scam. The entire set of stakeholders of the capital market viz. investors, intermediaries, entrepreneurs, government and the nation at large was surcharged with anger and dismay. The issues echoed even in Parliament and culminated in the appointment of a Joint Parliamentary Committee, the appointment of a new minister to head the finance ministry and rapid regulatory changes.

This book is neither a history of the securities market of those years nor a chronology of events. Though the years were action-packed, the changes had the fury of a flood and there are numerous stories, only a few selected have been picked to illustrate the transformation of the capital markets of India. It is quite possible that some of the events or actions may appear insignificant and/or irrelevant now particularly in the face of democratization of communication technology and proliferation of social media. Waive that for the myopic view of the author.

The format chosen deliberately is of storytelling. However, a conscious attempt has been made to neither moralize nor pontificate. Jargons have given way to simple English to obviate theorizing the stories and help readers to relate to actual market events that happened then and keep happening albeit in the modified forms.

The book is arranged broadly in five frames. The first frame deals with paving the path for re-engineering. It begins with my appointment, grappling with the responsibilities and covers the image of SEBI then as also inadequacy of its empowerment. The second part of the book unravels the re-engineering of the market microstructure aimed at minimizing the operational risks. The chapters in this frame include contracting the settlement cycle, introduction of the STT, solving broker fees issues, dealing with market meltdown following the General Election results and helping the government with a public offering et al. Next frame deals with managing systemic risks and covers inspiring corporate governance standards, raising the bar of transparency, breaking news, dealing with media, the other 'Dabbawalahs', the stock market black economy and enhancing surveillance. The fourth grouping unveils overhauling the market macro-structure with a view to minimize structural risks and incorporates issues of regional stock exchanges, eliminating the conflict of interest—corporatization and demutualization of exchanges, BSE-IndoNext and enhancing regulatory depth through self-regulation, Central Listing Authority etc. The final part of the book described as weaving dreams, filling up the market structure gaps like retail debt market, Real Estate Investment Trusts includes consolidation of derivatives' market and internationalization of India's capital market and Indian Depository Receipts.

For me it was a journey of great learning—language of regulation, nuances of capital markets, theories of financial economics, behaviour of economic agents and the verbosity of trumpeters. I have attempted not to push those learnings to write a drudgery of a read. I suggest readers open the book as a light read.

1

BIG DECISION, LITTLE TIME

It was late evening on Friday, 14 February 2002. I was relaxing, almost half asleep in a hut in a game park in Kenya, when I was awakened by a knock at the door. Trying to shake off my slumber and almost stumbling to the door, I walked up and saw the managing director (MD) and chief executive officer (CEO) of Ken India Assurance Company Ltd (Ken India) R.S. Bedi standing before me. Unlike me, he didn't look relaxed at all. He told me that the secretary, economic affairs (SEA), C.M. Vasudev, Government of India (GoI) had called up my office in Mumbai and wanted to speak to me urgently.

This was enough to make me fully awake. I wondered what it could be about. I looked at my watch and realized it was already past ten in the night in India, which is two-and-a-half hours ahead of Kenya. I felt it was not an appropriate time to call the secretary. Thanking Mr Bedi, I went back to my bed to rest a little before going to dinner. However, I could not relax. I began wondering what it was that the SEA wanted to speak to me about. I was then the chairman of Life Insurance Corporation of India (LIC) and could not visualize the reason why he should want to connect with me urgently.

Even at dinner, with my appetite lost, I was thinking about what might have prompted him to call me with such urgency.

But I could not see anything in the horizon that was extremely pressing. Moreover, I had spoken to the secretary before I left India on Thursday night and had told him I would be travelling to Kenya for the board meeting of Ken India, where I was a non-executive director as the nominee of LIC.

Ken India was a composite insurance company, a joint venture between LIC, General Insurance Corporation of India (GIC), GIC's subsidiaries at the time, and the locals of Kenya and Uganda. Whereas the board met every quarter, the company had a tradition of inviting the directors and their spouses for their annual meeting, which is invariably held on a Friday so that the following weekend is free for wildlife excursions or trips to the city. This exercise is alternated between India and Kenya. So, biennially, Indian directors get the benefit of taking their spouses to Kenya. Our trip to a game park in Kenya was a part of that privilege.

The place being remote, mobile phones were not working. I tried calling the SEA on Saturday from the hotel line, but India could not be connected. I gave up and decided to contact him once I was back at my desk in Mumbai. The moment I entered my office on Monday morning, my executive assistant announced to me that the SEA had called up on Friday and had wanted me to speak to him urgently. And, even before I could settle down fully, the SEA was on the line again. He announced that GoI was considering appointing me as chairman of Securities and Exchange Board of India (SEBI).

Even though the media had been speculating for a while as to who would be the next SEBI chairman, and even though my name had been mentioned in some of the newspapers as a prospective candidate, I was still surprised by the news. I still had 30 per cent of unfinished tenure as chairman of LIC and hadn't even begun thinking of my life post-LIC. However, from the phone conversation I had, I realized I had no choice. And I had very little time too. It was 17 February 2002, and my predecessor was retiring on 20 February. By evening things had pretty much been settled.

However, after the conversation with the SEA that day I got busy with business as usual and almost forgot about it till the morning of 19 February, when I again got a call from the SEA. He asked me to stay put in my office as he had deputed the additional secretary (insurance) to personally get the necessary clearances from various authorities, like Central Vigilance Commission (CVC), etc., for my appointment as SEBI chairman. He said the gazette notification appointing me as SEBI chairman was likely to be issued that day itself. In the evening, at around 7 p.m., while I was still in office, I got a call from the joint secretary, capital market division, department of economic affairs, to inform me that the notification was being issued and that I would have to hand over charge as chairman of LIC that very day. Indeed, in a few minutes a copy of the notification was received in my office.

I was by now mentally prepared to move into the new role, but there were many things I needed to do before I left, so I requested the SEA to relieve me on 21 February instead of on 19 February. There was a pre-scheduled board meeting of the LIC, and five strategic propositions, where I felt my presence was critical for the projects to be taken forward. This was not a big request and should have been easy to fulfil but for one small caveat—the post of SEBI chairman could not be left vacant. I was disappointed, as these projects had been close to my heart. In my absence, I felt they wouldn't get the kind of boost needed, and might go off the LIC radar. However, the SEA was a kind gentleman; he understood my dilemma and assured me that he would take care of those agenda items. GoI has a representative on the board of LIC, usually the secretary-in-charge of the insurance division (which, along with banking division, now forms the Department of Financial Services). Thus I was made to handover charge at LIC on 19 February itself.

On 20 February, I had a commitment to inaugurate a seminar on pension at the National Insurance Academy (NIA), Pune, where international delegates were also participating. I had requested the GoI to allow me to at least fulfil that commitment, which was reluctantly agreed to, on the condition that I join SEBI latest by 5 p.m. that day. I left Pune in good time to be in the SEBI office well before 4 p.m., but the Mumbai traffic was bad and there were several delays along the way. Eager to reach on time, I asked the driver to rush, and we met with a minor accident on the way. However, I was able to take charge at SEBI on 20 February at 5.00 p.m., as its fourth chairman.

Having been put in the position, there was little I could say. When I look back I remember that I wasn't very keen on the job. My reasons were two-fold. First, after the major capital market misconduct led by Ketan Parekh, many horror stories were being published every day in the media about the stock market, the intermediaries, entrepreneurs and investors. Unfortunately, even the SEBI staff had not been spared. And, even as the stories about the staff eventually turned out to be highly exaggerated, if not false, I still wondered if I wanted to be a part of it all. To add to my dilemma, a Joint Parliamentary Committee (JPC) had been appointed to look into the mess, and this would make the situation political. Second, the reason my new posting was a little heartbreaking for me was that I was doing considerably well as the LIC chairman and was being complimented by all our stakeholders. LIC had taken significant leaps, and there was a need to consolidate them and take further steps to leave the organization in good shape for my successor. In fact, during my entire tenure as chairman of LIC, I never once thought about my life post-retirement. I was so involved that I thought of nothing else, much to the consternation of my family, who thought I was super-obsessed with my job.

There was also this doubt in me, as to whether I was the ideal choice for the post of SEBI chairman. So far, all the

SEBI chairmen, since the time SEBI had become a formal regulatory body, had been ex-civil servants—former IAS officers—except for S.S. Nadkarni, who had been chairman of ICICI and IDBI. A SEBI chairman's job involves the legislative work of framing regulations and enforcement, in addition to maintaining the rhythm of the stock market. SEBI is the first Indian experimentation of economic governance through a regulator. During its first decade, this body mostly focused on development of the stock market, while in its second it targeted regulation as well as development. A regulator is a mini-state having quasi-legislative, executive and quasi-judicial responsibilities. Legislation, including subordinate legislation, is an outcome of policy think. Policies have to be designed or re-engineered to ensure the efficacy of the market and efficient outcomes. The market failure at that point in time when the Ketan Parekh scam happened necessitated several changes in the macro- and micro-economic policies. In a democracy like India, it is imperative that the broad objectives of economic policy be such that they prevent market failures and enhance growth while also improving distributional justice and efficiency. I was unsure if I would fit the bill, not having had much experience in either legislation or enforcement.

Additionally, I felt I did not have the rapport and ease of working with the ministries of GoI that an IAS officer normally acquires in the due course of his or her job for pushing macro-economic policies to re-orchestrate micro-policies, transforming the micro-market structure and filling the gaps in the markets, etc. A political gridlock can be a serious challenge to regulatory transformation, although inroads can be made mostly through one's links with the bureaucracy and legislators. Also, my relationship with the finance minister of the time was very formal. The inadequacy of my political capital became apparent right at the beginning, when I was pushing certain important amendments of the SEBI Act.

It is my belief that liberal markets enable greater individual freedom, culminating in higher creativity and more innovation. Freedom brings out the best in every person. It allows everyone to participate in and contribute to the economy. It enables a person to undertake any economic activity or business of choice, in the manner and scale that he is comfortable with, helping him realize his full potential to innovate, invest in and contribute to the economy. It is empirically well established that economic freedom and economic performance have a very high, positive correlation. Countries having a high level of economic freedom outperform countries with lower levels of economic freedom. The thrust of reforms, therefore, has to be the provision and protection of freedom. It is for the same reasons that free markets bring about higher GDP growth and enhanced prosperity. Unfortunately, regulators oftentimes do not consider the adverse impacts of policy changes on market efficacy. I was unsure at that time as to whether SEBI's resources and structure would provide me adequate inputs to prevent knee-jerk reactions to policy changes, especially in the light of the recent Ketan Parekh scam. Would I be able to justify the costs with the likely benefits that the market may reap, albeit in due course, even though such justification cannot be the sole consideration while bringing about the changes? This was also one of the questions on my mind.

Even though my academic background is of economics and finance, having acquired a bachelor's and master's degree in commerce, I had spent my life learning and managing the life insurance business. However, I did have a fairly good understanding of capital markets, from having superintended the investments of LIC in my various capacities including as chairman, as director on the boards of several public financial institutions, such as GIC, ICICI, UTI, National Housing Bank, etc., and as non-executive chairman of National Stock Exchange (NSE). Although a qualified lawyer too (being a law graduate), I had hardly used my legal background, even for LIC work. I had heard about the nexus between entrepreneurs, fund managers and brokers in the stock market. In fact, connivance amongst the various operators in the market, which was to some extent coupled with regulatory forbearance, was the foundation of the mess in the capital market at that time. I had also heard about the widespread culture of short-termism (seeking immediate gain notwithstanding possible medium to long term harmful consequences), self-dealing and peddling of conflicts of interest, inspiring hype and stimulating hubris. The regulatory framework could not withstand large-scale, multi-pronged misconducts. My hesitation—or indeed, reluctance—to take up the post stemmed out of my own sense of inadequacy. I was not confident about my ability to efficaciously supervise the Indian capital market, given the precarious condition it was in. I knew that India's growth hinged on capital.

The economic agents operating in the capital market are widely networked and wield enormous power, not only to disrupt the efficacy of the market but also to influence even policymaking. The skill of assessing their strengths and anticipating their moves is essential for regulatory management.

A little over a couple of weeks into my new job, Tamal Bandyopadhyay, then resident editor of *Business Standard* newspaper, came to meet me. He asked me how I felt about my change of post from being chairman LIC to chairman, SEBI (regulatory operating manager); my response was that from being a player I had now become a referee. As a player, my every good stroke was applauded, but as a referee, my every decision will be fumed at or frowned upon by one or other section of the stakeholders! In fact, already, one important decision I had taken within a few days of my joining had been denounced vehemently by a prominent and vocal industrialist in an official meeting. In my journey of transforming market practices, I had the same experience over and over again.

However, since the impact of the SEBI leadership is greater on the economy of the country, I had resolved that I would strive harder to make a contribution.

I would champion the cause of investors and would pursue reforms and enforcement in a non-partisan way. Professionalism, honesty and industry would be my tools. I began my tenure with this single-minded approach. On no occasion during my tenure did I allow my reluctance to overwhelm my enthusiasm to contribute. In fact, when I look back now, I realize that I got emotionally engaged.

2

WHAT WILL YOU DO, GYAN?

By now you know that I took charge as chairman, SEBI, on 20 February 2002 in the evening, at around 5.00 p.m. The handing and taking over of charge at a government job involves the formality of signing of a form by both the outgoing and the incumbent officers, as having handed over and taken over charge, respectively. However, in the case of the chairman of SEBI, as is the case with the governor of Reserve Bank of India (RBI), an oath of secrecy is also signed.

While signing during taking over at SEBI, a question flashed in my mind, 'What will you do, Gyan?' I knew I was in a different setting with different set of responsibilities. I knew I would probably face situations and choices I hadn't faced before in my career, and was also cognizant of the fact that I and my decisions would be much more in the limelight here. Therefore, this question to myself. 20 February ended with a farewell to my predecessor. I went home that day to sleep over this question.

The next morning, as I was searching for an answer to that big question, I recalled what the great academic authority, Malcolm Sparrow, has said in his book, *The Regulatory Craft: Controlling Risks, Solving Problems and Managing Compliances,* about the approach to regulation, which should not be 'nitpicky, unreasonable, adversarial, rigidly bureaucratic and incapable of applying discretion sensibly'. I knew I was going to adhere to that and made some guidelines for myself: I will approach market regulation with the coordination of all stakeholders, with deep commitment to efficacy, candour of thought, action, and with the foresight of an academic. I will build pragmatism, enforceability and perspectives in regulation. I will also prevent the human behaviours that are likely to endanger the efficacy of the market and cause serious inconvenience to its participants. This, on deeper thought, looked like a broad answer to the question that had been plaguing me.

At the same time, I also started thinking about where and how I would begin my journey. And once again, Malcolm Sparrow's instructions came to mind: '. . . pick important problems and fix them'. With this resolve, I started exploring the starting point, and hit upon my goals.

Deconstructing SEBI's Mission

The preamble of the SEBI Act describes the objectives of SEBI:

–   To protect the interests of investors in securities
–   To promote the development of the securities market
–   To regulate the securities market

It is to be noted that unlike in other jurisdictions globally, the responsibility of SEBI is not limited to regulating the securities market and protecting the investors. It extends to promoting the development of the market, which essentially means inspiring the market participants to introduce new ideas and thought processes. In case the economic agents do not discharge their role of market development adequately, SEBI has to step in and lead the development. One also needed to understand that the comfort of status quo and resistance to change would make the development an exercise in persuasion and push, and at times require a bit of exercising of one's authority too.

In the year 2002, when I took charge at SEBI, the Indian capital markets were significantly behind global markets in terms of products, systems, processes and practices. Therefore, the agenda necessarily had to encompass everything that would help SEBI fulfil its mission, as outlined earlier.

SEBI has been empowered by the SEBI Act appropriately under four broad frames: (a) legislative, (b) executive, (c) quasi-judicial, (d) development.

- **Legislative** – design and promulgation of regulations, general orders and guidances
- **Executive** – Registration and monitoring of intermediaries and transactions
- **Quai-judicial** – passing of enforcement orders on ascertaining delinquencies
- **Development** – modernization of the market, including introduction of new instruments for facilitation of investment; and investor protection; bridging the gaps in market structure

The organizational structure of SEBI is quite simple, with the members at the helm and the chairman and his team below them.

Things were beginning to take shape in my mind, and I was eager to start my day on a high note, on the lines of the strategy I had thought up. Next morning, however, when I reached office at 9.30 a.m. as usual, I learned to my disappointment that there was only one whole-time member, Prof. Jayanth Varma, at SEBI, and that he too had sought early relief from his post to go back to academics. Since he had already made up his mind there was little I could say to make him stay, and within a few days he had left. Thus the important hierarchical link of whole-time members (WTM), which connected the functions of the executive directors (EDs) and the chairman, was now vacant.

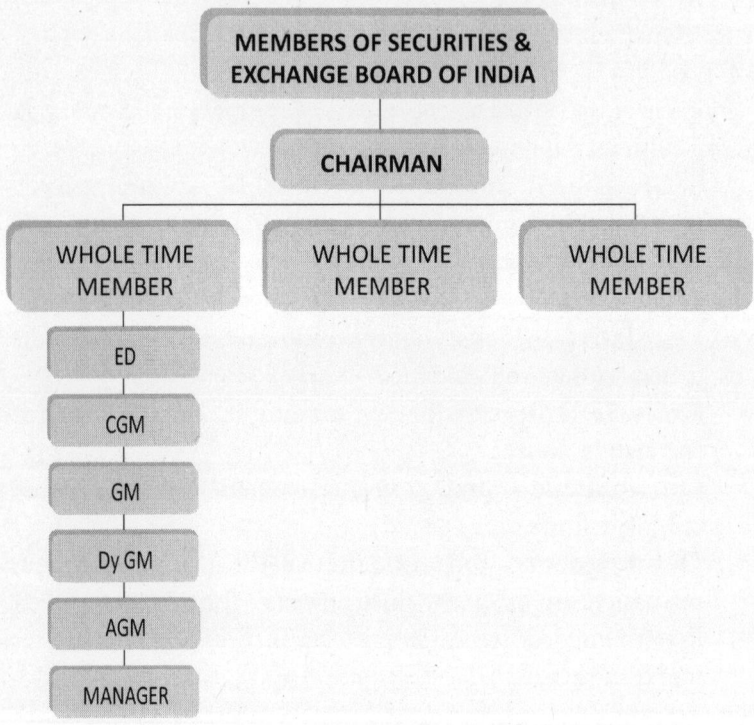

The organizational design of SEBI at the time was woven around its functional areas. This means the organization was structured and operated by its members according to function. This structure integrates people, information and purpose. It includes plans and processes. Its level of efficacy determines the quality and quantity of the innovated processes and products. The commitment of people to strategies and the organization's state of efficiency is also shaped by the organization's design. In short, organizational design is the frame of the edifice of the organization. It also delineates roles, responsibilities and accountability. I needed a peep into the institution's history to understand the process of evolution of this design, its relevance and impact. Pratip Kar, executive director, a highly competent and knowledgeable officer, was now the only person who could help me. We sat together to understand every nook and cranny of the structure.

Its in-depth examination made me feel that it needed significant re-engineering, as timely innovations were not happening, delineation of responsibilities was unclear and accountability diffused. There appeared to be no teamwork, as each person in the organization knew only what he or she was doing. Any conversation within departments and functions was negligible. There were open rifts and hidden wars between the insiders (SEBI-recruited staff) and outsiders (those brought in on deputation from elsewhere)—each denouncing the other for incompetence, inefficiency and even inefficacy. Congruence and coordination were missing. The organizational chaos was visible, but only to the discerning eye.

Added to this were the media horror stories appearing post the Ketan Parekh-led scam which involved major, widespread market misconduct. (This scandal was widely referred to as Scam 2001). There were stories about the functioning of SEBI, including accusations of inefficiency against SEBI officers, their inadequacy of skills, lack of commitment and even corruption. The impact of those stories was writ large on the faces of the officers. That they were demoralized was obvious. As a result of their intense self-doubt they were hesitant to open their mouths even on mundane matters.

Over the next couple of days I met a fairly large number of senior and middle-level officers. Their faces bespoke disappointment and dejection. The professional manager in me was in a state of daze. As one who had always assumed the leadership role with alacrity, responsibility and accountability, and had led from the front, the obvious concerns got me acutely vexed: How am I going to restore the comprehensively shattered confidence of all the stakeholders in the Indian capital markets with a demoralized army? No general wins a war if the army he leads lacks enthusiasm, confidence and determination. Inculcating all that among the SEBI staff was the first and foremost challenge to start setting right the market ethos.

A few days later I went to Delhi to meet my political boss, the finance minister, to understand his expectations. Even though, legislatively, SEBI is an autonomous body and the chairman is independent, he has to coordinate with, if not report to, the finance minister in the discharge of his responsibilities. While on my way to Delhi, at the passengers' lounge at Mumbai airport, I happened to read Sucheta Dalal's column, 'Different Strokes', in *Indian Express*.[1] Dalal, one of the foremost financial journalists and opinion makers in Indian capital market affairs, had the instincts of an astute journalist. In her article addressed to me, she had made some acute observations about SEBI. She had also rendered some advice as to what I should do as SEBI chairman. She'd warned me, '. . . the capital market is all about transparency and full disclosures. There is nowhere to hide. Every action and every silence has immediate consequences and immediately attracts comment. This intense attention, flattering initially, can soon become exasperating.' She also gave me some credit stating, 'You have already made a good beginning. The fact that you found time to meet every official in SEBI, shake their hands, ask their names and to talk to them on your first day, has already gone down well with the organization that is crying out for a sensible Human Resources policy . . . As far as discipline goes, in one respect you are already leading by example. Your executive directors, who had developed the habit of strolling into office well past the official time, have suddenly turned punctual.' As I was considered a rank outsider and a novice in the craft of dealing with the capital markets, I was inundated with advice from colleagues, friends and well-wishers about the financial system.

I had a good meeting with the finance minister, Yaswant Sinha. He treated me well. He made it abundantly clear that I had been selected with a mission to clean up and develop the market. He did not give me an elaborate discourse on what I should or should not do, but the enormity of job was manifest in the few sentences that he spoke. I must confess here that I had mixed feelings of elation and apprehension. The happiness emanated from the treatment Sinha meted out to me and the confidence that he and the prime minister, Atal Bihari Vajpayee, reposed in me. My apprehension had its moorings in the immensity of my responsibility and in my own doubts about whether I had the skills to manage a regulatory apparatus of the most dynamic segment of the financial market.

Some years later, at a meeting, P. Chidambaram, finance minister, had remarked to me, 'Bajpai, the RBI governor gets three months' time (the monetary policy stance was released quarterly then) but the SEBI chairman has to react instantaneously as ethos changes with the speed of light.' Even though I heard these prophetic words only midway through my tenure, in my subconscious probably, I was currently worried as to whether I would be able to respond to market developments competently. In fact, in the early days of my tenure, during a chance meeting with Chidambaram (he was not a minister then) on a flight, I had asked him what I should focus on. He had suggested looking into the regulations and quasi-judicial orders, which he felt weren't adequate.

After my meeting with Sinha, I met my friend of more than twenty-five years, Balbir Punj, then member of the Rajya Sabha. Even now, I meet him whenever I am in Delhi. Post the pleasantries, I sought his advice on my role. Punj is an intellectual of eminence and has a reputation of utmost integrity— intellectual and financial—which I deeply respect. He had been a professional journalist, had been writing on national politics and economics for several years and had a broad understanding of the state and the functioning of the financial markets. I had on many occasions sought his counsel, which helped me greatly on many a momentous occasion. His advice to me was to clean up the system and develop the market. 'Keep your equanimity and integrity as ever and make a success of a level that benefits the economy substantially.' I kept his words in mind all through my tenure at SEBI.

Now, flying back to Mumbai, my thoughts were entirely centred on one, and only one, subject—how to usher in confidence and enthusiasm in the rank and file of the SEBI team. And I decided to do the following:

1. Hold a town hall meeting of the entire staff, do a bit of eloquent talking and lift their spirits
2. Ensure that in interactions even in smaller meetings and one-to-one discussions, nobody denigrates or undermines the role of anyone, either as an individual or as a group
3. Create conditions that will help improve the skills of SEBI personnel
4. Create a structure for participative management
5. Define timelines for every action/job/decision SEBI has to undertake
6. Bring about transparency in the functioning of the organization to minimize opportunities for subjective action
7. Minimize the risks in the capital markets
8. Create an agenda to raise India's capital markets to the level of those of mature economies

Having laid all this down, I dedicated the entire week that followed to giving shape to the action points and also deciding how, when and in what manner these actions would be organized. At that point I did not want to deal with organizational design, which I didn't believe worked fully. I felt that might stir up a storm, the weather being already rough. This was the time to take everyone along, irrespective of their perceived competencies and incompetencies. It was more important at this stage to unite the staff into a team to optimize the available resources.

I began the process with a town hall meeting, where I made an impassioned opening speech about the significance of SEBI to the economy of the country through the creation of a vibrant and effective capital market. I went on to talk about the sterling role that each SEBI employee had played so far in building the regulatory framework and in developing the market. This should continue unhindered, notwithstanding what the media or the opinion makers may write or talk about. I did indicate that some of my colleagues had not conducted themselves appropriately, but the majority, I believed, has slogged at their job, and has been honest, responsible and committed.

After my speech I allowed the audience to raise questions, seek clarifications and even make observations. I also gave every officer an opportunity to summarize his achievements, suggest ideas and make observations on improving the effectiveness of the regulatory regime. More than two dozen officers from various levels spoke in that meeting, giving their opinions as to how we should go forward.

At the end of the question–answer session, I summed up the discussions, concluding the meeting by assuring everybody that we would meet regularly, and in smaller groups from different departments and sections. At the end of this session, I felt the employees' sense of being incompetent, corrupt and outcast was mitigated somewhat, at least among some of them and to some extent. The manager in me had overtaken the policymaker.

Over a period of a couple of months, we instituted systems that saw a sense of urgency, and the ethos of responsibility, accountability and objectivity starting to take shape. We also began holding regular monthly meetings of the division chiefs and weekly meetings of the EDs to ideate and follow up on the actions to be taken.

In fact, the whole exercise of creating an efficacious monitoring mechanism as well as the re-engineering of systems and processes began with my taking a relook at the chairman's office itself. When I had joined, this office consisted of just two secretaries, who were only responsible for controlling the movement of files and fixing up appointments and meetings. They weren't expected to coordinate the agenda of the meetings, including board meetings, to provide context or references to the matters put up before the chairman, or to even create a document by themselves.

I believe every chief executive deserves to be adequately assisted by his office to help him monitor the functioning of the organization with the use of tools like management information system (MIS). The office must do the coordination work for creating the agenda for meetings, provide briefs on the matters placed before him and collect information on matters that visitors were expected to discuss, besides promoting the direction of the organization. I decided the chairman's office would consist of officers with operational experience, with an executive assistant (EA) heading it, a position similar to that of the executive assistant to the RBI governor. I shortlisted and interviewed several general managers and chief general managers, and finally decided on P.R. Ramesh for my EA. I also chose three other officers— Ankit Sharma, Anupam Tandon and Manish Bansal—and two secretaries.

My expectation from the secretariat was to ensure, among other things, the efficacy of the monitoring mechanism. Organizing meetings with WTMs, heads of departments, division chiefs, other officers as well as visitors, were regularized. Proper agendas were created. I also needed inputs for my many different meetings, and for the functions where I was expected to speak. In fact, over a period of time, the entire mechanism became so effective that movement of files and matters got speeded up and reminders were issued where actions had been delayed.

Following this arrangement, I held regular meetings with the division chiefs (DC). The monthly meetings of the management committee—an informal structure—ensured that everybody was engaged in re-energizing the organization and creating the roadmap for the initiatives SEBI had to take in the next few years. In the first such meeting, a vision statement for SEBI was discussed, and the SEBI officers unanimously agreed that it would be for SEBI to become a 'globally respected regulator'. These DC meetings, as they were called, were scheduled every month, and in the first few meetings a strategic action plan (SAP) was drawn up. The SAP listed out the initiatives that every department would take, both on the market development side and the regulation side. The SAP also included clearance of the huge backlog of investigations, adjudications and quasi-judicial proceedings, along with the files, matters and issues that were pending at various levels. These meetings brought in the involvement of every officer in the organization, as each was now directly participating in its functioning. The meetings became a great motivating force. In fact, every senior officer looked forward to those meetings. All the division chiefs were asked to hold similar monthly meetings with their teams to inform them about the DC meeting plans, and to seek their views and build enthusiasm among them.

I also started the practice of offsite meetings, which built further enthusiasm and an increased level of participation among the employees.

Once the dust of the initial measures had settled, I took on the task of modelling a new organizational design. I asked my team to study the regulatory organizational designs in various developed markets, and based on their report I requested the United States Agency for International Development (USAID), who was advising India on its Financial Institutional Reforms project through the ministry of finance, to submit a detailed report on an organizational design for SEBI that would help ensure the efficacy of the market. We discussed the proposed organizational design with the heads of the divisions. Drawing upon my experience in running a large organization like LIC, I finalized the new organizational design, the broad features of which were:

1. Homogeneous units—for instance, all matters relating to listing of companies, like Initial Public Offerings (IPOs) or post-IPO activities, like takeover, delisting, buyback and corporate restructuring, were headed by the same ED.
2. Mitigating conflicts of interests—the division licensing the intermediaries was not involved in inspecting and supervising the intermediaries.
3. Segregation of surveillance, investigations and enforcement, as enforcement requires people with a strong legal background.

The new organizational design was taken to the SEBI board for approval, and was finally implemented in October 2002, seven months after I became chairman. The organizational design was slowly but steadily implemented; purpose, people, plans and processes were integrated.

I imagine that at this stage SEBI transited from being a personality-driven body to a systems- and process-led organization. Institutionalization of learnings, the seeking of feedback—internally and externally—and use of the collective wisdom in framing and re-engineering regulations and enforcement processes were driven constantly. The organization shifted gears and moved to collective leadership and teamwork, while at the same time not undermining the role of the team leader. It turned into a more transparent, confident, open and friendlier organization.

3

LOOKING INTO THE MIRROR: SEBI'S PUBLIC IMAGE AND GETTING THE BEST OUT OF PEOPLE

I was highly aware of the burst of media reports following the Ketan Parekh scam. They highlighted three facets of SEBI's shortcomings. It pained me greatly that SEBI's image had suffered and that there were so many uncomplimentary views about the organization floating around. I decided to pay attention to the main points on which we could work, and came up with three.

First, SEBI was accused of being incompetent and inefficient. 'A little like the police as pictured in many of the movies that are churned out by the Mumbai-based film industry, the Securities and Exchange Board of India (SEBI) arrived at the scene of India's largest stock market fraud after all the action was over,' said *Frontline* magazine.[1] 'Speculators are confident that reluctance, inefficiency and incompetence would keep the regulator (SEBI) from acting against them,' said Sucheta Dalal in her blog titled 'SEBI Now Needs a Change of Leadership'.[2]

Second, SEBI was being called corrupt. *The Hindu* wrote, 'Watchers of BSE, SEBI knew of one thing—the existence of a businessman-bureaucrat nexus . . . The regulator [SEBI], of course, was a mute spectator of Mr Parekh's actions for reasons unknown.'[3]

Third, SEBI's practice of having bureaucrats (particularly from the revenue, IT and customs departments, IAS officers, etc.) on short-term deputation to manage its operations also came under the scanner. 'Regulation and supervision and the quality of on- and off-site supervision can be strengthened only through professionals, not through bureaucrats,' wrote *The Hindu*.[4]

And then there was what I call free *ka gyan* (free advice), both from some genuine experts and some self-proclaimed ones. Some of them said only a complete revamp of the organization would salvage its reputation, and some of the others said there was an urgency to re-examine the institutional structure of SEBI.

There was much drama accompanying these accusations, but I knew there was an extremely genuine and serious challenge in front of me. It was to revamp SEBI's image to that of an efficient, agile and independent regulator. And for that, I knew I had to concentrate on strengthening the cornerstone of the organization—its people.

Key Human Capital Issues at SEBI

Inadequacy of staff

The human capital of SEBI comprised the board of directors, the chairman, whole-time members, executive directors, and others in the hierarchy, as described earlier in the book. At the time of my joining, we had 350 employees, 200 of whom were of officer level, and 150 of staff member level. The numbers were wholly inadequate.

The Joint Parliamentary Committee (JPC) which probed the securities market scam also brought out this point in its report that was submitted to the Parliament was also published by the *Financial Express*: 'Due to the inadequacy of staff, the number of inspection of brokers carried out by SEBI has been gradually coming down from 157 in the year 1997–98 to 80 in 1999–2000.[5] The committee (JPC) urges that SEBI augment its staff strength if need be, and progressively increase its coverage of inspection of brokers.'[6] SEBI, in its own report on the scam, admitted that 'the staff strength and infrastructure of SEBI in the areas of surveillance, investigation and inspection of the stock exchanges and intermediaries need to be urgently strengthened for achieving proactive and improved oversight . . .'

In addition to the inadequacy of people at SEBI, the staff was not fully SEBI's own. Some of the executive directors and senior officers were on short-term deputation from other government departments, such as revenue, income tax and customs. The JPC pointed this out in its report published December 2002. It said, 'SEBI needs to be professionalized with adequate in-house manpower having a sense of belonging and commitment to the organization. There should be adequate manpower assessed on scientific basis to man various positions in SEBI.'

I realized that if SEBI had to function to its fullest, it could not run on borrowed human capital. We needed more good lawyers, investigators, chartered accountants, administrators and other skilled officers to bridge the deficiencies in surveillance, investigation, enforcement, administration and other functional areas. Also, I was convinced that an organization like SEBI must have its own dedicated pool of expert in-house professional administrators and thinkers.

However, it was not easy to enhance the quality and quantity of staff. Even if I managed to attract some talent (the challenge and thrill of working at SEBI were not a bad pull, after all) at SEBI's pay scale and train them, it would take a long time to build an adequately large enough pool of competent staff.

Filling such an enormous skill gap was going to take a long time. I began to think of ways to go about it. The only way to do it was to prioritize the requirements. 'Which are the functions where I have serious challenges?' I asked myself. The first was in legislative affairs, mainly in the area of drafting regulations. If regulations weren't drafted well, they would frequently fail the test of judicial review in the courts and SEBI would lose its credibility. Further, the regulations may sometimes be suitable only for the market dynamic of the day, but a fast-moving business environment demanded that the regulations be evolved proactively. The second area was in regulatory function—enforcement and protection of market efficacy. With these two functions in place, we could commence the journey of re-engineering and reinforcement.

I decided on a two-pronged approach. One, to hire quality professionals, introduce sound human resource practices, organize appropriate training and development. We also had to mould the leaders of tomorrow from the current workforce. Thus, we would add numbers in the short run, meet our immediate needs and build, in the long run, an in-house talent force of competent senior employees.

At the same time, I immediately needed a qualified and experienced think tank at the top, especially in the areas of regulation design and market development, at least for the duration of my tenure. For this I thought up a short-term solution, which I discuss later in the chapter.

So, beginning with the legal team and then moving on to the other teams, SEBI started hiring additional full-time staff. During my tenure of three years, employee strength increased by 103 at SEBI—by 33 per cent on a net basis (i.e., new hires minus those who resigned). Looking at the records, one could see that the total employee count had increased by only seventy over the past five years. I changed that, and during 2003–04 alone employee strength increased by 100, making it possibly the highest year-on-year increase in manpower in SEBI's history till date. A larger increase in numbers was not considered desirable, in the face of our limited capacity to educate, train and assimilate employees into the emerging new culture of efficiency and ethics.

Among these additional 100 employees, SEBI managed to get qualified professionals, such as MBAs, lawyers, CFAs, MFCs, chartered accountants and company secretaries. It was very satisfying that this quality manpower was entirely hired without making any exceptions to the usual SEBI pay scale.

Training and Development

Now began the next phase. Hiring quality people had to be followed by equally good training and development opportunities for them. An important change I brought about was to send our people—other than the chairman, WTMs and EDs, which had been the norm earlier—to attend a range of domestic and international conferences, seminars and training programmes. During my tenure, every officer at the level of division chief, i.e., CGM, GM or DGM, got at least one opportunity to participate in a global conference, seminar or training— some as participants and some as speakers. They gained invaluable global exposure from this, and the knowledge they gained was passed on by them to their respective teams. This is a practice that continues to this day. It hadn't been possible earlier, when only the chairman, WTMs and EDs were attending these events.

I also introduced a scheme for deputation of SEBI officers to overseas regulatory bodies and multilateral organizations. A few of them were sent on deputation to the Capital Markets Authority, Sultanate of Oman and to Bahrain Monetary Authority. My successors found this useful, and continue to follow the exercise.

We also started the practice of inviting guest speakers to SEBI from time to time. All officers up to the rank of division chiefs were invited to attend these talks. The intention was to bring some high-level expert understanding and perspectives on matters of interest. This series was kicked off with a talk by Dr Y.V. Reddy, governor of RBI, at the SEBI board room on his visit to the SEBI office.

We introduced a staff suggestion scheme to receive suggestions from our employees for improving the functioning of SEBI. This increased employee participation, ushering in a greater sense of commitment and responsibility among the staff in the running of the organization. We approved the SEBI (Payment of Gratuity to Employees) Rules, 2003, to reward employees who had put in long service and to encourage in them a sense of belonging to the organization. The performance appraisal systems were revised to include key result areas, self-appraisal, competency assessment and two levels of review, with effect from January 2003. We also introduced market-linked house rent allowance to officers, as I took a conscious decision not to make SEBI an asset-heavy organization. Instead of buying flats for accommodation at prices which were then sky-rocketing, we decided to pay HRA. This was a welcome decision, as this perk helped our officers take home loans and buy their own houses. In fact, even today this is said to have been one of the best decisions of benefit to SEBI officials.

The increase in the quantity and quality of manpower helped in filling up the understaffed areas, particularly the surveillance, investigation and enforcement departments. The quality of our investigations and quasi-judicial orders improved substantially, and continued after my tenure. This was recognized by the Securities Appellate Tribunal (SAT). Besides, we were also on track in training our newly acquired talent and preparing them for bigger roles at SEBI. Many of them have now reached the levels of Dy GM, GM and CGM. In fact, career planning was done for all levels of staff, including the secretary level, and I learn that some of the secretaries have been promoted to the level of Dy GM now.

Having filled the vacancies and having put in a structure for future leadership to sprout, I now had to think about getting officers of high-quality skills, talent and experience. They were for strategic and macro-level roles, and needed to be people with grey hair and domain-specific knowledge and expertise. The issue was, hiring such experienced people was prohibitively expensive, and could not just happen suddenly in a government organization. The employees who were currently being trained would take years to acquire the necessary level of maturity. So if I could neither buy nor train the think tank, the only option left for me was to borrow them periodically for SEBI work.

The Short-term Solution

One of the projects close to my heart, and which turned out to be quite an eventful journey, was to build an all-experts, almost no-cost 'think tank'. I set about doing this department-wise.

Legal Affairs Advisory Committee

The frame of reference of this committee was to ensure that only first-rate regulations came out of SEBI. Every regulation needs to be laid before Parliament, whose Subordinate Legislation Committee scrutinizes it word by word. If a regulation is not drafted well it stands the risk of being amended under the directions of Parliament. Even worse, if a regulation is not drafted well it runs the risk of being challenged in the courts, the regulation being inadequate to serve the purpose for which it was drafted.

Also, a good regulation needs to be futuristic—i.e., it must be made not only keeping the present environment (technological, economical, business, political, etc.) in mind but also taking into account possible future developments. A good regulation is one which also has the ability to adapt faster than the changes in the environment.

To meet these sky-high standards in regulatory drafting, I needed a team possessing the following talent: A 'draftsman' who understood the nuances of legal language, an 'academician' who could foresee future challenges, a 'lawyer' who could argue for or against the regulations, and a 'judge' who could interpret a regulation as through a detached lens. Not wanting to settle for half-measures, I approached the best in all these fields, with an empty pocket but with tremendous self-belief, to form the legal affairs advisory committee for SEBI.

The draftsman: I approached Dr Raghubir Singh, who had then recently retired as secretary, legislative affairs, GoI. During the last six years he had concentrated mainly on drafting acts, rules and regulations for the government, and had the reputation of an expert. It was great to have him on board, and his enthusiasm was infectious.

The academician: For this role I approached Dr N.L. Mitra, a distinguished lawyer and educationist, whose CV included a senior partnership at a leading law firm, Fox Mandal, and vice-chancellorship of the top law school in India—National Law School India in Bangalore. He had also founded many other law schools in the country. In addition, he had also been vice-chancellor of Jodhpur Law University, advisor to the RBI governor, chairman of the RBI committee on bankruptcy, member of the RBI committee on financial fraud, and chairman of a host of public sector committees. These roles involved intersection of law and finance. He had also been head of various research programmes at national and international levels, and had been part of the reforms in the Indian judicial system, reforms in agricultural marketing, etc. He was author of more a dozen books and articles on law. He too was kind enough to agree to be part of the committee.

The lawyer: I approached the ex-additional solicitor general of India, Rafiq Dada. He is a man of few words, one of those whose reputation precedes them. He was famous for being part of quite a few controversial and high-profile cases. He was president of the Bombay Bar Association when I met him. He not only agreed to give his services and time but decided to do so for free!

The judge: I had none other than the eminent former Chief Justice of India, M.N. Venkatachaliah, in mind. He had been at the High Court of Karnataka, and then a judge in the Supreme Court before becoming Chief Justice of India. The self-effacing seventy-three-year old was acclaimed as much for his knowledge and experience as for his work ethics and impartiality. He was reputed to be one of the greatest living jurists of India. The people with whom I discussed the idea of taking Venkatachaliah on board greatly appreciated my choice, but they warned me that having retired now he would not be interested in taking up a role with SEBI. Yet I tried my luck. It took me two extensive meetings to convince him to join SEBI. He finally agreed, purely in the national interest. But before confirming he would join, he made two conditions: 'I will not take any money,' he told me. I smiled, 'I anyway have no money to offer you, sir.' His second condition was that he wanted a guest house to stay in and not a hotel (which the others had agreed to). Accordingly, an IDBI guesthouse was arranged for him. I wished things could always be so easy! In 2004, while still part of our committee, Venkatachaliah was awarded the Padma Vibhushan, the second highest civil honour in India.

This elite committee met on one Saturday every month. During my three-year tenure, most of the SEBI regulations were rewritten. Every regulation or its amendment had to pass scrutiny by this committee; they would vet it word by word and comma by comma before it was allowed to be put up to the board. The quality of our regulations improved dramatically. The committee worked for two-and-a-half years (starting from mid-2002), and the SEBI legal team benefited immensely from their association with these men at close quarters, learning from them the fine art of regulation making, apart from many other skills.

Market Development Advisory Committee

Another important area of focus for me, personally, was to develop the capital markets by introducing new products, refining the market structure and doing some futuristic thinking. And I needed a think tank for this. For this committee, I was looking for well-known economists. I was aware that most of the good Indian economists worked on international assignments outside India, so even though my team suggested a few names I wasn't convinced they could deliver. We needed people with some connection with us, or else, I feared, they would not agree to be part of the SEBI committee.

In the end, we managed to get the likes of Dr Raghuram Rajan, Dr Kaushik Basu, Dr Marty Subramanium, Dr Rakesh Mohan, Dr Arvind Vermani and Suman Beri for this committee. Dr Rajan was then a professor in Chicago Booth School. He would later become the youngest chief economist of the International Monetary Fund (IMF) and go on to become the RBI governor. Dr Basu was an acclaimed professor of economics with Delhi School of Economics, a professor at Cornell University and visiting faculty at MIT, Harvard and LSE. He later went on to become India's chief economic advisor, and later the chief economist at World Bank. Dr Marty Subramaniam was professor of finance, Stern Business School of New York University, and was an acclaimed expert in the derivatives markets. Dr Rakesh Mohan was then India's chief economic advisor (CEA); he later became deputy governor at RBI, and then ED at IMF. Dr Virmani too later became India's chief economic advisor and then a director at IMF. All-in-all, we were in august company.

The meetings had to be held through video conference, since all these honourable men were spread across the globe. The time difference also had to be accounted for, and we ended up having most of the meetings at odd times, like from 7 p.m. to 11 p.m., or in the very early hours of the morning.

Some of the important outcomes of this committee were: suggestions for developing the debt market and the derivatives market, and fund-raising for small and medium enterprises. In fact, it was this committee's idea to set up a separate, dedicated trading platform for small and medium enterprises (SMEs) to raise money—both debt and equity—and to provide liquidity to SME securities. Accordingly, BSE-IndoNext was set up as a separate trading platform under the BOLT trading system of the BSE for SME listing.

As in the case of the legal affairs committee, the market development committee too provided a wonderful opportunity to the senior officers at SEBI to observe, interact, work with and learn from distinguished luminaries.

Capital Market Institute Committee

I have talked about the Securities Market Institute later in the book; suffice it to say here that a world-class committee was set up.

We were able to collect the wisdom of the world to improve the functioning of the organization whose reputation had been severely ravaged in 2002.

An Institution Ready to Lead

These efforts yielded results, and today SEBI's talent, I believe, is comparable with that of any other global regulator's. Its employee strength currently stands at about 750. It is full of people passionate about the financial markets. The employee force includes top-class CAs, CSs, MBAs and lawyers, etc., from tier-I colleges. Innovation leads the way in almost all spheres of its activity.

SEBI is now being looked upon as a globally respected, mature regulator, and is taken seriously. Sadanand Dhume, in 'Dragging India Out of the Muck', an article published in *Wall Street Journal* in November 2010, observed: 'Unlike many developing countries, India has a record of sustaining credible institutions, among them the Supreme Court, the Election Commission and the Securities and Exchange Board of India.'

4

LEGISLATIVE EMPOWERMENT: SEBI GETS SOME TEETH

'SEBI is a toothless tiger', was an often repeated statement by a former colleague in response to the accusation of failure on SEBI's part to prevent Scam 2001. Apparently, the enforcement powers conferred by the SEBI Act, 1992, were wholly inadequate to the task of tackling such a scam.

Whereas SEBI had been pursuing the matter of strengthening its powers with the government for some time, little progress had been made. Some of the recommendations included increasing SEBI's search and seizure powers and monitoring the telephone calls of suspected manipulators and getting their telephone records.

Scam 2001 shook the policymakers and pushed the agenda of SEBI reforms to the front desk of the establishment. It expedited the introduction of a bill of amendments to the SEBI Act. However, this bill was still with the department of company affairs (now ministry of corporate affairs) for their concurrence. This was required in the light of duality of jurisdiction on quite a few matters relating to regulation of listed companies.

My predecessor had been pursuing the matter rather vigorously, but with little success. Having studied the situation, as also the proposals, I felt that amendments to the SEBI Act were immediately required. On my second meeting with the finance minister, I took up the matter. He was kind enough to assure me that he would speak to the minister in charge of Department of Company Affairs (DCA) to expedite it. A week later the finance minister told me that the minister of company affairs had agreed to push the matter, and that I, the secretary of economic affairs and the secretary of DCA should meet to sort out our differences and discomforts with the DCA over the bill and build a consensus.

The meeting was quickly arranged, the contentious points discussed and a broad agreement reached. In order to build consensus, I agreed to drop some of the amendments intended for strengthening the broader framework of SEBI. However, more than a month passed after our meeting, and nothing had happened. The draft bill still remained pending. I reminded the finance minister about it, and still I heard nothing. In the meantime, in a Cabinet reshuffle, Jaswant Singh was appointed minister of finance, with the added responsibility of DCA. When I called on him I requested him to expedite the process of amendment of the SEBI Act. I also briefed him as to where the draft bill was held up.

Jurisdictional tug of war is quite common across nations, and so it is in India. Even though there was an honest attempt on the part of SEBI to compromise in a few areas, DCA, maybe for plausible reasons, still hesitated to clear the bill.

I sought an appointment with the finance minister to discuss several issues, one of them being amendment of the SEBI Act. Before meeting the minister I called on U.K. Sinha, then joint secretary (JS), (divisional head), of the capital markets division. I raised the matter with him to get his suggestions. He advised me to propose the ordinance route for amendment of the SEBI Act.

Later, when I met the minister, I spoke to him about the amendment, making a polite submission that the file did not seem to be moving. I made my suggestion, 'Kindly issue an ordinance.'

After a minute of silence, the minister said, 'I will have to talk to the prime minister.'

I said, 'Sir, kindly do,' and left the room after wrapping up my discussions on the agenda in a few minutes.

Within half an hour of my leaving the minister's room, the JS called me up on the mobile and said, 'The minister has asked me to immediately prepare for an ordinance.' He was surprised at the speed with which the minister had decided on the ordinance route. This is an eloquent testimony of the decisive approach of Jaswant Singh.

The Indian Constitution envisages, under Article 123, the power of the President of India to promulgate ordinances during recess of Parliament. The Constitution says: 1) If at any time, except when both the houses of Parliament are in session, the President is satisfied that circumstances exist which render it necessary for him to take immediate action, he may promulgate such ordinance as the circumstances appear to him to require; 2) An ordinance promulgated under this article shall have the same force and effect as an Act of Parliament but every such Ordinance must be approved by the Parliament within six weeks of its meeting post issue of ordinance.

Since there was only one week left for the next session of Parliament, the JS and the entire division had to gear up to get the ordinance issued in the next three or four days. The capital market division must be appreciated for its speed and hard work in organizing the issue of the ordinance before the start of the next Parliamentary session.

Thus the SEBI Act was amended. Its powers were enhanced and the effectiveness of its enforcement improved. Whereas everything that was asked for in terms of enhancing the authority and powers of SEBI was not approved, significant additions were made through this amendment to the SEBI Act. In addition, the corresponding provisions of the Securities Contracts (Regulation) Act and the Depositories Act had also been amended by the ordinance. Demutualization (privatization) of stock exchanges had been given statutory sanctity.

Policymaking in any vibrant democracy is a slow process. The goals of a policy influence—both positively and negatively—other goals being pursued, and all these goals have to be appropriately synchronized before a new policy can be laid down. Further, implementation of policies for achieving the stated goals creates positions and authorizations, and opens opportunities for rent-seeking, which at times culminates in the creation of vested interests, both inside and outside the legislature. The inherent apathy to change is another important factor in India. Eventually, a variety of moving parts emerge whenever a policy change is initiated. The ability of the promoter of the policy change lies in the efficacious understanding of the moving parts and in creating a positive energy. However, at times, an authoritarian push becomes necessary when pragmatism proves incapable of navigating the rough weathers.

A Regulatory Intervention (The Dividend Distribution Tax)

The Union Budget for the year 2002–03 was presented in Parliament on 28 February 2002 by the finance minister, Yaswant Sinha. Among the proposals in the budget was dividend distribution tax (DDT) at the rate of 10 per cent, to be paid by the company disbursing the dividend. DDT would be effective from 1 April 2002. It created a bit of a ruckus amongst the entrepreneur and manager fraternity. They, quite obviously, did not want to pay DDT and started looking for ways to save tax, at least for one year.

The broader suggestion among the community was that an interim dividend—of approximately the rate of total dividend payable during the year 2002–03—be disbursed before 31 March 2002. This would save them DDT at least for the year 2002–03. Since the regulatory process called for the holding of board meetings for consideration of dividend with a minimum notice period, many dividend-paying corporations rushed to the exchanges asking for the minimum notice period to be reduced. Declaration of any dividend has to be approved by the company boards, as their annual general meetings for final dividend were held only sometime between July and September. The intent of such haste on the part of the corporations was commented on in the newspapers.

The finance minister, concerned and apprehensive that the proposed dividend distribution tax would not bring in the revenues envisaged in the Union Budget for 2002–03, called me up to discuss ways and means to stop this unseemly corporate behaviour. I agreed with the minister's views on DDT. I directed the exchanges not to grant corporations any reduction in the minimum notice period required for holding board meetings. The fundamental logic in my mind was that relaxation in regulatory checks and balances should not facilitate tax avoidance.

In the process of soliciting and galvanizing the views, opinions and recommendations of all stakeholders in the design of systems applications and processes (SAP) at SEBI and building an environment of confidence, I had called a meeting of the top twenty industrialists and business house heads to get to know what they felt about the environment in the capital markets. The attendance at the meeting was 100 per cent. After my opening speech I invited suggestions from the participants. An outspoken head of a business house opened the discussions with an accusation of venality against me. 'You have paid the price of your appointment as the SEBI chairman. On the instructions of the finance minister, you have directed the exchanges not to grant remission in the time required for issue of notice for board meetings,' he said. I listened patiently without interrupting the gentleman. When he was done, I said something along these lines: 'Before joining as chairman, SEBI, I was a sitting chairman of the largest financial institution in India. I was not only enjoying my job but also being complimented by all the stakeholders. And I still had more than a quarter of my tenure at LIC left. I was not a retired executive looking for job post-superannuation. I had not applied or appeared for any selection interview or sought the appointment at any time at any level. In fact, even to me it was kind of a surprise, to be appointed as SEBI chairman. There is a member of the search committee in this assembly who can testify to this.

'I do understand that you, as a likely beneficiary of the proposition of avoidance of DDT by short-circuiting the regulatory system, should have a natural grievance. I fully appreciate that. However, I serve the country. I am not only empowered to promulgate subordinate legislation but also have the obligation to uphold the country's legislation. Hence, I cannot be a party to short-circuiting, in disobedience of the proposed legislation. What is within your right and authority you are entitled to do as the chairman of your company. You have the authority to hold board meetings, but if the law requires a minimum notice period for that and the authority is not with you but with the regulatory apparatus—the stock exchanges (they are the second-line regulators in the securities market)—why do you expect the apparatus to be a party to your tax avoidance? I certainly cannot allow that.

'If you have a grievance against DDT, here are the following four options in the order of sequence:

1. Approach the minister to revisit the proposition and persuade him to withdraw the proposals; failing which
2. Go to the prime minister and to the Cabinet to advise the minister of finance not to push this proposal for approval in Parliament; failing which
3. Persuade the members of Parliament not to approve the proposal of the finance minister; failing which
4. Build public opinion against the proposal of the finance minister so that the current political executive is booted out in the next round of elections.'

The gentleman who had raised the issue was dumbfounded, and the audience too stunned. He had neither bargained for nor was used to such strong, spirited and stout rebuttal. In fact, he was used to getting away with his outbursts.

The issue was buried then and there in the meeting room. The entire exercise of attempting to avoid DDT for the next year was abandoned by the corporate world forthwith. I believe the incident also sent the signal that I was a 'no nonsense regulator'. Since I do not harbour ill-will, prejudice or rancour against anybody, I was happy to help the gentleman when, six months into my tenure, he made a genuine request concerning his company.

There were several discussions like this with a variety of economic agents during my tenure, and my responses were forthright, leaving no scope for anybody to promote as a public good something he was ineligible for.

Architecting Global Cooperation

In 1983, eleven security market regulators from the countries in North America and South America came together to form a global cooperative body of security market regulators. This body came to be known as 'The International Organization of Securities Commission' (IOSCO). Over the years, IOSCO expanded its membership to include regulators from outside the Americas too, and by the time I joined SEBI, IOSCO boasted of 150-plus member nations, including India.

Over the years since its inception, IOSCO became a torchbearer of international benchmarks for security market regulations and their effective implementation across countries. Post the tragic event of 11 September 2001, a need was felt in the financial world at large to deepen the cooperation among financial agencies, including the capital market regulators, to curb the movement of money used for funding terror, other criminal activities, general fraud and misconduct. This was thought to be possible only if there was an appropriate and timely exchange of information among the financial agencies of the concerned nations, including the capital market regulators.

IOSCO is segregated into two parts: the technical committee and the emerging markets committee. All members of Organization for Economic Co-operation and Development (OECD) countries are members of the technical committee, and rest are the members of the emerging markets committee. In fact, membership is determined on the basis of a country's GDP per capita rather than the state of development of its capital market. All guidances issued to members, including decisions on international benchmarks, are made by the technical committee, proposed in the general council, and approved almost without question. Changes in guidance, if any, are decided by the technical committee. The role of the emerging markets committee was limited. In fact, the whole organization was dominated by the developed market regulators, led by the US. During my tenure, we engaged them in all new frames of cooperation. In fact, initially, I was elected to lead the corporate governance committee of the emerging markets committee. Even though there were discussions in the technical committee for appointment of a separate committee for corporate governance, it was objected to by Japan, which argued that India was capable of leading the corporate governance committee of IOSCO and not just the emerging markets committee. Thus the corporate governance committee became an IOSCO committee rather than of its emerging market committee.

However, there was the overarching influence of the US Securities and Exchange Commission (SEC) and the European regulators, like those of Germany and the UK. Nevertheless, SEBI representatives were able to create enough noise on various areas of discussions, which was noticed and acted upon. The signing of the multilateral memorandum of understanding (MMoU) made SEBI's position in IOSCO stronger.

The MMoU

In 2002, IOSCO came up with the 'multilateral memorandum of understanding' (MMoU) to facilitate appropriate and timely sharing of information among the capital market regulators of the countries that were part of the MMoU. India, on more than one occasion, had been the victim of terror, criminal activities, frauds, misconduct, etc., the funds for which in some cases were suspected to have been routed through the global capital markets channel. There was also rampant circulation of black money in India through the capital markets route. Naturally, SEBI wanted to be part of this MMoU to be able to share as well as receive information to help curb such anti-social funding. In fact, when the MMoU was discussed at IOSCO, SEBI was at the forefront of getting the idea currency to help it become an instrument of global cooperation.

SEBI was a member of IOSCO, but not every member of IOSCO could automatically be part of the MMoU. There were eligibility criteria to be fulfilled, which was tested through a questionnaire. Basically, once you are a signatory of the MMoU, you could obtain information relating to any suspect activities taking place globally, right from terror and crime funding to fraud and misconduct (related to insider trading, misrepresentation of information, solicitation of investor funds, activities of market intermediaries, etc.). The signatories could share all kinds of information to help reconstruct a proper trail of the transactions and money routing to help identify the beneficial owner of various suspicious accounts, and even take a person's statement under oath regarding a potential offence. The questionnaire would test the applicant country's as well as its regulator's technical ability, their legal scope and their intent to maintain and share such information with foreign authorities.

Answering this questionnaire turned out to be an uphill task for SEBI, as the answers required had to be exhaustive. Then there were a couple of requirements that we at SEBI were not adhering to, and a solution had to be found to that. However, we took up the challenge and immersed ourselves in becoming a signatory of the MMoU.

As a first step, I quickly managed to convince the Indian government about the advantages of our becoming a signatory to the MMoU and get its permission for that in a record time of one month. Then the entire legal department, including my EA, Ramesh, started working on the questionnaire. As already mentioned, the major focus of the questionnaire was to ascertain whether we were technically capable of maintaining money and stock movement trails, the records of our exchanges, details of account holders, etc. The questionnaire asked to know if India's laws permitted us to share such information with the regulator of a foreign country even when we did not have any interest in the matter, if we could keep the information shared with us confidential, and if we would allow foreign regulators to use such information for investigation, enforcement proceedings, criminal prosecutions, etc. Anybody could ask us for information. IOSCO's bigger concern was whether SEBI could provide the required information when needed.

Well, we quickly submitted our answers in the very first round itself; at that point only twenty of over 150 countries had submitted their responses. From the emerging markets, we were the only regulator to have submitted our responses. The rest of the respondents were all from the developed markets, such as the SEC (USA), the erstwhile Financial Services Authority (FSA) (UK) and BAFIN (Germany).

As expected, our responses were studied by the IOSCO team with a magnifying glass and every word scrutinized. The IOSCO team came back with a set of queries, as they wanted to understand our systems and processes better. This time their queries were difficult to comprehend. They were too technical in nature, and for some we had no clear answers. Our team, which comprised junior and mid-level officers, struggled to come up with suitable responses. So, eventually, I had to step in to guide the team and collect the relevant inputs from different departments. To SEBI's credit, once the initial approval from Government of India was received, the government was not involved in any further part of the exercise. All responses were provided to IOSCO independently by SEBI. There were multiple rounds of back and forth between IOSCO and SEBI, with IOSCO relentlessly digging deeper and SEBI replying with equal vigour. Finally, we were required to do a conference call with the IOSCO team to iron out the few issues that remained, and we at SEBI knew very well that this could be the call that would decide our fate with respect to the MMoU.

On the conference call were five international regulators from the developed world. And I recollect that one of the key questions they were time and again emphasizing was regarding the sharing of information. Well, presence of mind and awareness of our powers came to our rescue, and in a few seconds, on the call itself, we were able to tell them, citing a clause from the SEBI Act, that SEBI had the authority to share information for the efficient discharge of its functions. We argued that SEBI could independently issue any directions in matters concerning securities. On the strength of this call, combined with our earnestness and persuasive powers throughout the process, SEBI managed to convince the five international regulators on the call and the entire IOSCO team that it was as competent as the regulator of any developed country to sign the MMoU.

After going through all the rigour and churn, SEBI finally signed the MMoU in April 2003, making India among the first from the emerging countries to do so (even countries like China and Indonesia had to revise their applications on account of inadequacies in their responses). At the time, only nine regulators (including SEBI) had signed the MMoU, and, barring SEBI, the rest were all from the developed world. We had taken the lead, overcome all obstructions and scrutiny with our sincere attempts, and managed to be a signatory to the MMoU. A new era of international cooperation had begun for SEBI, and history is witness to how this agreement has been immensely valuable for our national security, given the rise in international crime and terrorism.

What Did We Do Differently?

I think the fact that SEBI is genuinely empowered and has been set up as independent authority helped a lot. The IOSCO people could see from their evaluation of SEBI that we were indeed capable of sharing all the necessary information and that we were fairly independent of political interference. On top of it all, the SEBI team worked very hard, and were sincere and honest in their replies, persuasive where required, and approached the whole exercise with a winning attitude. And win it did, with flying colours!

And we were rewarded. It so happened that within just a month of SEBI signing the MMoU, it started investigating people behind the money flowing into India in the form of investment in participatory notes (P-notes) part of the requirement of the JPC report on Scam 2001. Since SEBI was now a signatory of the MMoU, it could easily get in touch with regulators from the UK, Hong Kong, Singapore and even the US to share with us information on these P-note holders and other suspected stock market manipulators sitting abroad. Invaluable information was received from these regulators on this matter.

With the signing of the MMoU, SEBI had also enhanced its respectability. Earlier, SEBI was just another third-world regulator whose views did not matter, but now, no IOSCO or any other global investor conference would start without SEBI's presence.

Today, 100 regulators are part of this MMoU. Every year since the signing of this MMOU, SEBI has been receiving from and providing information to foreign regulators about mischievous activities globally. In fact, SEBI has become renowned in global regulatory circles for the promptness of its response to information requests and has a record of zero complaints in the matter of cooperation. A couple of years back, SEBI had helped SEC bust a major investment scam being run by two Indians through online social media platforms. The capital market regulators from Canada and Hong Kong too provided their inputs. This was possible only because SEBI and the other regulatory bodies were part of the MMoU.

Overall, the return on investment from the efforts SEBI put into the MMoU turned out to be quick, huge and long-lasting. In stock market terminology, its investment was a 'multi-bagger'!

5

RE-ENGINEERING THE MARKET MICROSTRUCTURE: APPROACH TO AGENDA FOR ACTION

The initial efforts were addressed to preparing the organization for the journey of reforms and reengineering. The next step was to design the agenda. While appearing before the Joint Parliament Committee (JPC), I had inter alia stated that there are three kinds of risks in the capital market: (a) Structural, (b) Systemic and (c) Operational and assured the Committee that my efforts will be to minimize those risks.

It is true that human behaviour is sought to be governed by legislation/subordinate legislation. Hence laws are enacted to control and/or limit the behaviour of the people. But can a law actually reform the behaviour of the people has been the subject of the researchers of this area? Law can only demarcate the behaviour but it cannot demarcate the mind of individuals, which is prompted by a variety of sentiments like duty, fear, anger, trust, self-interest etc. In fact, 'Regulatory Response Theory' in the regulatory jurisprudence is still evolving. The responses to regulations are generally of three kinds:

1. Natural Behaviour: follow law in letter and spirit

2. Purposeful Action: stemming out of ignorance, incompetence, incapacity or misunderstanding
3. Motivated Action: motives not to comply

I was looking forward to ensuring that the structures, systems and processes are orchestrated so as to promote human behaviour to be acting naturally and if acting otherwise the impact to be limited. This would demand re-engineering, refurbishing and restructuring the entire gamut of the regulatory frame.

The structure of the market is defined by the institutions and participants and the linkages between the institutions and participants. In the case of the securities market, the institutions could be listed as stock exchanges, issuers of securities, investors and intermediaries. The intermediaries would include a range of the institutions like depositories, registrar and transfer agents, investment bankers, mutual funds, brokers et al. The linkages will be the methodology, which facilitates intermediation. This I would like to describe as the Macro-Structure of the Capital Markets. The potency of all these institutions including their methods of conduct and behaviour has got to be appropriate to deliver the expected outcomes in an efficacious manner. Deficiencies in the design of these institutions and also the methods of their interconnection in the market place create structural risks.

Systemic risk is often described as the risk, which can lead to the collapse of the entire market and/or financial system as a whole. In other words, the risk, which envelops the entire market or a segment of the market, is a systemic risk. These relate to the basic foundations on which the institutions of the Capital Market as mentioned above would be created and operate. Hence, the areas, which can create a systemic risk to a capital market are Accounting and Financial Reporting Standards, Disclosures (in a disclosure based regime), Governance framework including

Code of Conduct etc. In any market when any of these frames become substantially inadequate to sustain the efficacy of broader market, a risk of market wide failure and even the failure of the entire financial system surface besides the black swans events that can never be ruled out.

The operational risk relates to the actual conduct of the transactions, which encompass people, processes, systems etc. The Basel Committee defines the operational risk as, 'The risk of loss resulting from inadequate or failed internal processes, people and systems or from external events.' The often quoted example of operational risk bringing the collapse of the oldest investment bank known as Barings Bank is that of infamous Nick Leeson, a former derivative trader who in the absence of supervision and without proper authority fraudulently and unauthorizedly traded massively on Singapore and Tokyo Stock Exchanges. There could be other similar outcomes like settlement failure etc.

In fact, Scam 2001 to my mind was a fusion of all the three risks—Structural, Systemic and Operational. I evaluated the entire Macro & Micro Market Structure of Indian Capital Market; spoke to quite a few knowledgeable professionals and experts as also some of the financial market economists. Collating all the inputs received, I started thinking of the areas that SEBI will have to revisit so that eventually structural, systemic and operational risks are minimized and an environment of efficacy and confidence prevails.

This was the underpinning of Strategic Action Plan and all the thought processes that followed thereafter. The areas of re-engineering, refurbation and reorientation were far too many and with three years tenure, I became a man in a hurry. This treatise is an attempt to help the readers appreciate the anxiety of a man committed to his assurance to JPC and to the nation at large. Fortunately, ditching the decennial trend, no market scam has occurred so far.

Mitigating Operational Risks

Stock markets are a meeting point for issuers of securities and investors, who in turn are linked by intermediaries. Each of these constituents is a prisoner of general human behaviour, and has an inherent tendency to be self-aggrandizing—mostly in an ethical way, but given the opportunity, in unethical ways too. Unethical profiteering practices accentuate systemic and operational risks, lead to undue advantage for some players and compromise investor protection, jeopardizing investor confidence in the efficacy of the market. It is here that the mission of SEBI to 'regulate the market' and 'protect investor interests' comes into play, to bring in order and ensure the efficacy of the market.

The ground rules, regulations, general orders and guidance to legislations and their effective enforcement shape market behaviour and efficacy. The participants in the capital market have to be closely monitored for their strict adherence to the ground rules. Whenever a breach is observed, cognizance must be taken of it and investigations carried out. If a participant is found guilty of misconduct, apt and timely action should be taken. 'A stitch in time saves nine' is a potent proverb to go by. To address these responsibilities effectively, SEBI has four distinct frames of authority.

When I took stock of SEBI's functioning and priorities, one area that particularly bothered me was its quasi-judicial function. Thousands of enforcement actions were awaiting closure, some on matters as high-profile as the Ketan Parekh scam. Ineffective enforcement was the apparent verdict, of stakeholders and opinion makers alike. In fact, just a couple of months after my joining SEBI, P. Chidambaram (who was part of the Opposition then) had made a scathing remark about SEBI at a Confederation of Indian Industry (CII) conference. He said, 'SEBI, over a period of [last] seven years, became so complacent, self-praising, smug and non-transparent'.[1] He stated further, 'we are a punishment-free society. Nobody except petty offenders are punished, and that too for petty crimes. What is the use of SEBI if people like Harshad Mehta and Hiten Dalal are not punished even after 10 years of their committing scams that robbed millions of their savings? Even if they are punished after 10 years, they get those sort of punishments that are generally given for traffic violations.'[2]

Then, just a few months after my joining SEBI, a senior journalist had lambasted SEBI's judicial abilities, saying, 'G.N. Bajpai has taken charge of SEBI at a difficult time. Over the last seven years, SEBI has lost all credibility as an effective supervisor, allowed a huge backlog of cases to pile up in almost every department, has deliberately changed its rules to favour market participants and has been open to allegations of favouritism or worse.' The negative fallout on investor confidence was real. I had a mountain to climb, but I was ready for it.

A quasi-judicial order (like the ones issued by SEBI) is a method of enforcement. Formal inquiries and hearings are preceded by investigations to ascertain culpability of delinquency. The investigation involves determining what rules were broken, how they were broken and who broke them. It also involves collection of maximum evidence of delinquency. Even if the investigation establishes that rules have been broken willingly and/or maliciously, an important process has to be followed before punishment can be dispensed. This is the process of giving adequate opportunity to the accused to be heard and present his version of the case in defence of himself. He can do this through a representative too.

It is to be kept in mind that the Constitution of India guarantees that Indian society shall function in a cogent manner, that all citizens shall be treated equally in front of the law and that no one will be punished without being given an opportunity to defend himself. The right of the accused to be heard and to present his defence is a fundamental right, the gravity of the misconduct notwithstanding. Even otherwise, both civil and criminal jurisprudence envisage giving an opportunity to the accused before the verdict is passed. The SEBI process actually resembles that of typical judicial proceedings in India, but without lengthy court procedures.

Expert bodies like SEBI are created by a statute (law). All the three functions of the state—legislative, judicial and executive—are entrusted to SEBI in the sector it oversees. The need for creation of such bodies was recently emphasized by the Hon'ble Supreme Court in the *Tata Cellular vs Union of India* case. To quote Justice Neely of US Federal Court, 'I have very few illusions about my own limitations as a Judge and from those limitations I generalise to the inherent limitations of all appellate courts reviewing rate cases. It must be remembered that this Court sees approximately 1262 cases a year with five Judges. I am not an accountant, electrical engineer, financier, banker, stock broker, or systems management analyst. It is the height of folly to expect Judges intelligently to review a 5000 page record addressing the intricacies of public utility operation.'[3] I like to quote this judgment when discussing or talking about SEBI's quasi-judicial authority.

The word 'quasi' means 'not exactly'. An authority is christened as 'quasi-judicial' when it has some attributes of judicial function but not all of them. A judicial function involves the following: (a) a dispute between two parties (b) taking evidence on oath, (c) strict legal procedures, like the civil procedure or criminal procedure codes (d) payment of court fees, (e) the judicial discipline of following precedents set by higher courts (f) not acting as judge in cases involving itself. However, in the case of quasi-judicial proceedings, a, b, c, d and e need not exist or be followed, and f, too, can be relaxed. Thus a quasi-judicial authority has the paraphernalia of a court, but in reality is not a court. The important points to understand are that a quasi-judicial authority can be its own judge, is not bound by the procedures of taking evidence, but has the discretion to pass orders. The exercise of this discretion, therefore, becomes a fundamental issue in all quasi-judicial orders. In fact, Bombay High Court has laid down an elaborate procedure, and also limits, for quasi-judicial authorities, which are binding in the case of SEBI too.

Judicial Hierarchy

The normal civil and criminal judicial systems in India are hierarchical—cases go from a lower court to a district court, then to the High Court (HC) and finally to the Supreme Court (SC). For SEBI, the quasi-judicial hierarchy goes something like this: SEBI to Securities and Appellate Tribunal (SAT) to High Court to Supreme Court. Thus, if a parallel is drawn between the two systems, SEBI is the equivalent of a court subordinate to the district court, and SAT a district court. And this is where, precisely, lay the problem. SAT was the equivalent of a district court and subordinate to the High Court, whereas, actually, SAT was well placed to handle securities market-related cases.

SEBI and SAT dealt with securities market-related violations, which deserved a treatment different from that reserved for the usual civil and criminal offences, as this example illustrates. Say there has been a murder in which a gun was the weapon, and say there is a suspect. No court in India will convict the suspect unless it is proven beyond doubt that a shot was fired by the suspect using that gun, which resulted in the murder. It would not be sufficient to only prove that the accused had owned such a gun; it has to be further proved that the accused actually fired a shot using that gun. Hence, incontrovertible evidence is demanded in such cases. But securities market-related violations are decided by SEBI on the basis of the principle of 'preponderance of probability' described as evidence that persuades a judge or jury to lean on one side as against evidence beyond a reasonable doubt, which is necessary for criminal trails. In the case of a civil liberty or criminal offence, proof beyond reasonable doubt is required, whereas in the case of economic liberty, preponderance of probability or rule of reason is sufficient.

Even though the burden of proof varies from case to case, under Indian law the burden of proof normally rests with the complainant. However, it is a settled principle—on the strength of a number of Supreme Court judgments—that in administrative and quasi-judicial actions, the onus of proof sometimes shifts to the party challenging the validity of the orders of the administrative or quasi-judicial authority like SEBI. In fact, it works on the maxim of '*Omnia praesumuntur rite esse acta*', which means 'all things are presumed to be done in due form' and that the evidence of preponderance of probability is enough for the authority to have passed its order. This is in significant variance from what obtains in civil and criminal proceedings in the courts.

To explain this further, take the example of insider trading, which can invoke both civil and criminal punishment. Insider trading is when a person is privy to some insider information about a company and does not use this information to trade himself but passes it on to a friend, who acts on this insider information and executes a trade. In this case, if it is established that the person executing the trade has no way of getting the information from any other source but from the person in possession of the insider information who could have shared the information with him, it becomes sufficient grounds for holding both parties guilty of insider trading, so far as civil liabilities are concerned. It is not required to go to the extent of proving through incontrovertible evidence that the information was actually shared. However, for criminal liabilities, the case has to be remanded to a magisterial court to establish the '*mens rea*' (criminal intent or knowledge of criminality of act) with irrefutable evidence of when and how the information was shared, along with evidence of the actual act of the suspect making use of that information.

The functioning of the securities market and interpretation of the securities laws are rather technical subjects, requiring a specific skill and a suitably trained mind. SAT was exclusively dedicated to deal with securities-related offences and had a distinct advantage in the understanding and interpretation of the securities related laws. Also, HCs were flooded with cases of all kinds and, as a result, could not expeditiously deal with capital market cases. SAT, on the other hand, did not take much time in handling them. So my first thought was to see how this (High Court) leg of the SEBI-judicial hierarchy could be skipped and the quality of judgements improved to bring them in line with the spirit of the securities laws so that SEBI cases could quickly culminate in the ultimate verdict.

Contracting the Layers

As jaw-dropping as it may sound, the best way to wade through the HC bottleneck was to eliminate the HC portion of the hierarchy and to make SAT the equivalent of an HC so that cases could go directly from SAT to SC! The thought at that time was indeed a bold one, and admittedly we were not fully confident of succeeding in getting the government agree to it. The law ministry was then headed by Arun Jaitley, a strong modernist and futuristic thinker. As a former additional solicitor general and senior advocate before joining the Union Cabinet, he took it upon himself to push the proposal. It was entirely his efforts that brought the amendment to the SEBI Act (October 2002), which made SAT the equivalent of an HC so that SEBI cases could move directly from SAT to SC and the HC leg could be totally removed from the judicial hierarchy of the securities market. This was as innovative and significant as it was bold, and will go down in the history as an important judicial reform, fully to the credit of Arun Jaitley. Simultaneously, SAT was also upgraded from a single-member bench to a multi-member bench, and the presiding officer of this multi-member bench had to be a serving or retired SC judge or a judge or Chief Justice of HC;

and adjudicating officers at SEBI in a way, became equivalent to district judges.

The positive outcome of these developments is that the whole process of a SEBI case reaching finality shortened drastically. Since SAT's status was elevated, in most of the cases SAT itself became the final decision-making authority. Only those SAT decisions involving a substantive question of law (i.e., one involving a debate over interpretation of a certain law) were challenged before the Supreme Court. For the rest of the SAT decisions, lawyers avoided knocking at the doors of SC.

SAT was quick to give verdicts, and very few cases went to SC. So far, so good. But there was another leg in the whole process where the verdicts were taking time—SEBI's own investigations and hearings. So, next, I focused on setting my own house in order.

Setting My House in Order

On analysing what was going on, I discovered that there were a number of pending cases that were to be disposed of by SEBI itself. They were pending either because investigation had not been taken up, or had been taken up but remained inconclusive. Then there were the cases where the investigation had been completed but the final enforcement actions were pending. Many such completed investigations that had to be heard had piled up because of our restrictions on who could conduct the hearings.

If the investigation revealed violations that deserved a suitable punishment (for instance, cancellation of license of an intermediary, suspension of a company from trading, or debarring an entity from the stock markets), the hearing had to be undertaken by either the SEBI board, the SEBI chairman or a whole-time member who was part of the board. The logic behind this was that the SEBI board had the legal authority to punish, and this authority could not be delegated to anyone more than one step below the board. This would have been fine, except that we did not have any WTMs until a full year after I joined; and surely the SEBI board (consisting of the chairman and several independent members) could not be called upon to undertake the hearings. So the entire workload of hearing cases fell to me. However, imposing only monetary penalty could be done by the adjudicating officers, who need not be chairman or WTM. And we are talking of cases not in the hundreds but in the thousands!

On top of it, I had joined at a time when one of the most high profile cases in the history of SEBI—the Ketan Parekh scam of 2001—was also awaiting closure. This case, fresh in everyone's mind, was in the constant public and media glare, with everyone looking up to SEBI to provide an appropriate and quick closure, which was an added pressure. And as the SEBI chairman, I had many other areas to take care of: legislative work, revision of regulations (the scam had necessitated the tightening of SEBI regulations, guidance and directions) and general market development.

To put it in another perspective, my total tenure of three years had just over 1,000 days (including all weekends and other national holidays); that meant on an average I would have to close hearing of at least two cases every day, that too only if I worked on all the 1,000 days and focused only on closing hearings and nothing else! This was unrealistic.

To sum it up, I was hard pressed for time to do justice to all my obligations as chairman. The situation demanded strategic planning, smart prioritizing and focused execution. It may sound surprising, but I found this pressure-cooker-like situation piquant.

Execution

First I asked the team to classify all pending cases and found that they fell into three categories—takeover cases, IPO cases and miscellaneous cases (pertaining to general market misconduct, etc.). This classification helped me tackle each type of case using a customized approach, which helped us fast-track many cases, as described later here. Also, I kept experimenting with various strategies to achieve maximum output.

When I first started hearing the judicial cases, I would usually stretch my working time in office to twelve hours to be able to hear them as well as deal with other matters. Then I came up with what I thought was a better strategy: to dedicate one day of the week (either a Wednesday or Thursday) completely to judicial work. It worked for some time, but soon enough I realized that just one day a week was not enough, since lawyers usually take a long time to argue their cases. I often was not able to finish even a single case in one day. Besides, even on that one day, various other unexpected matters cropped up, distracting me from the judicial work.

Then I decided I would keep the weekends for hearing cases. Although this meant that my workdays increased from five to seven a week, I took it in my stride as I was determined to fast-track the clearing of various long-pending cases at SEBI. Weekends, I felt, were the best time to dedicate fully to quasi-judicial work as one was free from the pressures of other work. But, funnily enough, the biggest opposition to my weekend plan came from the lawyers, who did not wish to spoil their weekends. I put my foot down, saying 'this is the only time I have', thinking, rather naively, that I was the one who was driving the quasi-judicial process. Reality soon struck, however. Many of the cases involved huge penalty or punishment, so companies and individuals not willing to take chances had appointed the best of advocates, some of whom refused to work on weekends.

So once again I had to refine my strategy. I decided to continue with my judicial work on Saturdays (many lawyers were still ready to work on Saturdays) and only sparingly on Sundays when the advocates were available. I also heard cases on weekdays. The weekdays got even more busy after the weekends, because once a hearing was completed on the weekend, the related paperwork (drafting of orders, etc.) was done on the weekdays with help of the officers in the legal department, often after office hours and on Sundays.

This seven-day-week schedule continued for a year before I got two WTMs, who too, on their own, started hearing cases. Here I could have taken a breather, having worked almost round the clock for almost a year. But then, I thought, if I show that extra commitment it would set an example for my colleagues to work harder and expedite the cases. In fact, together we came up with various innovations to close the cases.

Some of them were:

1. For takeover and IPO cases, which usually had a standard set of defaults, we prepared a broad framework under which we gave the accused options to 'confess and pay a standard fee or fine'—an amnesty for quick decision making, or something akin to a Lok Adalat—which saved both parties unnecessary legal hassles and the costs that go with them. We concluded a large number of cases (in the thousands) this way, and I authorized many officers to do this. As mentioned earlier, this was where classifying the cases helped us. SEBI came up with a formal consent and settlement mechanism in 2007. The SEBI Act was amended to provide for settlement in 2014 and a formal regulation by SEBI was issued in the same year. The initial settlement process pursued during my tenure was a precursor to this formal mechanism.

2. Where the cases involved only monetary penalty, we started adjudication proceedings, for which many SEBI officers could be designated, thus reducing the burden on me and the WTMs.

Overall, my efforts paid off, and during my tenure of three years SEBI passed a record 1,200 judicial orders i.e. on an average more than one order a day. Fortunately for me, being a law graduate helped greatly. However, this practice (of the chairman being a significant part of the quasi-judicial work) was not continued once I left. My successors, maybe for good reasons, have not undertaken any quasi-judicial hearings and have fully delegated that work to the WTMs.

Making SEBI Orders Public

As mentioned in the other chapter, we started making SEBI orders (complete with details of the investigations conducted, etc.) public from the beginning of 2003. This gave a wonderful opportunity to those adversely affected by the order to throw unwarranted and unfair criticism at us, mostly through proxies, under full media glare. Some even persuaded journalists and lawyers to write stories against the logic of our orders and the rationale of the punishments. However, I was indefatigable. I was sucked into the mission, and nothing could dampen my enthusiasm.

Arguably the most high-profile case that was handled by me personally was that of Ketan Parekh. The scam happened in March 2001, about a year before I joined SEBI. I made the very first hearing in the case, and the last one too. The hearings continued for three months, and many advocates at various levels made appearances. The final order that I wrote was roughly 1,200 pages long. It debarred Parekh from the markets for fifteen years—a kind of a life sentence. The order was upheld by both SAT and the SC.

Another high-profile case that I handled involved a collective investment scheme—Golden Forest Scheme. Between the mid and late nineties, this scheme had collected thousands of crores of rupees from about 25 lakh investors, promising them sky-high, unrealistic returns. It was a promise the scheme was unable to fulfil. My order directed Golden Forest to register as a Collective

Investment Scheme (CIS), and on their failure to do so, refund all the monies collected, with interest, to investors. Soon legal proceedings for refund were initiated against the company. The matter continued for a few years before finally reaching the SC. It was during my tenure that the apex court appointed a committee under the chairmanship of a retired Chief Justice of India, along with one representative each from RBI and SEBI, to take into custody all assets owned by the scheme and simultaneously call for the claims of the investors and scrutinize them. When last heard of, some of the assets of the scheme had been auctioned and the rest were in the process of being auctioned off.

Then there was another high-profile case involving Tata Capital, from which I had to recuse myself because one of my sons-in-law was then an MD in a Tata group company. Since I decided to stay away from the hearing of this case and there was no WTM at that time in SEBI, the case could be heard only by the SEBI board. The board, though initially reluctant, agreed to hear the case but was unable to fix dates for the hearing as all members were required to be present. Finally, the case came up for hearing only after two WTMs joined SEBI. All this delayed the hearing, which did not go down well with the Tatas. So one day, the finance director at Tata Sons asked for an appointment with us. At the meeting he conveyed that Ratan Tata, chairman of Tata Group, felt SEBI was dragging its feet on taking action in this particular case. When I told him the real reason for the delay, he appreciated it but was surprised to know that my son-in-law was working for a group company and that he was not even aware of it, even though he was a director on the board of that company! He said, 'But he never told me.' I requested him not to mention this conversation to my son-in-law. 'He is a man of self-respect and a proud individual who does not like to take favours,' I said.

The decisions of all the regulatory bodies are reviewed by an appellate body mostly created under the same statute or law. Above all, there is a constitutional judicial review of all the decisions of all the administrative bodies. However, there is a need to develop regulatory jurisprudence which should include a sector specific regulation, autonomy in its functioning, power to legislate to match the market dynamics including licensing, quick regulatory reaction and effective enforcement actions. The quasi-judicial orders are part of this enforcement and licensing. In the process of evolution of the regulatory jurisprudence, consistency in decision making and predictable actions and reactions play a very important role. This is what I tried to achieve during my tenure in order to develop the regulatory jurisprudence.

I am proud to mention that I maintained an impenetrable Chinese wall between my professional and personal duties and strived to maintain the quality of my orders. On various occasions, we were actually praised by SAT for the quality of our orders.

6

CRUNCHING
THE SETTLEMENT CYCLES

The most significant operational risk in the capital markets lies in the settlement of transactions. Customers buy and sell through intermediaries, i.e., brokers on the trading platform of the exchange. There are five parties who can cause failure of settlement, either jointly or separately. These are: (a) the two customers—buyer and seller, (b) the two brokers, on the buy and sell sides and (c) the settlement agent—i.e., the clearing corporation or trade guarantee fund. Whereas a number of scientific risk management measures have been laid down and applied to ensure that none of these parties fails to fulfil its commitment, there can always be unforeseen events to retard the ability of one or other party to fulfil its obligations. The uncertainty stems from the time gap between the actual trade and its settlement. This is known as settlement time. Such buy and sell transactions take place in the millions on the trading platform every day. Each and every transaction cannot be settled individually. Therefore, exchanges create a cycle for all the transactions to be aggregated and settled together. This, in capital market terminology, is called the 'settlement cycle'.

The Settlement Cycle

The settlement cycle is the period from the time of a trade to the time of its settlement—i.e., from the date the trade is actually undertaken to the date when the actual exchange of cash and securities takes place. The longer the cycle, the larger becomes the open positions of the brokers for settlement. To illustrate this, suppose a trade is executed on 1 September and the exchange settlement takes place on 15 September, the brokers on the two sides would have accumulated open (unsettled) positions of trades for fifteen days. In that period, the financial condition of the brokers and/or their clients can turn adverse, which can lead to failure of the broker/s to meet their commitment to pay or deliver securities, and eventually derail the order during settlement. This may happen notwithstanding the risk management measures undertaken, because no risk management measure can foresee all future eventualities, which keep changing with time and the environment. It is, therefore, desirable to have the shortest possible settlement cycle, which, ideally, would be $T+0$ or $T+1$, where T is the date of trade. In order to minimize the settlement risk in the Indian capital market, I decided to bring down the settlement cycle to the minimum possible.

History of Indian Trade Settlement

It might be worthwhile to recall the history of settlement of trades in the Indian capital market. Before technology took over, the shares and money had to be exchanged physically. The system in operation was to settle the trades periodically. For years this period was thirty days, and then it was reduced to fifteen days, i.e., $T+15$. In the late nineties, the concept of dematerialization (electronic form of securities) was introduced. Even though it did not require so long to close trades after this, the $T+15$ cycle continued.

For a long time, India had the *badla* system (explained later). This supported speculative traders who (regularly) misused it to create false liquidity in the market, which led to a lot of controversies. At times, even badla on the sixteenth day was deferred. On paper, the settlement cycle was T+15, but in reality it was 'T+ anything'. Another description used by some of the foreign institutional investors (FIIs) for the Indian stock market was 'snake pit'. I had personally experienced the pitfalls of badla in my previous job at LIC, where after selling shares, we received the money for it after three months sometimes, as the badla kept getting deferred fortnight after fortnight. Badla had been banned in 1993 by SEBI, but was brought back in a slightly stringent format later because of pressure from the broker community. It took a full-blown Scam 2001 before this system was banned for good by SEBI in July 2001 and was replaced by derivatives, with adequate risk management measures. The much-needed reforms were also brought in, and the settlement cycle was reduced from the old T+15 to T+5 and then to T+3 in April 2002.

T+2, the Stepping Stone

In April 2002 (a little over a month of my joining), the Indian capital markets joined the league of the developed markets of the world, such as the US, Canada, Japan, Hong Kong, Singapore and even the European countries, as SEBI introduced the T+3 rolling settlement cycle. I would like to credit my predecessor for most of the groundwork done for the epoch-making transformation of the settlement cycle from the T+15 and T+5 account period settlement to T+3 with rolling settlement. My role was limited to pushing the change hard to ensure a smooth transition and to thwart any move from any quarters to delay implementation, which was not insignificant either.

The developed markets had set timelines of around 2004–2005 to move to T+1. I did not want India to be playing catch-up this time.

There were other reasons too, besides the major domestic reason mentioned above. When the world was becoming increasingly global and when markets could turn volatile with the speed of light, what to say about a period of three days! Market volumes were growing by leaps and bounds in India, FIIs had become very active, the economy was by and large completely open now, and any laxity in the capital market could threaten economic growth and dent India's image as a preferred investment destination among the global community. A shorter settlement cycle fuels quicker churn, increasing the depth and efficiency of markets. It sets a positive cycle in motion and results in increased investor confidence.

Over and above all this, shares are considered to be liquid assets. But what good is a liquid asset that takes three working days after trade, i.e., more than half a week, to truly liquidate? If someone trades during the latter half of a week, his position will not be settled until early next week, which actually increases the settlement cycle to five days (including the weekend). A person banks on his liquid assets in times of emergency, and clearly no emergency can wait for so long.

With such high stakes, my decision was firm—to reduce the uncertainty from three days to only one day. The same sentiments were echoed by the finance minister of the time, Jaswant Singh, on 31 July 2002 in Parliament. Accordingly, a deadline was set to achieve the T+1 cycle. It was March 2004. The stepping stone was to reduce it first to T+2. In fact, in one of my many conversations with Ravi Narain, MD and CEO of NSE, he had suggested that instead of straightaway jumping to T+1, we should approach it gradually from T+3 to T+2 and then to T+1. But, was the infrastructure ready for this?

Building a Consensus

It was not easy to bring even the SEBI staff on the same page for further contraction of the settlement cycle. Accordingly, a committee was constituted to create a blueprint for this. The report was put up on the SEBI website for feedback, which was aplenty. Brokers particularly opposed this vehemently. There was resistance from bankers and from RBI too. So I had one-on-one discussions with a variety of senior functionaries representing a multiplicity of interests, including the governor of RBI. These discussions threw up a couple of genuine problems, including some which were more systemic.

A valid concern was about the speed of money transfers in India at the time. In fact, two things needed to move faster for implementation of shorter settlement cycles—securities and money. Securities (99 per cent of which were already dematerialized) in demat format could be transferred at the speed of light. At least, this was feasible, but not easy. Systems and processes had to be transformed. But any time less than two days was not possible in the case of money movement because of the technological inadequacy of the banking sector. Real Time Gross Settlement (RTGS) had not been introduced then, and SWIFT was being used, but not very widely. To appreciate this fully it is important to understand what a typical trade cycle looks like.

Transactions in the secondary market (for example buying and selling of shares in the stock exchange) pass through three distinct phases: trading, clearing and settlement. A trade is initiated by clients through their registered brokers on the trading platform provided by the exchange. The exchange then passes on the trade details to its clearing corporation (CC) to determine the funds and securities obligations of the respective brokers. This happened on T+1 and marked the end of the clearing process. The CC takes the counterparty risk on itself and ensures that trades are settled through the exchange of obligations. To settle a trade successfully, it takes the help of the broker's bank and the depositories.

Once the obligations were fixed on T+1, there were an additional two days for transfer of securities and money to the appropriate accounts through the CC. These additional days could be reduced to one or even zero for securities, but doing this for money was a genuine challenge. For securities, we needed to get consent from the depositories, depository participants (DPs) and the stock exchanges—independent entities in their own right but still very much under the regulatory jurisdiction of SEBI. For the other leg of movement of money, we had to knock at the doors of a totally different regulator—the RBI.

Depositories, DPs and Exchanges

Multiple meetings were held with these intermediaries. We wanted them to prepare for T+1 and not T+2, although T+2 was a stepping stone. T+1 required eliminating manual intervention completely. An immediate next-day settlement meant DPs and depositories had to respond within an extremely short lead time on the day of the trade itself, and that warranted a fair amount of systems upgradation. In fact, that meant depositories and DPs had to be connected in real time and respond in real time, in lieu of what was hitherto taking more than a day with the two depositories in the country—National Securities Depository Limited (NSDL) and Central Depository Services Limited (CDSL). That these two institutions were run by different managements that had to talk to each other in real time made the challenge greater. Depositories were used to going against the tide. Their establishment itself was to challenge the status quo of the time. They agreed to be ready by December 2002/January 2003 for T+2, and gradually thereafter for T+1. The major hurdle was to create interoperability between the two organizations. NSDL had reservations. It took some time but we persuaded them to come around.

Even exchanges were required to overhaul their existing systems to ensure that clearing corporations take confirmation and assign obligations to brokers on T+0. It also involved taking into account the cascading effect of their default handling mechanism. Hence, even those procedures had to be streamlined. However, like the depositories, the exchanges agreed to support a smooth transition from T+3 to T+2 and finally to T+1. The BSE management needed a bit of cajoling because some of the brokers in the management were opposing the change tooth and nail. With the securities market participants broadly confirming their support, the only aspect left was that of movement of money. And for that we were dependent on RBI.

Broker Resistance

As a community, brokers were opposed to the shortening of the settlement cycle beyond T+3. Their objections largely centred on the improbability of monies and securities moving so swiftly. During the numerous meetings we had with them, it transpired that their resistance emanated from the two underlying issues:

a. They would have to upgrade their technology infrastructure and skill up their staff, which meant extra expenditure.
b. They would not be able to use retail customers' monies and securities, which they were rampantly doing now.

It took numerous meetings for my pressure on the broker community to start showing its effects. They got a strong sense that I was going to push T+2 in the market anyway, and they were using various channels—the media, opinion makers and political executives—to advocate deferment, if not abandoning, of the initiative.

In fact, some of the international participants expressed scepticism about it, and some of the stock exchanges scoffed at the idea as being a fancy of SEBI's.

RTGS (Real-time Gross Settlement)

Today it is hard to imagine the world without RTGS and electronic fund transfers. But that was the reality when we were trying to bring about this revolutionary change—a change that even developed countries had not implemented at the time. Intuitively, one would believe that the banking industry is the torchbearer of the financial markets. Banking is a bigger, more widespread need than trading in shares. In the developed world, banking is ahead of the securities market in the matter of development and reforms. However, in India, it was the securities market that was pushing for fast-track reforms, such as RTGS.

I was in constant touch with the RBI governor on this issue, and he was very helpful. Clearly, there was pressure on RBI even otherwise. But RBI could not allow the implementation of T+2 to be delayed because of them alone. RBI had a problem. It had specified the list of clearing banks, and to trade in the markets brokers were compulsorily required to have accounts with those banks only. There were thirteen such banks, comprising both the major public and private sector banks. It was not possible to introduce RTGS countrywide in such a short span of time. RBI agreed to introduce the electronic funds transfer (EFT) facility in fifteen centres for all the specified bank branches by January 2003, and to extend the facility to 100 centres covering roughly 400 cities and towns by April 2003. This would by and large cover all the bigger places. When I got the names of these centres I was elated. At the 1,000 places that had online trading terminals, 95 per cent of trades would be covered by EFT! Brokers', or sub-brokers', offices were anyway located at these centres. So I pushed to speed up RTGS in these places. I had a personal meeting with the governor of RBI, who agreed to push the process fast. In a few days RBI was ready with RTGS, and we were almost ready to roll out T+2, except that the brokers had one more concern.

The Middleman Syndrome

The concern was that small retail investors do not have the means to pay in such quick intervals of time and would need more time. That additional day, if taken away from such investors, would increase pressure on brokers. Besides, in their view, this could even repel the affected investors, considering the urgency of funds for each transaction. It pleasantly surprised me that the parties that actually had to change their systems— which were the depositories and the exchanges—bringing in additional technology, upgrading the skills of their staff . . . in effect, deploying more financial resources and really increasing their workload . . . agreed to accept the change without much resistance. Ironically, the brokers, who had to just follow the system, albeit in an efficient manner, were the most aggrieved interest group. This efficiency of the market would have only helped them in multiple ways—closing trades faster, bringing additional business and in general lifting the market sentiment. It was a classic case of '*unknown fears*' playing on the mind.

A very well-regarded name in the securities market, whom I respected greatly as the father of automating the exchange business, was clearly convinced by the disguised vested interests. He advised me not to mess around with retail investors as they were the most sensitive of the lot. In his opinion, T+2 would definitely push the retail investor out of the market. I took his counsel and started pondering over it, and then it struck me— almost all the parties in the market had given their opinion on T+2 except the end investor for whom all this was being done. So, to decide the matter it was important that we conducted a survey, the results of which put to rest all confusion. In 99 per cent of the cases, investors were paying money in advance or giving securities in advance to their brokers. In no way was introduction of T+2 going to have an adverse effect on them. On the contrary, it only made sense to provide investors their securities or money at the earliest. Clearly, the most affected parties were the brokers themselves.

T+3 meant the advance collected from investors could be rotated for one full day, still leaving the brokers two days to settle the trades. In T+2, there was practically no time for rotation of money. When T+5 reduced to T+3, there were a few issues raised, but nothing major. This was partly due to Scam 2001 having increased everyone's appetite for big-bang reforms, and raising a voice against reforms would have been counterproductive. Besides, T+3 still provided some time margin to brokers to play around with investor funds. In short, the capital was being taken away from the rightful owners (investors), and these owners were getting their purchase late (T+3), and this capital was being used by someone else (brokers) to earn a little extra money. The markets could often be truly about greed, I thought! This practice was clearly a risk to settlement itself and could not be a reason to delay T+2.

But the brokers had not given up just yet.

FM Intervenes

With no respite in sight, the brokers decided to seek political refuge. This was a clear sign of desperation, showing that all their logical arguments had failed to support them. Some prominent brokers had access to the finance minister. Even otherwise, brokers are often liberally granted appointments by the finance ministry as they play a key part in the securities market machinery. They are the actual bridge between markets and investors, and hence indispensable. They have existed since the time the first exchanges in the country were established almost a century ago and have been synonymous with the markets. They are powerful economic agents, and their clout may be underestimated only at one's own peril.

And so, one fine morning, as I went about trying to make this world of bulls and bears a little better, I got a call from the finance secretary. After the customary exchange of initial pleasantries, he came to the point, 'Chairman, why are you taking decisions (transition to T+2) without our approval?'

To defuse the situation a little bit, I jokingly asked, 'Who are you . . . ?'

He said, 'We are the government.'

I replied, 'I am an independent regulator, and you, Government, will have to use Section 16 of the SEBI Act and give your advice in writing.'

He took my jibe in the right spirit and said that brokers had been granted an appointment with the FM and wanted him to intervene in the matter of T+2. He also told me that that the FM was anxious about the initiative being pushed down their throats. I told him not to worry and that I would explain to the FM the why of the initiative.

Incidentally, a day later, I happened to talk to the FM on some other matters. Sensing an opportunity, I also explained to him what we were trying to do with T+2 and how it would bring various risks down considerably. He heard me out calmly and was apparently satisfied with my explanation. He said, 'In that case, I will not meet the brokers, Chairman,' and added, 'you hear them again.' The appointment given by the FM to the brokers was cancelled and they were advised to meet the SEBI chairman, who would sort out the issues agitating them. Once again, Jaswant Singh's decisive approach to issues was demonstrated.

The brokers came, we discussed the matter, and we settled it for good. We issued a strict timeline for moving to T+2. Sufficient transition time was given, and it was eventually implemented by April 2003. There were no hiccups, no problems in settlements. And, as they say, the market lives happily thereafter. Some sections of the media even praised our efforts to finally implement T+2. *The Hindu Business Line* said, 'This is definitely a singular feather to the regulator's cap. Today, as the Indian Capital Market gets into doing final closure of transactions within a span of three days (the day of transaction committed or T and two days then on +2 when pay-in, pay-out on the transaction take place) it is SEBI's ardent pursuit of liquidity and transparency that has paid off.'[1]

It is heartening to note here that the transition from T+5 to T+3 to T+2 in a very short time of just over a year of my joining SEBI was achieved without any hiccups, setbacks in traded volumes or in the functioning of the exchanges and intermediaries. These disruptive changes were navigated without stirring up a storm in the marketplace.

Ancillary Reforms

Straight Through Processing (STP)

As mentioned earlier, our primary aim was to reach T+1, which required full automation of the trading cycle. No stone was being left unturned to simultaneously prepare for this even while T+2 was being sorted out. As a precursor to T+1, we introduced STP—a mechanism that automates the end-to-end processing of transactions. In other words, STP is electronic capture and processing of transactions in one pass, from the point of trade initiation to the final settlement. Even T+2 required manual intervention for data entry at some stages, which was not only slowing down the process but also making it prone to errors. STP would reduce manual intervention to zero. So we implemented STP some time in November 2002 on a voluntary basis to test the waters, as also to smoothen the process for implementation of T+2. NSDL was appointed to take the lead on this, and four STP service providers were appointed. If an investor was interested in using STP, he could take the services of one of these service providers. This happened even before RTGS became widespread. However, there were a few technical challenges initially, like non-availability of uninterrupted connectivity, and it was decided to not make STP compulsory for all participants immediately.

The implementation and undertaking of operations on a voluntary basis helped the service providers, as also users, to find solutions to the issues and challenges that came up. These were of two kinds: (a) technical bugs and hitches (b) re-skilling and redeployment of the surplus staff who were providing the manual intervention in the operations. The service providers and users sorted out their issues rather quickly, and a kind of economy and efficiency of operation was achieved.

In fact, the whole idea of STP had come to my mind when I visited the USA officially. One of the engagements during that visit was with the Securities Market Industry Association. During the meeting with the leaders of the industry, a presentation was made by an Indian businessman settled in the USA. The US industry proposed to implement STP by 2008, at a cost of over US$ 8 billion.

I now wanted to implement STP as a compulsory measure. So a consultation paper was put up on our website, and comments invited. Some comments came; they were read and notes taken. The brokers' delegation met me on this issue and explained their problems. The senior officers at SEBI had already had a couple of rounds of discussions with them, and had sorted out the minor issues that were raised. During the meeting, I noted the brokers' apprehensions, of (a) expenses on upgradation of technology and (b) re-skilling or redeployment of staff as a consequence of redundancies.

We then organized a seminar on the subject to meet all the market participants as a group. The only real and genuine issue was non-availability of Internet connectivity, especially for individuals, and particularly in far-flung areas. All the companies had connectivity. The brokers' head offices were only in the metro centres, and they were in any case trading electronically and making use of computer-to-computer link software (CTCL). So making STP compulsory for corporate trade would not be challenged. However, after the seminar I felt a bit hesitant. While going down to my car, I had a couple of mid-size broking company heads walking alongside. They said they were going to implement STP whether SEBI mandates it or not. It would save them at least their runner costs—runners used to carry the contracts to customers—and make operations error-free. I had no hesitation left now. Next day, I got instructions issued for compulsory STP for all corporate trades. Thus it was that in July 2004, STP was made mandatory for institutional investors alone. I understand this continues till date, even though many individual traders too are using STP for all trades.

Other Areas

'Trade for Trade'

There were about 1,600 companies which still did not have their shares in demat format, and appropriate steps had to be taken to bring trading in their shares too in line with T+2. Settlement of trades in the securities of these companies was taken out of the normal settlement and was settled separately on 'Trade for Trade' basis, which, of course, could not be T+2. This decision had two impacts: (a) it took the thorns out of the normal settlement system and (b) it encouraged further dematerialization.

Automatic Disablement of Terminals, etc.

Measures such as strict real-time monitoring of broker positions, dynamic upfront margin systems and automatic disablement of broker terminals were also implemented. These acted as a curt reminder to the brokers to take appropriate action in case of insufficient funds. By their very nature, FIIs dealt in huge volumes in individual trades. For such large volumes, even a day's difference meant a huge opportunity for cost reduction. Hence, FIIs were permitted to earn proportionate interest on the amount lost in the process. A significant but manageable issue raised by brokers was to do away with the issue of physical contract notes. The reduction in days was going to keep them busy and electronic contract notes were far more convenient. The exchange bye-laws were modified accordingly to enable this.

A Dream Fulfilled

We were the first country to move to T+2, barring Israel. Israel had T+1, but it also had the advantage of being a smaller geography. India is a sub-continental geography and has a complex demography. It also has a large number of brokers, intermediaries and investors. Interestingly, Canada, Japan, Singapore and Australia, all have T+3 even today. The UK and most of the European markets have moved to T+2 only recently in January 2015, after having learned their lessons in the 2008 financial crisis. We were also the first country to introduce STP. This was a technological breakthrough in its own right.

Amidst all the loud voices, the investors were silently happy, and that is what mattered to me most. For them, T+2 and STP were a bonus, an unexpected gift. While travelling by local train my colleague, Ramesh, once heard an investor say, 'Hey, this T+2 is fantastic. We get money or securities in two days after trade.' This was heartening, considering it was coming from a common investor.

The best part about trying out new ideas is that often they bring benefits not considered earlier. Who would have thought that our endeavour to make the securities markets more efficient would also prove to be a game changer for another industry, banking, and also benefit a host of people not in the securities markets? While RTGS would have been introduced sooner or later, our ambitious target of T+2 definitely pushed it to sooner rather than later. T+2 also helped in ensuring smooth trade settlement even in the face of volatile events, when markets went up and down substantially, by between 5 per cent and 20 per cent.

In the end, all our efforts gave a tremendous fillip to SEBI's image on the international as well as domestic stage. SEBI had become a globally respected regulator. Our respect as a proactive regulator, which does not wait for scams to bring changes, went up a notch higher.

A Dream Outstanding

We could not implement T+1 at the time, as it required an almost fully automated system, 100 per cent penetration of RTGS and complete demat of securities. On these technical grounds alone we had to defer its implementation. But these bottlenecks can be managed now, and somebody needs to take an unpopular stand and fight it out, the way it was done more than a decade ago for T+2. In my opinion, in the current times even a two-day gap poses a significant operational risk, and a truly liquid asset must not take more than a day to liquidate. T+1 further reduces the risk of counterparty insolvency and brings savings in operational costs as processes become fully automated. The excuse that cheque payments continue to be widely prevalent, particularly in tier-I and tier-II cities, will forever be made to thwart T+1. What is required is to make a resolve to fulfil a dream and then push others along towards it. I strongly feel that SEBI once again stands at the threshold of a brilliant opportunity to take the lead to further minimize operational risks.

Minimising IPO Time and Delisting

Making IPOs time-bound

Initial public offerings (IPOs) have a special significance in any stock market. For companies, it is an avenue to raise resources. It also makes them answerable to the public at large for everything it does from then on. For investors, it brings the excitement of having a new product in the market to be assessed, evaluated and invest their surplus resources in. For stock exchanges, it means a new revenue source. However, for a considerable period of time, IPOs were being mismanaged, much to the frustration of investors. Here is what was happening: The SEBI Act was passed in the early nineties. The IPO market was then controlled by the Controller of Capital Issues (CCI), which observed a merit-based regime. From a corner office in the finance ministry in North Block, the office of the CCI decided everything—whether a company can raise funds, the type of instrument (equity, debt etc.) it could issue, their quantity, price, premium, rate of interest/dividend, duration of the instrument, and the like. Once all these parameters were decided, the usual process followed—the issue opened at the pre-decided price, interested investors subscribed, the issue closed, proportionate allotment of shares/debentures and refund of excess money was calculated, physical certificates and refund demand drafts dispatched by post, the exchanges approached and final listing of the shares done. However, between all these processes, there were problems aplenty.

Pricing of issue

To begin with, there would often be a huge mismatch between the price fixed for the IPO shares and the price the management of company and investors expected it to be. This was because the price of an issue was decided unilaterally by the CCI and was not driven by market-based valuation. During boom time, issues would be underpriced, and during a bear phase they would be overpriced. Naturally, if during boom time an issue is underpriced, it would be oversubscribed, which would result in a whole lot of refunds. This brought a set of problems.

The grey market

The process of issue of shares also took a lot of time. From the opening of the issue till allotment of shares and refund of money, the time lapse would be as much as 120 days, i.e., approximately four months, after which the listing would take place. In fact, the listing often took place a month after the allotment of shares or refund of money. During this month, share certificates and refund demand drafts would be dispatched, and the exchanges' approval taken for listing (exchanges used to take as many as fifteen days to consent to a listing).

This entire wait was obviously very frustrating for investors. In addition, during the thirty-day time period between the allotment of shares and their listing, the investors who were allotted shares (this would be known from the exchanges) would get impatient and start speculating on the price at which the shares would list on the exchange. The shares being not yet listed and the physical share certificates not necessarily having been received, a sort of (grey) speculative market developed during the time gap between post-allotment and pre-listing. Thirty days were also enough for macro- as well as microeconomic factors related to a stock to change, providing further impetus for speculators to heighten the grey market. The investors whom the shares were allotted to would start trading them informally outside the BSE building, not waiting for the shares to be listed on the exchanges. Obviously, such informal trading was undesirable on many counts. It bred speculation, leading to fraud and unaccounted secondary market transactions.

Exchanges declining to list

At times there were even cases of exchanges refusing to list a stock, even after the allotment and refund process of the IPO was complete. This was a huge waste of effort, money and time for all the market participants, not to mention a disappointment for the investors who would lose the opportunity to own and trade the shares that had been allotted to them. This happened because the company, when filing for the IPO, would take approvals from the CCI and/or SEBI, but was not required to get the 'go-ahead' from the exchanges before commencing the IPO process. And the exchanges took their decision on listing (or not listing) a scrip only after allotment was done.

Theft of share certificates and demand drafts

Then there were other reported malpractices taking place between the opening of an issue and listing of shares. Till about 1996, there was no concept of dematerialization of shares. All share allotment took place with physical share certificates only. Now, these share certificates would be dispatched through Indian Post, and sometimes the postal department became a breeding ground for a huge racket. There were instances when, at Nariman Point, Mumbai, arguably the financial nerve centre of the entire country at the time, physical share certificates on their way to being delivered to the allottee by the postal department were stolen. The envelopes would be torn open, the share certificates taken out and sold to other investors by unscrupulous persons. Thus, share certificates in many cases never reached the intended buyer, and when the original buyer applied to the company for duplicate share certificates, he would get the news, to his shock and dismay, that the shares have 'apparently' been sold off by him.

Other issues

Another prevalent practice was that investors subscribing to shares in an IPO had to pay the entire subscription amount upfront. And when the excess amount, if any, had to be refunded to them, 'demand drafts' would be issued in their names and dispatched through Indian Post (these were the pre-electronic-transfer days). Here too, unscrupulous elements, at times with the connivance of the postal department, played mischief. They would steal the demand drafts and deposit them in a fake bank account opened in the name of the investor mentioned on the DD. It helped the mischief mongers that the demand draft mentioned only the name of the investor and no bank account number. In those days a bank account could be opened in anyone's name, particularly in cooperative banks, as there were no stringent KYC norms (no photographs or photo IDs, etc., were required).

The result was that SEBI used to have one lakh to two lakh complaints pending at any point in time, and expectedly, most of the complaints would be IPO-related—about non-receipt of share certificates and/or non-receipt of refund.

Reformation

After enactment of the SEBI Act in 1992, multiple ways were tried to streamline the whole IPO process and make it more investor-friendly. Some of the experiments worked, some did not, and some worked but partially.

First, the merit-based regime gave way to a disclosure-based regime, and IPO pricing was no longer dependent on the CCI. Companies could decide the issue price on their own, based on their estimate of market demand and supply. This was a welcome change, but companies going for IPOs started misusing this freedom. The issues were usually overpriced, resulting in a loss to investors on the date of listing itself. In good times, overpricing also furthered overselling and oversubscription, resulting in the huge grey market before listing. Eventually, it was the small investors who were at the losing end.

To counter the problem and make IPO pricing more transparent, SEBI introduced the book-building process (a process by which investors bid for the shares at a price within the given band and thus build the book of subscription) from 1999 onwards. The book-building guidelines were introduced by SEBI in 1995. However, while book building became an accepted practice in the market for private placement of debt securities, it did not apply to the public issue market, despite the regulatory framework being in place. Only in 1999 was the book-building exercise conducted for the first time for an IPO, and during that year five IPOs were made using the book-building route. India is the only country where the entire book is kept transparent during the bidding period. The greatest advantage was that qualified investors, who have experience in valuations and pricing of equities, were the ones contributing to arriving at an almost correct price for the equity on offer. The small investors or retail investors rode on the expertise of these qualified investors. Thus, this method of book building, unique to India, went on to be a great success in the due course. In this process, the pricing of an IPO was decided by market forces, except that there was a price band—the upper and the lower limits of the issue price—set by the company beforehand. This was a significant improvement on what used to happen earlier. I improvised on the book-building process further during my tenure.

The time between the opening of an issue and the allotment of shares and refund of money was reduced to forty-five days from over 120 days earlier. Now the opening of an issue, subscription to shares by investors and closing of the issue— i.e., the bidding process, took only fifteen days. The allotment process—calculation of allotment of shares, dispatch of physical certificates/refund of money and listing of shares—was given another thirty days to be completed. If T was the date of closure of an issue, T+30 was the outer limit for the listing of shares. By 1998–99, these timelines were brought down to three days and fifteen days, respectively. Basically, the bidding (which was now happening through book building) reduced to three days, and the entire allotment process reduced to fifteen days. However even these fifteen days were sufficient for the growth of a strong grey market, and nothing prevented exchanges from refusing to list shares even after the allotment was done.

Additionally, as the concept of dematerialization of shares had been introduced, a shift from physical shares to 'demat' shares was gradually taking place, although it was not made compulsory for investors,. The switch to 'demat' also eliminated the theft of share certificates, as mentioned earlier. However, since dematerialization of shares had still not been made compulsory (either in the primary or secondary markets) the problems arising from theft of physical share certificates continued, albeit in lower numbers.

To overcome the problem of money refund, SEBI experimented with the concept of 'stock invest', which essentially required an investor subscribing to the IPO shares to deposit the requisite amount in a bank account and to generate proof to that effect. The particular account would only be debited if that investor was allotted shares. This practice did away with the requirement of refunds. But unscrupulous investors found a way around this too. Investors would not deposit the entire amount (required for the number of shares subscribed for) into the account but only a fraction of the amount instead. They would then have an arrangement with the bank to generate false proofs of their deposit of the full amount. So 'stock invest', being not very efficient, was not popular and was later scrapped altogether. While the book-building process reduced the unnecessary oversubscriptions, which in turn reduced the administrative burden of refund of money and thus the related frauds, there was yet no proper substitute for refund of money other than in physical form. Electronic money transfers were unheard of then.

In short, by the time I joined SEBI, things had improved from earlier, but there was tremendous room for improvement still, in areas such as the book-building process, curbing the grey market between closure of an issue and its listing, taking exchanges into confidence before an IPO, complete dematerialization of shares and doing away with refund of money in physical mode.

Remedies

While internationally book building was always through a 'closed book', India was the only market where the entire book, including the QIB portion, was open—anyone intending to know the subscription levels in any IPO could see the degree of interest at various price points on the online terminals of BSE and NSE. This transparency was sometimes going against the interests of the issuers and the merchant bankers, because if there was lack of interest from QIBs owing to the price band, there would be no interest shown in the last minute either by retail investors. The issue would then fail, or the merchant banker would have to underwrite a large portion of the issue and bear a loss on listing (which was a more probable scenario).

There was tremendous pressure from merchant bankers to keep the book building a closed process. That would give them room to create an artificial demand in case the IPO was not taking off. Since book building was an open process and investors could clearly see the subscription amount and quantity in real time during the three days when the offer was open, the merchant bankers were not able to create any artificial situation around the issue. This was the extent of transparency we had. Although it made several people unhappy, it is a matter of pride for us that till date the concept of an open bidding process for an IPO exists only in India in the entire world.

Another step was taken with regard to the book-building process. Earlier, the price band was to be disclosed in the Red Hearing Prospectus (RHP) itself and the issue would open after about a month. This gave sufficient time to mischievous parties to play on investor sentiment by planting news that influenced investor judgement on the issue and its price. We permitted companies to disclose their price band closer to the opening date to protect their IPOs from getting affected by vested interests.

Next, I focused on shortening the entire issue process— from the opening of an issue to its closure, allotment and dispatch of shares/refund and the final listing. To facilitate this SEBI made it compulsory for anyone subscribing to an IPO to have a 'demat' account into which shares allotted to that person would be transferred. That did away with the inconvenience of dispatching physical certificates, which reduced the number of days in which the subscribers got their shares. Then we brought in the concept of obtaining a prior clearance from the exchanges for an issue before its opening. Exchanges had to give their in-principle approval to the listing at the prospectus stage itself. This further reduced the uncertainty about exchange approval for listing of the shares issued. This too reduced the time limit required for listing.

To shorten the timeline, we had to shorten the money collection and refund process, which involved significant time and effort. At that time, in 2003 there was no RTGS, and there was no electronic transfer of money. The securities markets were ahead of banking technology. The banking sector was still catching up. We could not immediately make both collections and refunds electronic. However, we managed to put pressure to initiate the process of making electronic payments to applicants. We made it mandatory that all refunds shall be made directly into an individual's bank account only. No more would there be the bother of sending demand drafts of refunds. The entire refund process now became smoother.

All these efforts reduced the time from closure of the issue to actual listing of shares from T+15 to T+12 and finally to T+6, which continues till date. Within six days of closure of an issue, the stocks get listed and start trading. As intended, this killed the pre-listing grey market completely and led to better price discovery, as listing happened quickly. Further, the compulsory 'demat' accounts for shares and direct refunds into individual accounts completely eliminated the transition frauds.

In between, we also brought in the innovation of using secondary market techniques for primary market offerings. What happens in the secondary market is that sellers put in their bids to sell a certain number of shares at a certain price, and buyers put in their bids to buy a certain number of shares at a certain price. When the price and quantity match, trade takes place. All this happens on the broker's terminal, and there are no lengthy procedures to follow or paperwork involved. So we thought of using this mechanism for the primary markets too.

The innovation was that the issuer of shares (equivalent to the seller in the secondary market) would seek bids for his bulk shares at a certain price range (just as in book building). The subscribers (equivalent to the buyers in the primary markets) would mention their share quantity and price (within the price range). Thereafter, the allocation of shares would be calculated as usual by the system, and shares allotted to the relevant buyers. We wanted to do a quick delivery-vs-payment settlement just the way it happens in the secondary markets—do the price discovery, pay across the table instantly (RTGS) and get your shares in 'demat' format the same day. So the aim was to bring even IPOs under a T+2 settlement regime.

In the secondary markets, every transaction is backed by the settlement guarantee fund (SGF) or Clearing Corporation (CC) of the exchanges, which ensures that no transaction fails, as the SGF or CC takes the counterparty risk. However, the SGF and CC refused to take the counterparty risk under a similar mechanism for primary market transactions, as the amounts involved in any IPO were huge and required altogether different settlement guarantee calculations. Then there were objections against this mechanism from other sections involved in the IPO, like the sub-brokers and registrars, as they stood to lose their fees. However, with countrywide RTGS in place, the mechanism stated above is possible for the primary market. Subscriber accounts can be blocked for the amounts the subscribers apply for, similar to what happens in online secondary market transactions.

In fact, when Google got listed in the USA in August 2004, Google did it through the book-building process using this secondary market mechanism. Global Media reported that Google was the first company in the world to do this. A few days after the issue, an article in the *Financial Times*[2] said Google was not the first company to use the secondary market mechanism for a public offer, and indeed it was already being used in India!

Today, IPOs in India happen seamlessly, without any hiccups. And I can proudly claim that there are three broad things that SEBI did in 2002–05 to lay the foundation for this. It implemented a price-discovery-enhancing mechanism, reduced IPO timelines substantially and, finally, pioneered the use of technology to eliminate fraud in allotment of physical share certificates and refund of excess money, virtually killing the rampant grey market.

7

THE STT SAGA

Upfront Taxation on Share Transactions

The first two years of my tenure were spent focusing on bringing in reforms like T+2, STP, fast-tracking quasi-judicial proceedings, and letting the hurricane of Scam 2001 calm down. It is only in the latter part of my tenure that I started making the rounds of investor forums across the world. I went to Singapore, Hong Kong, New York, London and other international financial centres to market the India growth story to FIIs. After all, the Indian capital market was competitively efficacious and was growing by leaps and bounds. It provided ample opportunities to investors to profit from the continuing economic reforms in the country. And I was also aware that our presence at the global forums was low-key compared with that of other countries.

I wanted to send out a message saying how strong we were. In 2004 the UPA came to power and P. Chidambaram became the finance minister, and therefore also a member (as India's representative) on the Board of Governors of World Bank (WB), Asian Development Bank (ADB), IMF, and the like. He made it a point to be there at all global forums, like the WB, ADB and IMF meetings. He raised the level of India's participation in investor forums by attending them himself, and SEBI became an inseparable part thereof. Consequently, my presence too increased at various global investor forums. As we will see, this turned out to be quite helpful, and the practice is continued even now.

The Taxation Issue Faced by FIIs

For the first global investor meet, an informal forum with fund managers in New York, the FM asked me to join him too. I was a little tied up with some pressing matters and tried to wriggle out of it. But he was not pleased by my reluctance. So I decided to join the New York and London forums and travelled there just for a day each. These forums were attended by many investors, FIIs and some big broking houses like Merrill Lynch and Morgan Stanley. After the formal talks, there were one-to-one meetings, where two groups of fund managers focused on the subject of taxation. One issue regarded the capital gains tax that FIIs were required to pay on their share purchases and sales in the Indian stock markets. They did not have an issue with the tax per se, but they had complaints about its timing. Capital gains are taxed, as the name suggests, when a gain is made, and gain is known when a transaction is complete. The completion of a transaction may happen after a gap of many years, and the exact tax liability remains unknown till well after completion of the transaction and assessment of liability by the assessing officer. This is owing to the fact that there is generally a gap between filing the income tax return and the assessment.

In a typical transaction, the FIIs buying/selling shares in Indian markets through Indian brokers complete their usual Indian tax return formalities for the year at the end of the year, pay their self-assessed liability (on a tax consultant's advice) and go on about their normal business. (It is to be noted that no tax was required to be paid at the time of transaction). After a few years, when assessment is made, capital gains tax liability (in most cases additional) springs up on these FIIs. This put FIIs in a bit of a jeopardy.

FIIs are institutions executing securities transactions on behalf of customers or investors who are the persons liable to pay tax. But most of the time, these customers having cashed out and gone, it becomes well-nigh impossible for FIIs to recover, after several years, the tax levied on them by the Indian Tax Authorities from their end investors. Since the investors represented by these FIIs have closed their transactions with the FIIs, made their profits and moved out, there was no way that FIIs could deduct the tax liabilities from their payments to these investors. This was because the actual (not estimated) liability was not determined before the end customers closed their transactions with the FIIs. And even if these FIIs went back to those investors to recover the tax, the investors would not oblige them, leaving the FIIs to bear the tax burden.

The suggestion towards a solution was to levy something upfront, at the time of the transaction. The FIIs would then deduct the tax liability from their investors and then pay the Indian tax authorities. We heard them out and came back to India, determined to solve the problem. Later, I also got to know that there was a number of pending legal cases in India which were pertaining to such tax issues between FIIs and the investors they represented.

Until I started attending these forums myself, I never got to know about these taxation issues. What the FII representatives told me was a common complaint at many such global investor forums. Even domestic institutional investors (DII) in India had the same complaint. Now, since the FM himself was present at most of these forums, he too understood the problem and started exploring ways to tackle it.

The Idea of STT

The thought of introducing this upfront taxation in the form of Securities Transaction Tax (STT)—a charge of a certain percentage of the transaction amount at the time of buy/sell, as a replacement for long-term capital gains tax—came up. Where the shares were held for less than a year, since STT had been paid, capital gains tax would be reduced to 10 per cent from the earlier 33 per cent, it was mulled. This would promote long-term holding and discourage short-term speculation. For example, if an investor buys shares for Rs 100, then he has to pay STT of (let's say @ 0.01 per cent, only for the sake of example) of Rs 0.10 upfront. Now, if the investor sells the stocks after more than a year at Rs 110, the entire gain of Rs 10 goes tax-free. But if he sells it within a year for Rs 110, then there will a tax of 10 per cent on the gain of Rs 10, which means a short-term capital gains tax of Re 1, in addition to the STT charged. The STT similarly applied to the selling of shares. The STT would remain unchanged even if a share transaction resulted in a loss to the seller/buyer.

In economics, such a levy is called a 'Tobin Tax'. This was proposed by a Nobel Prize–winning American macroeconomist, James Tobin, in the seventies, with the intention of putting the brakes on short-term currency speculations in the Latin American countries. This concept had its fair share of critics, who argued that the tax increased costs uniformly for everyone, irrespective of whether they made a loss or profit in their currency conversion transactions. Eventually, this meant that the cost of transacting in the market would go up, and may make the market uncompetitive, shifting trades to other markets with lower costs. The verdict on STT by some of the well-known Indian economists was similar.

To me, however, STT provided many benefits. It was easier to implement and administer, and a much cleaner and efficient instrument than the tax system of the time for collecting taxes (almost zero-cost) from the financial markets, as the collection would be centralized through the stock exchanges. I also felt that if the right percentage of STT was applied, it would in all likelihood increase tax collections from the capital market—the investors, intermediaries and speculators, some of whom were notorious for blatant tax evasion by exploiting the loopholes in the existing tax system. Third, STT would incentivize long-term holding of shares and act as a deterrent to unscrupulous speculators and short-term traders. Internationally too, many markets like the US, UK, Belgium, France, Singapore and Hong Kong had the concept of such a 'financial transaction tax', and some of them had been successfully implementing it for decades. The appropriate rate of tax, though, would not increase the cost of transactions significantly. From my point of view, for the Indian stock markets, STT was an idea whose time had come.

Getting STT into Budget 2004

At the time of preparing Budget 2004, the finance minister, Chidambaram, who had obtained inputs from other sources, in addition to SEBI's recommendation too, asked my personal opinion on the matter of STT. I fully supported the tax. I then went on to emphasize the advantages of STT to the FM, even offering to ensure that the stock exchanges would pay the entire STT amount collected to the tax department without charging any administration costs for its collection. In contrast, the administration costs of the Income Tax department in collecting capital gains tax was significant. I gave the FM some rough estimates by mentally multiplying the current volume of transactions with some rough rates, projecting future numbers also on the basis of the growing rate of increase in the volume of transactions. We spoke for a while, and the FM finally seemed convinced about the idea.

It was agreed to introduce STT in the upcoming budget of July 2004. As far as the rate was concerned, we did not discuss the specifics, but I remember requesting him to keep it nominal. I thought it was a closed chapter and that everything was going to be fine. Then, on 8 July 2004, when the budget was presented by the FM, the STT was introduced at 2 per cent. This rate was anything but nominal, and I had no role in fixing this. However, I was sure of a backlash from the broking community and, eventually, upheavals in the market.

Fortunately, when the budget was presented the markets were closed, and we were spared the immediate knee-jerk reaction from the market to this high rate of proposed STT. However, there was a furore in the evening on all the news channels, and everybody expected the markets to collapse the next day.

I realized that the markets could react very badly the next day unless some preventive measures were taken. So the next day I woke up earlier than usual, got ready quickly and by 6.30 a.m. was on my way to the office. I also asked the other team members in my office to rush to work as there were only three hours left for the markets to open and even less time for us to do something to prevent a possible market fall. I also fixed for the brokers' association representatives of both BSE and NSE to meet me immediately.

On my way to the office, I got a call on my mobile phone from the finance minister, from Delhi. He too seemed very worried, so I told him about the action I had already taken by calling the brokers' association heads. 'I will tell them that whatever the rate of STT, it will be applied only after it is approved by Parliament, and the Finance Act signed by the President of India and notified, which is a few months away, so why panic now. They may calm down, they may not, but I will have to work out something with them,' I tried to reassure him.

I also told him, 'I will ask the brokers to make a representation to you to reconsider the STT rate. From your side, if you can issue a statement before the markets open, that you have received the representation from the brokers and are looking into the matter . . . Please also add that in any case the STT will be applicable only after it is approved by Parliament, signed by the

President of India and a notification issued, all of which is going to take time and will not happen in this Parliament session.'

This seemed to be the sensible thing to do, and the FM agreed.

Meanwhile, as I reached the office, I noticed that the brokers' representatives too had arrived. Expectedly, they were angry and expressed their rage at the proposed STT rate. Such a high rate was unfair and the market would collapse unless STT was taken back or the rates drastically reduced, they said.

I calmed them down and gave them a solution, 'Look, I have already spoken to the finance minister. You make a representation to the FM with your demands. I will send it to him immediately and the FM will go on record to say that he has received your representation and will consider the same.'

The representation was drafted immediately and faxed to the FM's office. We managed to do all this before the markets opened for the day, and when the markets did it was business as usual. In fact, on that day the BSE Sensex closed approximately 180 points up and NSE Nifty roughly 36 points up from their previous close!

Revision in the STT Rate

Next day, when I met the FM in Delhi to discuss the next steps on STT, he discovered that I had not been consulted on the fixing of the STT rate.

The FM was angry and anxious with the turn of events. We spoke for some time on the possible rate options. Finally, the rate was decided at 0.15 per cent on each transaction, half to be paid by the buyer and half by the seller, or 0.075 per cent each. Before the new rates could be announced the situation got a bit political too, but that was expected.

To soothe the situation, the new STT rates (of 0.075 per cent each for buyer and seller) were announced finally in the next couple of days in Parliament, and eventually STT came into effect from 1 October 2004.

In general, we found a lot of supporters for STT too, especially from the financial advisor community. 'The pundits, who were predicting that the Securities Transaction Tax (STT) would dry up trading volumes in the short run, were stumped on Friday by the soaring Sensex. The benchmark index shot up 91 points—its highest since July 9, a day after the union budget,' said one media report.[1]

Vallabh Bhansali, chairman, Enam Securities, said, 'The introduction of turnover tax is a welcome move even for the FIIs. This will help to reduce speculative activity in the market. The fall in volumes is only short-term, as one section of the market participant is likely to take a hit. However, going ahead volumes will pick up.'[2]

'Implementation of STT will have no major impact in the market . . . The trimming of short-term capital gains (STCG) tax and the complete abolition of long-term capital gains (LTCG) tax will be a positive step for the market on a long-term basis,' said Krishnamurthy Vijayan, CEO, JM Mutual Fund.[3]

'The market is clear about the tax and the payment mechanism. There was no indecision in the market that can be attributed to the transaction tax,' said a broker. STT is proving to be a lot better than many had expected. 'STT leaves no scope for tax avoidance and is easy to administer. All categories of investors/traders will be taxed uniformly,' said another media report,[4] a month after STT became effective. Still another media report congratulated the FM for daring to contemplate a radical proposal for revenue mobilization with his STT.

Over the last decade, STT has spread its benefits in multiple ways, made tax collection easy and hassle-free for the government, eased out the tax issues faced by FIIs and domestic institutional investors, and acted as a deterrent for fictitious trades by creating a trail, thus helping retail investors and leading to market efficacy.

However, there has been some misuse of the provisions of STT in the capital markets. Some misguided elements have tried to convert their black money into white through the capital market route under the shadow of STT.

Eternal vigilance is the fundamental principle of regulation. Malicious economic agents are always on the lookout for kinks in the regulatory framework to use them for their misconducts.

Today, STT has blended so well into the entire stock market functioning that it seems strange that its introduction had to be forced. Similarly, today, the fact that long-term capital gains (gains on shares held for more than a year), where STT is paid, is exempt from tax is so taken for granted that people forget that there was a time when this was not the case and that some persons actually fought for it.

In the budget for the year 2018–19, Long Term Capital Gains tax has been reintroduced albeit of a low rate with a grand fathering provision. Hopefully this measure will help in plugging the loop holes and garnering some additional revenue for the government.

8

THE DELICATE ART OF PERSUASION, THE FINE ART OF PERSEVERANCE

Ensuring SEBI's Financial Autonomy

Financial autonomy is one of the fundamental pillars of strength for a regulator. If a regulator has to depend on the government for its financial resources, its ability to act independently is jeopardized. Financially dependent regulators willy-nilly become subservient to the bureaucracy in the government, not to mention having to kowtow to its political masters. I had therefore committed myself to ensuring the financial autonomy of SEBI right from the commencement of my tenure.

Regulators like RBI, SEBI, Insurance Regulatory and Development Authority (IRDA) and Pension Fund Regulatory and Development Authority (PFRDA), in particular, play a critical role in ensuring that industries like financial services operate efficiently and serve the best interest of all stakeholders. Considering the criticality of the role of these regulators, it is important that their operations are conducted effectively, transparently and neutrally. This objective is constantly under threat because multiple forces like the government, politicians, heavyweight industrialists, industry lobbies, intermediaries and even the media are always trying to influence the regulators. It is a regulator's relation with the government—among all the above-mentioned influencers—that is the most conflict-ridden; in the case of financial sector regulators, while the government is interested in the good health of industries and appoints the chief and other top functionaries of the regulator, it also participates as a player through public sector enterprises (PSUs). Regulators, though created to function independently, often struggle to strike a balance between bringing in effective policies and giving an ear to the influencers.

In a Parliamentary democracy, regulators cannot be totally independent. However, it is imperative to reduce the extent of external influence on their decision making. One of the fundamental factors leading to interference by the government in the functioning of regulators is their dependence on government funding for their sustenance. For a regulator, financial independence can be a significant step towards achieving independence.

The SEBI Act of 1992 allowed SEBI to have independent sources of revenue. From 1988 to 1992, SEBI as an administrative authority was in set-up mode and was funded by the development bank, IDBI. Subsequently, the government granted it an interest-free loan, to be repaid in instalments. Other than what brought SEBI income were the annual fees from intermediaries except brokers. There was other meagre income flowing from registration of exchanges, depositories, merchant bankers and the like. I felt this flow of incomes would not ensure SEBI's financial autonomy for even its current needs and what if it were to increase its manpower, modernize, expand its infrastructure, offices, buildings and technology, and also invest in building capacities on an ongoing basis. The biggest intermediary, the broking community, remained outside SEBI's purview as a potential revenue source. The issue of SEBI charging brokers a fee had been the subject of battle for a long time—for over twelve years, and without any resolution. In fact, Scam 1992 got exposed because the exchanges were shut in protest against the proposed levy of broker fees by SEBI. My tenure came to be destined to give me this wonderful opportunity to play my part and see this matter turn in SEBI's favour. I believed that this would ensure our financial autonomy forever. But first, let's step back to see what the matter was really about.

Levy of fees from brokers brought three benefits, intended and unintended:

a.   It exposed the Harshad Mehta scam of 1992 and consequently cleaned up the system.
b.   It paved the way for all regulators to levy fees, as it established that the fees levied by SEBI were not tax and that SEBI was entitled to levy them.
c.   It made SEBI self-sufficient.

Historically, the SEBI Act of 1992 conferred widespread powers on the regulator. Among its first steps was to mandate registration of securities market brokers with SEBI. Till then, the brokers were registered only with the stock exchanges. The reforms under the SEBI act were intended to rein in the brokers a bit and to facilitate SEBI to have better control over their activities. Now that SEBI was also to provide a plethora of services to all market intermediaries (including brokers), a registration fee and a turnover-based fee were proposed to be charged. All hell broke loose. Quite naturally, the brokers reacted strongly.

Initially, the fee was a fixed one, but it was later revised to a mix of fixed fee and a certain percentage of the broker's annual turnover. This was done to accommodate the brokers' demands. Yet there were strikes demanding complete withdrawal of any fee on them, and trading remained shut for days. Finally, a committee was set up under the chairmanship of R.S. Bhatt (founder of UTI and a pioneer of the mutual fund industry in India) to suggest an effective method for calculating broker fees, and this committee recommended something similar to what had been proposed by SEBI. Consequently, SEBI made registration mandatory for brokers around the end of 1992 and notified the fee structure. Please note this was also the time when the Harshad Mehta scam was happening.

The furious brokers took legal recourse and filed cases in various courts, including multiple writ petitions in many high courts across the country. It was estimated that there were over 400 such cases in different courts in different geographies. The cases continued for almost over a decade and finally reached the Supreme Court. Only in February 2001 did the apex court pass its judgment, clearly stating, inter alia, that SEBI was very much within its rights to charge a fee and should be paid the fees with interest of 18 per cent on arrears. It, however, advised some modifications in the calculation of turnover, based on the recommendations of the R.S. Bhatt committee. SEBI accordingly issued a circular detailing the procedure for computation of fees and demanded the money from the brokers. The agitated brokers once again found themselves pushed to the corner, and the markets were in chaos for a few days.

In the meantime, SEBI held back its approvals for change of ownership, including change in the structure of a broking entity from a proprietary concern to a partnership or corporation, until the fee arrears were paid with interest, as ordained by the SC. Thus, any approval by SEBI in respect to brokers was delayed, and came with the condition of their paying up the broker fees.

The Right Thing to Do

When I joined, the situation was something like this. The brokers knew they had to eventually pay up, but they had differences with us on the matter of computation of fees. The interest rate of 18 per cent on arrears was the biggest bone of contention. Since both the fee and interest rates had been blessed by the Supreme Court, their reduction was not possible.

There was no clear solution yet in sight to the deadlock between SEBI and the brokers. The brokers' association's argument was that since the Supreme Court, in its judgment in January 2001 on the issue of turnover fee, had emphasized the rationality of the fee and did not mention any interest on fee arrears, SEBI should be flexible and take into account the ground realities while arriving at the final amount to be paid. I started talking to the brokers and negotiated hard. I told them it was not possible to reduce any outstanding fee but we could look at doing something about the interest part. After prolonged and protracted discussions the brokers finally agreed to pay the full fees with arrears, but with no interest. They were actually playing smart. The profits generated by the accumulated pending fees of over a decade was enough to take care of the fee they had to pay. They were actually not shelling out anything extra. The key point of negotiation was the interest on arrears. We too felt the interest rate of 18 per cent was atrociously high, when fixed deposits and lending rates had come down to below 10 per cent. But we could not reduce the rate as it had been sanctified by the Supreme Court. We wanted to waive a significant part of what brokers had to pay, which, in effect, would mean charging a lower rate of interest on arrears. SEBI would still receive a substantial amount.

I had the option to now let the issue drag on or accept the brokers' offer and close the chapter. I wanted SEBI to be financially independent forever, and felt this was our best chance. If I could successfully close this issue it would set a precedent, and regular payment of broker fees would become the norm. Along with the recurring fees coming in from various intermediaries, this would make SEBI financially independent forever. The potential revenue to be waived was also substantial. It was close to half the fees plus interest. In my opinion, the long-term gain from doing this far exceeded this short-term loss, which was not even in sight. But this meant being answerable to the likes of the Comptroller and Auditor General of India and the Central

Vigilance Commission, the risk of government intervention and later, politicization of the issue. These swords perennially hang over the neck of every public servant. A progressive decision made with good intent could be perceived as a 'wrong' move, and then all the swords could come down, vying for one's blood.

After much deliberation, I chose the option to settle, as I felt that was the right thing to do. I had become the chairman to close contentious issues and not to consign or keep them in cold storage. Given the way we were going currently, we would never resolve the matter. I got the SEBI board to agree to this. Now the two directly affected parties, SEBI and the brokers, agreed to the proposal. However, this was just the tip of the iceberg. Many more people had to be convinced and persuaded to agree.

CAG of India

The Comptroller and Auditor General (CAG) of India, a Constitutional authority, is one of the most powerful positions in the Indian bureaucracy; it is equivalent to that of a judge in the Supreme Court. It has widespread powers to conduct audit of government (state and central) expenses and receipts. The companies owned or substantially financed by the government also fall under its ambit. Unlike private sector statutory audits, a CAG audit extends to cover the propriety and prudence of financial decisions too. The CAG is the financial conscience-keeper of the tax payer's money. SEBI was very much under its purview, and I clearly did not want to be on the wrong side of CAG.

At the time, the position was held by a distinguished public servant, V.N. Kaul (Padma Bhushan awardee in 2014). The Maharashtra unit of CAG was first approached. It rejected our request outright, on the grounds that interest of 18 per cent had accrued, and in its view no authority except Parliament could waive it. This came as a blow to all of us. So I decided to approach the CAG in Delhi directly. I sought an appointment and got one hour to make my case. I managed to convince him. My arguments centred on the fact that since brokers had never agreed to pay interest of 18 per cent, it cannot be taken to have accrued. Further, the dispute had been raging for over twelve years and was not likely to be settled unless there was some give and take. And finally, SEBI would get a huge amount of arrears annually from this move. He was convinced by my arguments. The CAG asked me to write directly to him, covering all the points I had made, which I did. I again met him in Delhi, and this time I got an assurance that an approval was in the offing. Eventually, a few days later, a tacit approval was received in writing. The first milestone was achieved, but the saga wasn't yet over.

CVC—Central Vigilance Commission

Each government department has a vigilance section, which monitors and keeps a strict check on possible corrupt practices at the department. All individual activities of every department come under the direct purview of the CVC. On many matters, CVC follows up on the findings of CAG reports and conducts detailed investigations. The Central Bureau of Investigation (CBI) is the investigating arm of the CVC. The CVC had played a key role in unearthing the palm oil import scam in the nineties.

While the CAG may have given its go-ahead to us purely from the point of view of financial prudence, CVC could have taken note of it independently and could have taken action. That's the reason I decided to take prior approval from it.

By the time I approached the CVC, it had become a multi-member body, with a chief vigilance commissioner as chairman, and two vigilance commissioners as members. Janki Ballabh was a friend from the financial sector. We were contemporaries. When I was chairman at LIC, he had been chairman at State Bank of India. I explained to him in great detail what SEBI was doing in the matter of broker fees. Even though he told me that there was no way the CVC, as a monitoring agency, could approve any action of a public servant in advance, he suggested a way forward that would ensure the transparency of our decision.

Government

If CAG and CVC bring out something accusatory in their reports, the government has to respond. But they had been more or less convinced about our case. If the Opposition made an issue of the matter, the government would have to act, but the CAG and CVC could still stand behind SEBI. The government, being the ultimate authority, had the right to object to our decision, notwithstanding SEBI being an independent regulator. Hence I sought the concurrence of the government too. I approached the minister of finance. He agreed with my arguments and asked me to write him a letter. It took some time, but approval was received. U.K. Sinha, then joint secretary (capital markets division), who become SEBI chairman later, did play a crucial role in getting us the government approval. To close this issue for good, I had to not only get the government but even the Opposition to agree to it. In short, the approval had to be passed in Parliament. All our efforts so far would have fallen flat otherwise. But letting a revenue stream go would have provided a fighting point to the Opposition, resulting in a potential deadlock in Parliament. Nobody would appreciate the fact that the issue was getting resolved after more than a decade. I had found a way out; it was again somewhat tricky and exhausting, but effective.

To be fair, Chidambaram did not take credit for himself in his budget speech and gave SEBI due acknowledgement when he said: 'I am also happy to announce that SEBI has been able to resolve the long-standing issue of broker's fee and brokers may expect an announcement shortly.'

Within a week of this we made an official announcement on the issue, ending the long-drawn battle of nerves between the broking community and SEBI. SEBI came up with a scheme which enabled brokers to pay their fees within a timeline and avail of an 80 per cent rebate in interest liability. Here I must acknowledge the sterling role played by M.S. Sahoo, then CGM in SEBI, later to become WTM and now chairman of the Insolvency and Bankruptcy Board of India (IBBI) in resolving the issue. That year SEBI received the outstanding broker fees, and till date the broker fee continues to be an important revenue source for SEBI, going a long way in ensuring SEBI's unbiased image as a regulator. The corpus SEBI built on the strength of this helped construction of the new SEBI building (SEBI Bhavan) in Bandra-Kurla Complex in Mumbai, and a magnificent seventy-five-acre campus for National Institute of Securities Markets (NISM), all from its own financial resources.

9

BLOODY MONDAY!

Taming the Wild Beast

Every election is a turning point in the life of a nation. The results of the May 2004 general elections to the Lok Sabha came as a rude shock to many, and as 'Aha!' for some. The political pundits, the pollsters and the media had all predicted—and capital market investors and intermediaries expected—the NDA to come to power on the back of their continued progressive reforms agenda, high GDP growth, low inflation and interest rate regime and thriving capital markets. However, Thursday, 13 May, pitchforked Ms Sonia Gandhi to centrestage. The Congress had emerged as the single largest party in the Lok Sabha. Although it did not win an absolute majority, as a leader of the Congress party, Ms Gandhi had the right to be the first to be invited by the President of India to form the government. High drama followed, and the nation watched with awe and expectation.

Two things became clear on the same day: (a) there would be a coalition government (it came to be known as the UPA) at the Centre, and (b) leftist parties like the CPI(M) and CPI would occupy an important place in such a coalition. As if these developments were not enough, on the very next day, 14 May

2004, the prominent communist party leaders, buoyed by the NDA's loss and their own potential entry into the ruling coalition, vociferously demanded scrapping of, among other things, the PSU disinvestment policies actively pursued by the NDA during its tenure. In general, the left parties expressed clear opposition to many of the pro-market policies of the NDA government.

The market intermediaries and investors perceived this as a negative development, believing that the economic reforms would be consigned to the cold storage by the new government. The contrast from a day earlier could not have been more striking. A tsunami was brewing in the confident waters of the capital market. Optimism about a bright future for the stock market just the day before was now replaced by negativity and dampened enthusiasm. Economic growth and the health of the stock market indices appeared to be in jeopardy. The statements of the leftist leaders made the investors' and intermediaries' hearts sink in despair.

The stock markets, understandably, reacted negatively that day. 14 May 2004 happened to be a Friday. The BSE Sensex and NSE Nifty closed approximately 6 per cent and 8 per cent, respectively, below their previous day's close. The dip was significant, but panic was nowhere in sight; neither had the threshold for applying market-wide circuit breakers been hit, either for the Sensex or the Nifty. The next two days being the weekend, the markets were shut. The sentiment of alienation in the market was expected to settle down. The weekend was characterized by the trademark calm before the impending storm, which hit on Monday, 17 May 2004. That day the markets woke up to a tsunami, blowing everyone away.

Monday Morning Massacre

In hindsight, it appears the negative sentiments were churning the waves of disappointment and despair, and the markets, on opening, were hit by heavy selling and unwinding of derivatives positions from all quarters, particularly from FIIs. In a matter of just three hours, the Sensex and Nifty suffered intra-day falls of 842 points (approximately 17 per cent) and 290 points (approximately 18 per cent), respectively, from their previous day's close. The first circuit breaker was applied when the indices fell 10 per cent, and the markets were shut for an hour, as per SEBI's prescribed risk management system. When the markets reopened after an hour, the situation further deteriorated, and the Sensex fell by another 7 per cent, roughly, and the Nifty by another 8 per cent, approximately. Circuit breakers were applied again, and all exchanges suspended trading once more, this time for two hours! All this happened in a matter of hours of the market opening bell going off, and crores of rupees of investor wealth was wiped out!

To put it in perspective, this was the worst ever intra-day fall in the entire history of Indian stock markets until that day. This was much worse than any intra-day beating the markets witnessed even during the Harshad Mehta scam (1992) or the Ketan Parekh scam (2001). This was the first time that trading on both BSE or NSE was frozen twice in a single day! What followed next will be remembered in the history of the Indian stock market as one of its darkest phases.

Hundreds of traders and investors lost fortunes, their wealth evaporating substantially in a matter of just a few hours. With no respite in sight, they all helplessly took to protesting in front of the BSE building on Dalal Street, Mumbai. They shouted slogans against the leftist leaders, blaming them for their irresponsible statements which they believed drove the FIIs away. They felt this was the main reason for the deadly plunge in the markets. Even SEBI was dragged into this for failing to take any timely action and allowing markets to go into a free fall at the risk of investor money. They all demanded that some corrective action be taken, either by the government or by SEBI, to restore market stability at the earliest. Stories circulated about many investors, having lost all their savings, threatening to commit suicide if the markets did not stabilize soon. Many in the market suffered extreme anxiety attacks, high blood pressure, depression and trauma. Things spiralled a bit out of control when the angry protestors mobbed a television crew covering their protest and police had to resort to a minor lathi charge.

Amidst this intense drama, there was one thing everyone wanted to know—what is SEBI doing and where is the SEBI chairman? This was understandable.

As destiny would have it, I was about 4,000 kms away from India. IOSCO (International Organization of Securities Commission) had scheduled its annual general meeting in Jordan, coincidentally, for Monday—17 May 2004—and I was required to represent SEBI. Incidentally, SEBI was pitching for India as the venue for the next IOSCO annual general meeting, which is a prestigious global event that every regulator aspires to host.

Before leaving for Jordan, I had discussed and deliberated on the matter of my travel with the chiefs of the exchanges, the top brokers, my colleagues in SEBI and top government functionaries, including Jaswant Singh, who was the caretaker finance minister then. This was in view of potential instability in the Indian stock market on account of the general elections. As pointed out earlier, there was no panic in the markets on Friday, and so even Singh advised me to go. I can safely say that there was nothing, not even whispers (SEBI was geared to capturing even those) till Saturday, that could give us even a remote hint of the bloodbath that was to follow on Monday. Accordingly, we (one of the WTMs, T.M. Nagarajan, my executive assistant, Ramesh, and myself) left for Jordan.

On the fateful Monday morning at Amman, as I was getting ready to attend the IOSCO meeting, I felt I should check the television to see if everything back home was fine, purely out of curiosity. Since Jordan is 2.5 hours behind India, the markets in India had already opened. Switching on the TV, I saw both the Sensex and Nifty melting. They had already nosedived more than 10 per cent down from their previous close. The circuit breaker had been applied. After some time the second circuit breaker was applied. I stood there completely numb, watching the bloodshed in horror.

In between, I got a call from my wife, Asha, who asked me in a worried voice, 'Where are you? Everyone is accusing you of running away!'

I assured her that everything would be fine, although I was myself very uncertain that it indeed would be so. I was extremely disturbed and lost all interest in the meeting for which I had come all the way. I immediately decided to return to Mumbai without attending the meeting at all. But even before we had boarded the flight back, I was constantly receiving frantic calls from India to take the all-important decision, and almost in real time.

Racing against Time

Trading having been suspended at the exchanges for the second time, the BSE and NSE had been shut for more than two hours, and as per the rules prescribed by SEBI. They had to be opened for trading again, once the stipulated third hour was over. But no one was willing to take the decision to open them again, for fear of a further fall in the market indices. That would mean failure of settlement and sound the death knell for market participants. After all, the sell-to-buy ratio just before trading was suspended was at a mind-boggling 24:1.

Ultimately, it fell on me to decide whether we were going to strictly follow the rules and resume trading or go by the general sentiment and close trading for the day. I had about thirty minutes to make up my mind. The fate of our investor community rested on my shoulders!

During the short time before my flight from Jordan took off, I got several calls from the SEBI WTM, the FS, the CEA and the expenditure secretary (ES), all wanting to know whether the markets should be opened or closed for the remainder of the day. Both the CEA and ES were members of the SEBI board. The WTM who was holding charge at SEBI in my absence was also in similar discussions with various other people. Everybody whom I spoke to, except Ravi Narain, MD and CEO of NSE, were of the view that the markets should remain closed for the day, fearing further mayhem. I was warned of a repeat of a Scam 2001 like situation, where Calcutta Stock Exchange could not honour settlement of trades (amounting to a mere Rs 120 crore), if we dared to open the markets again that day. We were curtly reminded that after Scam 2001, the markets took three years to fully recover, and there were no IPOs during that time. Everybody warned me to close trading, but the responsibility of the final decision fell to me alone.

I attended all the calls (while in Jordan) and heard everyone out. I knew the easiest and safest route was to just keep trading suspended for the remainder of the day. I had enough explanations to back this decision, in case any questions were asked later. But I was still unsure of what to do, since a few contrarian arguments were running in my head too. I started weighing the consequences of keeping the market open. Now I had just about twenty minutes left to make my decision.

First, I felt that investors were misreading the situation, and hence overreacting to it. While it was true that the left parties would, in all likelihood, be partners in the ruling coalition, the government would actually be led by Congress, and the PM was going to be none other than Dr Manmohan Singh. It was not clear yet who would take over as the finance minister, but Singh was known to be a reformer. As a finance minister, it was he who had launched the new economic policy of liberalization and globalization under Prime Minister P.V. Narasimha Rao. After the initial hullaballoo and a break of more than two hours, I felt the markets would be able to see some merit in the appointment of Singh as PM and see that the original reformers would not let the spate of economic reforms die down.

Second, the economic fundamentals seemed strong. Overall, private consumption was high; the services sector was booming, companies were making profits, their balance sheets looked clean and robust, interest rates were low and lending was high. All in all, the macro- and microeconomic factors seemed favourable. The Indian economy was on the upswing, with GDP growth at levels of over 8 per cent. Our constant vigil had ensured that, unlike during boom prior to 1992 or Scam 2001, there was no froth in the market. Being an ex-LIC chairman, I knew there was a strong possibility that, in such a scenario, long-term investing organizations like LIC would very well pursue a contrarian path and buy when the markets were crashing.

I felt there could be others too who would, similarly, have the sense to go against the frenzy and find low stock prices a ripe opportunity to invest (what is called 'buying on dips'). Further, even if the ratio of sell to buy improved from 24:1 to 12:1, the markets would stabilize, if not go up. Third, the rules prescribed during my regime entailed opening of the markets after the second circuit breaker and to close them for the day only if they fell by a further 5 per cent. Closing the market after the second circuit breaker would mean changing our own rules.

Based on the above reasons, I had a very strong instinct that the markets would stabilize if investors were allowed to trade again. Even if the markets opened the next day, I realized, there was no guarantee they would revive. Hence the risk was inherent in either decision. But if I opened the markets and if stability returned (which my gut was telling me would happen), then it would turn out to be good for the nation in many ways.

To begin with, investors would have some respite from their anxieties. The settlement would be smooth. The SEBI rules, of keeping the markets open for trading after a cooling off period under market-wide circuit breakers, would be respected. This would reaffirm the robustness of SEBI's risk management framework. If the markets stabilized now, they would come across as naturally resilient, and as having the ability to bounce back on their own. With all this pondering, I became all the more certain to let trading be opened and allow the market participants decide their fate themselves.

All these thoughts ran through my mind in a flash. I also knew that if the markets revived that day everybody would be happy. But there would be many fathers for my decision and I would never get any credit for it. However, if my decision backfired, then my neck would surely be on the line. I was not worried about myself. I was worried about the economy of the country. I was worried about the investors and intermediaries. I owed them a responsibility. I was accountable to the nation at large. I had done my calculations and was willing to take that risk of backing my instincts to allow the markets to open again. With that thought, I took a two-minute breather, drank a glass of water to soothe myself, prayed to my gods and, against the advice of most of the well-wishers who had called, decided to follow the rule book. The markets opened.

As they say, the rest is history. It was indeed astounding how the markets rose, like a phoenix from the ashes, from their once-in-a-lifetime depths to finally settle at approximately 11 per cent (565 points) and 12 per cent (193 points below the previous day's close for BSE and NSE), respectively, by the end of the day. The markets shot up by approximately 6 per cent from their lows, relieving many tensed nerves, and my stand of allowing the markets to open was finally proven right. Today, though, people seem to have forgotten that such a nerve-wrecking decision had to be taken in a few minutes and that this resulted in the markets springing up from the unbelievably low depths they had fallen to.

After those tense minutes we boarded the flight, and on our way back to Mumbai, WTM T.M. Nagarajan and I were so unnerved that we hardly spoke. We finally reached Mumbai well past lunch time the next day and made ourselves available right in the thick of action at the SEBI office. We took stock of the situation and immediately began interactions with the chiefs of the stock exchanges and the SEBI teams. Our focus now was to ensure that on the next day settlement happened smoothly and our risk management processes worked. The SEBI team quickly analysed broker positions, the margins they had and the extended RBI line of credit. Overnight, we called tens of brokers who had large positions to confirm that they were confident of honouring their deals and settling smoothly the next day.

Our proactive actions yielded fruit, and next day the settlement of all trades happened smoothly, not requiring the markets to dip into the Settlement Guarantee Fund or take the backing of the net worth of the Clearing Corporation. We heaved a sigh of relief!

Setting the Right Precedents

The most noteworthy precedent established by these events was to trust the market to get up on its feet; to keep the ground rules robust; and watch from the ringside that the game was played fairly. Having laid the firm foundations, the referees—the regulators—should zealously guard the sanctity of the ground rules and reassess the solidity of the bricks of the plinth to ascertain that they are worthy of the faith that markets would bounce back on their own. This sets a benchmark for the action to be taken during future falls.

I had laid tremendous emphasis on developing an efficient risk management framework, consisting of upfront margining, real-time monitoring of broker positions and margins, extreme volatility testing, six-sigma deviation, reduced T+2 settlement cycles, straight through processing and the like. Risking unpopularity, I had fought to implement some of these measures.

The framework weathered the extreme, and was tested to their limits during that unfortunate market event of May 2004, emerging robust and reliable. While the failure of settlement amounting to a mere Rs 120 crore on Calcutta Stock Exchange had led the market to collapse like nine pins just three years ago, on 14 May 2004 settlement of trades of over Rs 3,000 crore (ten times the earlier amount) went smoothly. The risk management framework of the operations withstood the extreme test, and our assurance to JPC was fulfilled in letter and spirit. The market microstructure proved to be completely resilient.

Offering to Quit!

Even after the markets had revived, there was still a lot of clamour over the following days from various political quarters, particularly from the leftist party leaders, for my resignation. One prominent Congressman, a Rajya Sabha MP, wrote an article in *Economic Times* pinpointing my role in the high drama in the capital market. My critics said the markets had let the investors down by behaving strangely right under SEBI's nose. In their opinion, the SEBI chairman should resign on moral grounds.

After a couple of days I went to meet the newly appointed finance minister, P. Chidambaram, and at the end of our conversation I offered to quit. But Chidambaram graciously replied, 'Why do you even say so? Why think about it until I ask you to?'

During that first meeting we discussed the markets and other related matters, and as I was leaving, against his usual practice, Chidambaram came up to the entrance of his office and opened the door to see me off. There were quite a few media people waiting there for 'breaking news', and Chidambaram's gesture of seeing me off at the door blew over the speculation about my quitting, giving the media the message that I enjoyed the minister's confidence. The photographs in the next day's newspapers were quite vivid!

Chidambaram even tried to down-play the market fears and was quoted in the media as saying, 'Market will react to events. Market goes up and down. One should take it as it is. The Indian capital market is well regulated and even on the Black Monday there was no payment crisis.'[1]

In the end, the whole episode turned out to be an immensely gratifying experience for me. The regulatory body's faith in the investors' intelligence to read the situation correctly, and in its systems and processes, checks and balances, the efficacy of ground rules, had emerged victorious. The calculated bet I had taken had paid off. It reaffirmed my belief in the power of thinking with a cool head when everyone around is panicking.

> *If you can keep your head when all about you*
> *Are losing theirs and blaming it on you,*
> . . .
> *Yours is the Earth and everything that's in it,*
> *And—which is more—you'll be a Man my son!*

So said Rudyard Kipling in his famous poem, 'If'.

10

PUBLIC OFFERING WITH A TWIST: GOING BEYOND THE CALL OF DUTY

It is quite ironical that as a SEBI chairman my work involved monitoring entities owned by the very same government that had appointed me. The nature of the job, at times, demanded walking the tightrope—juggling between the role of a regulator of government-owned companies and an advisor or even aide to the government—and also switching sides as the situation warranted. With SEBI's legislative obligations including development of the market, this was bound to happen. I had the experience of managing conflicts, not in very distant past, as chairman of LIC. From my tenure as SEBI chairman, I cherry-pick one conflict—the disinvestment of Oil and Natural Gas Commission (ONGC) as a stand-out example.

The Public Offer

Disinvestment of government shares in PSUs was a major economic reform aggressively pursued by NDA-I during its 1999–2004 regime. For the first time, a dedicated disinvestment minister of Cabinet rank had been appointed. He was Arun Shourie. In the Budget of February 2003, Jaswant Singh, then finance minister, had set a target of around Rs 13,000 crore from PSU disinvestments for the fiscal year 2003–04. However, the

Supreme Court ruling of September 2003 against disinvestment without Parliamentary approval had slowed down the process. We were about to welcome New Year 2004, but not a single rupee had been raised yet from disinvestment. Failing to meet its target would have worked against the fiscal maths of the Union government.

Desperate to cover lost ground, the Cabinet Committee on Disinvestment (CCD), GoI, approved the sale of a portion of the government's equity in six select public sector companies, for which parliamentary approvals could be bypassed. This included a 10 per cent stake sale in ONGC. The sale was expected to raise more than Rs 10,000 crore—the highest for any public or private sector share offering in India till date. The ONGC issue was of prime importance, as approximately 80 per cent of the budgeted target was to be met through this alone!

The disinvestment secretary personally met me to emphasize the importance of these offerings, particularly of ONGC, and to seek SEBI's support. As a matter of courtesy, I agreed to extend full cooperation to the disinvestment. In fact, Shourie suggested the involvement of SEBI to the ministry of divestment right at the beginning.

Ideally, the SEBI chairman's duty is to ensure the unbiased functioning of the stock markets and to keep at arm's length anything to do with transactions. However, in this case I was specifically requested to get closely involved at every stage, particularly during the appointment of investment bankers and the pricing of shares. This could be tricky. It was only when I actually stepped in to do the task did it dawn on me that I had set my foot in quicksand. I got sucked deeper than I had imagined. But first, a little about the oil giant.

ONGC, the Behemoth

Oil and Natural Gas Commission dominated India's oil and gas exploration industry, with over 84 per cent of the market share, and was (and continues to be) one of the *'Navratna'* PSUs. About 84 per cent of its equity was with GoI (out of which 10 per cent was to be offered), 4 per cent with the general public (including employees) and roughly 12 per cent with Gas Authority of India Limited (GAIL) and Indian Oil Corporation (IOC). In effect, only 4 per cent of its shares was in the market. Financial performance-wise, ONGC was riding high. It was then the biggest company in India in terms of market capitalization (about Rs 90,000 crore), revenue (around Rs 35,000 crore) and net profit (roughly Rs 10,000 crore), and amongst the top ten oil and gas companies in the world in terms of market capitalization. With high dividend payouts year-on-year, it was one of India's biggest wealth creators. Naturally, the announcement of this offer for sale caused a flutter in the markets, with all stakeholders—government, bankers and investors—wanting to maximize their benefits from this once-in-a-lifetime opportunity. If markets run on fear and greed, this offer was going to test both in multiple ways.

The Investment Bankers (IBs)

The first key step was to appoint well-qualified investment bankers (IBs). For any offering in the securities market, IBs are mandatory intermediaries who will ensure that all the SEBI guidelines are followed strictly. In addition, they also help in discovering the price and size of the issue, its marketing, and, extremely importantly, its underwriting. Leading investment bankers of the country enjoy significant clout and influence in the financial world, and through that, in the economy and among managers of the economy too.

For their services, the IBs charge a certain percentage of the amount raised through the issue as commission. There was very little time left to complete the process, and hence bids (for the commission percentage) were called only from those bankers who had been involved in the earlier government privatizations and had the bandwidth to handle such a large issue. These were about seven in number, and included the top-tier Kotak, JM Morgan Stanley and DSP Merill Lynch. Since ONGC was going to be a landmark issue, they were all keen to get the assignment. So they started pressuring the ministry to award a collective mandate to all the players instead of making a bid-based selection. The government was, understandably, finding it difficult to resist these pressures. The ministry wanted my view and asked me to attend one such meeting, where the process of awarding the mandate was to be finalized. I recommended the bid-based process and deputed Ramesh as my representative. This caught the IBs completely unawares. They could barely hide their disbelief and shock at seeing the SEBI chairman's representative at the meeting. They also now knew that the battle was evenly placed, and if not, then slightly tilted in favour of the ministry. We were clear that the selection would happen through a proper bidding process alone. Accordingly, bids were received by the ministry and results announced.

For ONGC, Kotak was L1—the lowest bidder—at 7.5 basis points (i.e., it was asking for Rs 75 for every Rs 1 lakh raised, or Rs 7.5 crore for the entire offer of about Rs 10,000 crore), followed by DSP Merill Lynch and Morgan Stanley, who bid a fraction higher. The mandate was given to a consortium of investment bankers at Kotak's bid price. (All would get paid in that 7.5 bps of the money raised). It was a big sale, and it would have been extremely difficult for a single investment banker to handle. Besides, having a consortium also provided the government with multiple opinions and diversified the risk.

Although all the IBs wanted the assignment desperately, they started cribbing about the commission percentage after getting it. They knew there was no point in taking up the matter with the ministry as it would have to pass through me eventually. So they approached me directly. One famous investment banker, a thorough gentleman, talked to me separately and requested an increase of commission from the 7.5 bps. I was a little taken aback as a proper process had been followed and all this was coming up after the awarding of the assignment. But I knew I had to be direct. Any diplomacy might have been taken as a sign of weakness and hinted at possibilities.

SEBI's tough and clear stance helped the ministry follow their preferred process for investment banker selection and also get competitive intermediation fees. However, this was only the beginning of many more hurdles to be crossed.

The Twist

The matter of appointment of bankers successfully closed, we moved ahead. The bankers had suggested the following chronology to the ministry—draft prospectus to be filed with SEBI, thereafter with the relevant stock exchanges, followed by the book-building process. Typically, this process takes anywhere between two and three months if everything is in place. As the first step of preparing the prospectus, the IBs demanded that a due diligence must be undertaken on ONGC at the cost of about Rs 1 crore! Thus, an expensive, detailed prospectus was to come to SEBI for approval. But a closer look at the whole exercise suggested that the prospectus route could not be allowed in this case. This was not an IPO as this giant was already listed. It was not an FPO (follow-up public offering) either, as ONGC was not offering any new shares. Only for an IPO or FPO was a prospectus—an exhaustive document running into hundreds of pages—legally required, as per SEBI rules.

In the ONGC case, it was a mere 'sale of stake' by one of the shareholders of an already listed public sector company. All that government had to do was to advertise and sell its shares in the market to willing buyers. And, ONGC being a listed entity, all information about it was available in the public domain. There was no question of any prospectus or due diligence. Even if, under pressure from investment bankers, government and ONGC mutually agreed to get a due diligence done, we were clear about our regulatory duties here and would not permit it. We did not want to set a wrong precedent, lest tomorrow investment bankers should demand the full-fledged prospectus route and a due diligence every time a shareholder decides to sell shares in a company.

Ramesh raised this issue with the investment bankers and pointed to clause 36 of the SEBI listing agreement. They all panicked, as they had conveniently missed this point. Evidently, it suited their interests to suggest a detailed prospectus for the disinvestment, what with the high fees involved. The investment bankers raised the matter with the ministry too asking for the prospectus even though SEBI didn't feel the need for one. We struck down the prospectus/due-diligence proposal, and finally it was SEBI who gave a letter to the government explaining in detail that an advertisement-based process is to be followed for offloading their shareholding in ONGC. Also, a due diligence (which was unnecessary) meant the additional risk of delaying the issue. I thought, why take a chance? This way, we not only kept our regulatory duties intact but also helped the government save precious time and money.

Price Band Disclosure

Once the correct process was outlined by SEBI, work on the advertisement for the stake sale began in full swing. It was almost completed by end of January 2004. The book building, which essentially means inviting investors to bid at their preferred price and fixing the final price at which shares will be allotted (the price at which maximum revenue is generated), was to begin in the first week of March. This lay more than a month ahead. Typically, an advertisement for sale of shares had to provide the price range of the offer, and investors then get around a month to decide the price at which they want to bid under the book-building process. Meanwhile, the issuers would use this time to aggressively market the offer to the largest possible audience. The ministry had planned month-long roadshows, both in India and abroad.

However, as the advertisements were about to be released, there were wide fluctuations reported in the ONGC share price. This was not the best time to decide on the price range. The ministry wanted the market to stabilize and also wait for feedback from the roadshows before deciding on a final price band for the book building. They approached me to allow them to go ahead with the advertisements, but without the price range, which would be decided closer to the bid date.

To be fair, the problem seemed genuine. The markets were going through a technological leap—quicker settlement cycles, faster dissemination of information and shorter reaction time from investors, and the like. In such a scenario, a one-month gap between disclosure of the price band and the bid start date seemed a little outdated and open to being manipulated. Thinking a little ahead of the times, on this occasion SEBI went against its own rule and accepted the ministry's proposal. Later, as a validation of our decision, this became the norm. Shortly afterwards, the rules were revised and the price band/floor price was required to be disclosed only two working days before the bid opening.

Foreign Investors

The advertisements in order, the ministry now started hardselling the issue in India and abroad, particularly in South-east Asia, London and New York. Attracting maximum foreign capital was the key here, as that would promote the India Shining campaign and help the NDA in the next round of general elections in 2004. Fortunately, the offer was being received well abroad, considering which the ministry was open to issuing American

Depositary Receipts (ADRs) for ONGC, in case SEBI or the bankers advised them that the Indian markets would not be able to absorb this large issue of close to Rs 10,000 crore. In case ADRs were not going to be pursued, the bankers wanted SEBI to at least relax the disclosure requirements in the case of participatory notes (P-notes), which would help them attract more foreign investment in India. Otherwise, in their opinion, there was the risk of a lukewarm response from across the borders. This situation, the investment bankers very well knew, the government would do everything to avoid.

I met Arun Shourie, minister of disinvestment more than once to give my opinion on ADRs for ONGC. I told him that I did not think ADRs would be required. I had been the chairman of SEBI for almost two years now and had my ears to the ground. My reading suggested that the Indian markets would easily lap up a good offer. Once ADRs was ruled out, the ministry started pushing SEBI to relax the P-notes disclosure norms. Shourie had even commented, according to *The Hindu Business Line*, that, 'Participatory notes are mainly for getting big investors, not really to get retail investors. In this case, advisers (to the issue) also have contacts (abroad) and we want to use everybody's contacts.'

Now, this was a tricky situation. I knew the government wanted the P-notes relaxation badly, but this time I didn't side with the government and decided to wear the natural regulator's hat. I knew that there was a reason why the rule existed—to follow appropriate KYC norms and know what kind of foreign money comes into India. In fact, it was during my tenure that the strict disclosure norms for P-notes were brought in. This time, however, we did not budge, even under pressure, refusing to undermine our duties as a regulator by relaxing the P-notes norms. That would have set a wrong precedent. We were confident the offer would still do well, despite no ADRs and no relaxation in the disclosure norms for P-notes. In no way was it an easy decision to make. I knew I could come under fire if, for whatever reason, foreign investors chose to stay away from the issue. But I had made my decision and was willing to face the consequences.

Fighting for the Best Share Price

Everything else in place, the government was now focusing on fixing the price band at which the shares were to be offered for bidding. With the process moving on the decided lines, I thought my role was over and got busy with other commitments. I had to attend a meeting of regulators in Wellington, New Zealand. I went there on a short trip of just two days. After my long journey back, I had arrived late in the night and went to bed at 3 a.m. Early in the morning, at 6 a.m., Shourie called me up on the landline. Asha, who picked up the phone, informed him that I had arrived very late in the night and had gone to bed only at 3 a.m. If the matter was very urgent she would wake me up, she told him. Shourie, a gentleman to the core, told her to tell me to call him back as soon as I got up. Fifteen minutes later, Jaswant Singh, then finance minister, called up. Asha felt the matter must be very urgent for two Cabinet ministers to call so early in the morning in quick succession. This time she woke me up, and, probably to ensure that I did not get annoyed, jokingly said: 'Now your boss is on the line, better take the call and save your job.'

I took the call. Jaswant Singh said the ONGC offer for sale seemed to be in jeopardy. Before he could say anything more I told him that Shourie had called up a few minutes before while I was asleep. I would talk to him immediately to find out what the problem was and address it. I assured him of my very best efforts and also that the sale would happen. Jaswant Singh was extraordinarily courteous as he said, ' Chairman, thank you,' and hung up.

I called up Shourie immediately. He told me that the price of ONGC had been fluctuating lately, and had gone down to

Rs 600 from Rs 800. The investment bankers were advising the government to either call off the sale or to keep the offer price band very low. I told Shourie that the brokerage houses of these investment bankers were trading in the shares of ONGC and bringing their price down. We should not give in to their tactics and we should hold on to our stand of offering the shares at a fair price. I offered to send him the data about their trading, which I knew SEBI would have most likely gathered. He asked me whether I could come to Delhi as he was meeting investment bankers in the morning the next day, and suggested I find a way out to meet him before his meeting with them. We agreed that I would take a late evening flight to meet him the next day in his office. My meeting with Shourie was very brief. I repeated that some of the investment bankers seemed to be deliberately trying to bring down the price of ONGC shares through sales in the scrip being undertaken by their own brokerage houses. I supported my submission with complete data of each investment banker's brokerage house sales and purchase transactions in ONGC.

He was shocked. He agreed with me and said he would not succumb to their pressure and would carry out the process as decided. I also suggested that the bankers be given an alternative—that if they are not willing to conduct the sale of ONGC shares by GoI or not confident of its success, they could disengage and the government would hire another set of investment bankers. Shourie thanked me and very kindly walked all the way from his office right up to my car. Given that his office was housed in a huge complex, it was almost a mile-long walk for him. I don't know how the media got a whiff of our meeting, but over a dozen journalists, including television reporters, were standing near my car. They started asking me what decision had been taken. I quickly got into the car and told them it was the minister's prerogative to share the information, if any, and that the minister was just walking back and could be approached. While leaving,

I had requested Shourie to let me know the outcome of his meeting with the investment bankers.

Don't Meet the Target, Beat It

Shourie had been an investigative journalist in the early part of his career. In a way, he continued to be one at heart, even after becoming a minister. Once convinced by my argument about the downward price rigging in the stock market to bargain for a lower offer price, there was no stopping him. In his next meeting with the bankers, Shourie was a man on a mission. He showed them the data we had collected, which clearly exposed their hidden agenda. The meeting hardly lasted fifteen minutes and ended with the final word being delivered by Shourie; he told them that even at this stage the government could go with other advisors. He spoke to them in a language that crushed many egos. Not many could talk to the country's top investment bankers the way he did.

While I was still on way back, Shourie called me up to say that he had concluded his meeting in fifteen minutes flat and the investment bankers had all agreed to undertake the work at whatever sale price the government decided on. I asked him how he had achieved this in such a short time. Shourie gleefully told me, 'I gave them a piece of my mind!' He had laid all the data that I had given him before the IBs, and had made his own analysis as an investigative journalist. In fact, the data was fairly detailed because SEBI team had meticulously traced the sources as also the identities of those who were involved in the price manipulation.

A low sale price meant the favoured allottees would get very good shares with significant potentials of upside in the next couple of weeks itself. Investment bankers often do this. In this case, they probably also wanted to make up for the low commission (they had quoted to charge only 7 basis points, against the normal fees of 2–5 per cent). It appeared that the investment bankers were shocked to see what was shown to them and instantly agreed to carry out the sale. I was very happy that the process was on. I had also to make sure that the government did not, under any circumstances, agree to lower the price at which the market would eventually like to buy the shares. Happily, I replied, 'Mark my words, the issue will be subscribed in fifteen minutes. Do keep the price at the Rs 725 levels.'

I briefed Jaswant Singh too, making to him the same request—not to agree to a price lower than Rs 700, even if there was pressure on him.

Once the news spread that SEBI had intervened in the pricing issue, another gentleman and friend entered the drama—a TRAI chief. He called on my mobile and told me very categorically not to go ahead with the disinvestment, or the markets could crash. His opinion carried weight. In all probability, he had been approached by the bankers to soften me. I was probably the only person standing between them and an attractively low issue price. But I stuck to my view.

Thereafter, not a word was uttered on the matter and everyone agreed to cooperate. SEBI once again saved the government from being taken for a ride. The price band of Rs 680–Rs 750 was disclosed on 3 March, and the bidding opened 5 March onwards for ten days. The biggest issue the country had seen was oversubscribed in the first fifteen minutes of its opening, as I had predicted! I called up Shourie to tell him this. He was thrilled, and rushed to inform the PM of the issue's success.

Overall, the issue was oversubscribed six times! The offer split was 50 per cent to institutional investors, and the balance to individual investors (maximum 10 per cent allotment to existing members, a maximum 10 per cent to employees, a minimum 25 per cent to high-net-worth individuals [HNIs] and a minimum 25 per cent to retail investors). As many as 7.6 lakh retail investors and 350 institutional buyers participated in the issue. The international response was overwhelming too—about 88 per cent of the South-east Asian investors who participated in the roadshows made a bid. This figure was approximately 84 per cent for European investors and 67 per cent for US investors. Reportedly, two unknown Indian private companies had invested a total of Rs 1,600 crore in the issue. In between, there were even rumours of the legendary investor, Warren Buffet, showing interest in the ONGC issue. The good response to the offer of ONGC shares for sale even helped the markets in general, as can be seen from the chart below.

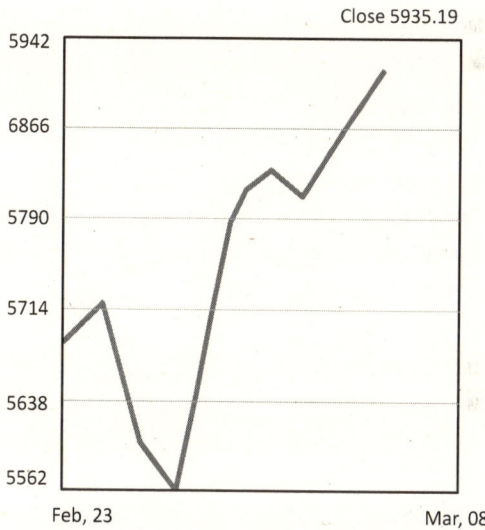

Our stand not to relax the P-notes disclosure norms had also proved right, as foreign investment still poured in generously. All categories, barring that of retail investors, oversubscribed to the shares reserved for them. The retail category was only marginally undersubscribed. The final allotment price was fixed at Rs 750, and the government managed to raise more than Rs 10,500 crore. It was one of those rare achievements, when a government target was not only met but also exceeded.

I am tempted to say—'And then everybody lived happily thereafter.' But the saga was yet not over.

Just as everyone was basking in the euphoria of the success of the issue, I got another distress call from the ministry. Not in my wildest imagination had I thought SEBI's involvement would be required yet again, at a time when the ONGC offer was almost over. What had happened was that MCS—the registrar to the issue—had made certain errors in the share allotment. Some HNIs got 100 per cent of the allotment instead of their rightful 70 per cent. This meant some others got less than their share. The government did not get the issue money. This goof-up threatened to take the sheen out of an otherwise stupendously successful issue. Tongues had already started wagging.

There were only two major registrars then—Karvy and MCS. The recent spate of issues had left MCS a little overburdened. We got Karvy to step in, and they agreed to help their competitor, MCS, at our insistence! Along with them worked the SEBI officers from the chairman's secretariat, led by Ramesh. They loosened their ties, rolled up their sleeves, got down on the shopfloor and resolved the error by perusing every single transaction! Ramesh spent a couple of nights in the MCS office, particularly to ensure timely recredits of government receipts. On one such day, SEBI even knocked at the doors of RBI to ask them to keep their books open beyond the account closing hours so that credits to government accounts (which were with RBI) could take place before the book closure. And the giant RBI willingly obliged!

SEBI was consulted at almost every stage, and the ministry's faith in SEBI paid off handsomely. I successfully dodged the double-edged scenarios of overstepping my bounds, helping the government, and also taking a stand as a regulator, refusing to budge from my principles when that was called for. I was particularly satisfied at having pulled off tricky calls, like disallowing the prospectus path, saying no to ADRs and not relaxing the P-notes rules, thereby putting my own neck on the line. I restricted the commission percentage, defied our own rule on price-band disclosure rather setting a new rule, and finally got a good value for ONGC shares. In spite of my firmness in these matters, I was not perceived to be rigid, as I went out of my way to help the government, in the national interest, wherever possible. SEBI had contributed beyond its defined role of a regulator by enabling a gainful and smooth disinvestment for the government.

Inflexibility and malleability are the two desirable elements in the regulatory approaches. The dynamics of the market dictate the tool selection, and the approaches. Discretion and judgement calls have to be sagaciously taken in the best interests of the market and the participants. That is when the competence and character of the decision maker is tested.

11

BREAKING NEWS:
DEALING WITH THE MEDIA

The flipside of ushering in the fast-paced reforms (quasi-judicial functions, transparency, T+2, demutualization, disclosures, RSE closures, broker fees, etc.) and the attempts at other reforms (MAPIN, REIT, SRO, FMC, IDR, etc.) had made SEBI a consistent source of fodder for the breaking news–hungry media. Amongst all the regulators (IRDA, TRAI, RBI), SEBI got the maximum coverage during those days. However, this extensive coverage was not necessarily always good.

As mentioned earlier, I tried to bring in greater transparency by making the SEBI orders public and setting in motion the process of improving the quality of orders too. Here, instead of being appreciated, we were unfairly targeted in the media. There was criticism that our orders were poor and that we even lacked objectivity. This criticism mostly came from people who did not even go through the orders or had 'scores' to settle with SEBI. The media response was similar when I tried to bring about policy changes, like improved disclosure norms, REIT, SRO, broker fees, MAPIN, etc.

There were times when I got to know about some 'poor' investigation done by SEBI only through the media, even though in some of those cases investigation had actually never taken place at all! As if this was not enough, certain media houses, in search of breaking news, accused SEBI officials of corruption without verifying this properly. Some media reports, including stories on listed companies, intermediaries and even investors, were so blatantly false and in bad taste that I lost my patience and responded strongly, refusing to take things lying down. I vividly remember three of my run-ins with the media, on issues ranging from alleged bad investigation by SEBI and bribery charges against us, to blackmail charges against a journalist by a stock broker.

Run-in 1: The Case of Imaginary Investigation

A prominent business news channel broadcasted the news that a big broker was being investigated by SEBI. This was not true, and SEBI had no intention of investigating the broker either. But this news created unnecessary panic among brokers in general and the management of that broking house in particular, who were on the path of pitchforking themselves into the league of biggies with big-time diversification. The television story also gave an opportunity to mischief makers to raise questions about SEBI's methods and intentions. Such false news had been spreading for some time now. So I cut through ranks and straightaway invited the No.1 at the channel for a cup of tea—this is a euphemism used by the regulator to summon someone (here a leading media personality) for counselling and to question him on the news about the SEBI investigation (which even I was not aware of) by his channel. The news head stuck to his report, insisting that an investigation was indeed being carried out. He also alleged that someone from SEBI itself had shared this news.

'Who told you this?' I asked, concerned. 'Tell me the name. I will get the man in front of you and then make him say it again,' I replied.

Naming his source, according to him, was not possible, and understandably so. However, it was not acceptable to me that fake news was being broadcast. I had made up my mind to take the news channel head on and go to court over it if need be. However, after some discussions the journalist reluctantly accepted that the news had been wrong; the error was regretted on his media channel. Interestingly, in spite of this incident, my relations with him continued to remain cordial.

Run-In 2: The Case of Imaginary Bribe-taking

One day I opened one of the prominent daily newspapers, only to find a news item to the effect that people at SEBI are corrupt and that SEBI officers take bribes. This was apparently a statement made by Ketan Parekh, who was in jail in Kolkata. Parekh was also saying that he had bribed SEBI officers, which he later denied. The article had made a very grave accusation but gave no proof or source for its claims. Once again I lost my cool. The editorial team of the newspaper was immediately approached and told to tell us who at SEBI were taking bribes. If they did not tell us, we would file a defamation case against the newspaper. We even sent a message across to them to apologize and publish a suitable correction negating the bribery accusations against SEBI officers. But everything fell on deaf ears. So SEBI issued a defamation notice.

The editor of the newspaper, (I got to know through someone and is unverified), was very angry about the defamation notice but was advised not pick up a fight with the SEBI. He was told that if SEBI filed a case and if the matter was dealt with by the courts, it would be the newspaper that would suffer greater damage as the people at SEBI were quite serious about the whole issue. But they could not produce the names of the bribe-taking officers because there were no such officers in the first place. So finally, with some reluctance, the newspaper regretted the news in their publication, saying the bribery accusations against SEBI officers were unverified.

Run-in 3: A Case of Blackmail

In another case, a broker came to me and told me that a journalist was trying to blackmail him; the journalist wanted Rs 25,000, failing which he would write a negative story about the broker. The scared broker had earlier paid a similar amount to the journalist, under the same threat.

I told the broker, 'It is between you and the journalist and outside SEBI's purview. SEBI won't be able to step in. But you may go to the CBI and complain.' He did not name the journalist or the media house. Even I did not ask him their names as the matter was anyway outside my purview.

A few days later, a journalist from a prominent economic newspaper was caught taking a bribe by the CBI. Whether it was the same journalist mentioned by the broker or someone else, I would never know. But these chain of events highlighted the practice of inaccurate, if not false, reporting by the media.

My biggest concern about the media, from the experiences I have described above, was that stories regarding the capital market, including those on SEBI, should be verified before they are published. I really had no problem if the stories were against SEBI or against me personally, as long as those were verified and correct. Stories alleging SEBI investigation against a big broker or a scrip, bribe-taking by SEBI, etc., create negative sentiments in the market and can lead to fluctation in stock prices, resulting in losses running up to crores of rupees. If these reports are not true, the loss they cause to honest investors would be completely unfair. Such misreporting could also be used as a tool by unscrupulous players in the market to make unfair gains at the cost of general investors. In any case, such false news in the media were becoming an operational risk, damaging the efficacy of the market, which we were building so assiduously. Widespread escalation in the frequency of false news has the potential of becoming even a systemic risk, albeit of low order. So something had to be done to stop such unverified reports.

I had set up a committee on corporate governance under N.R. Narayana Murthy (founder of Infosys). Even that committee had suggested issue of a code of conduct for media with respect to reporting on the capital markets. It said SEBI should take it up with the relevant authorities or media houses.

Putting a Stop to Unverified Reporting

Knocking on the doors of Press Council of India

To end unverified reporting by the media, I first decided to approach the authority which governs the conduct of print and broadcast media—the Press Council of India (PCI). I took an appointment with the PCI chief, and I was asked to file a complaint against the entire media!

I was aghast. First, I did not have any complaint about any particular story, media house or journalist. I had gone to the PCI to seek their help in charting out guidelines for verification of media stories before their publication, in the same manner that SEBI had laid down guidelines for true and accurate disclosure by listed companies for integrity of price discovery. Besides, a formal complaint, that too against the entire media, would make things messy between the media and SEBI and would not bring the desired results. It would also eat away much of my time from my core SEBI-related activities.

I thanked him for his time and came back. I felt this was a dead end as far as expecting anything from PCI went.

Knocking on the door of media houses

Next, I thought I should directly approach the various media houses, highlight to them the impact of false stories on investors and find a solution to the nagging issue. So I organized meetings in Delhi, inviting the heads of prominent media houses. I must state here that all the journalists I called were receptive to my invitation.

We had a good discussion at the meeting. The journalists all agreed that false reports can lead to price manipulation and must be avoided at all costs. In the end, they asked me for my suggestion for a solution.

'Have a common code of conduct,' I said.

We had three rounds of meetings with these media personalities. Every time we met we had very pleasant and incisive discussions on the state of the stock market, in particular, and on the economy in general. There was a consensus that false media reports had to be avoided at all costs. It was also decided that the draft of the common code of conduct would be prepared and circulated by them.

In the second meeting it was decided that SEBI would prepare a draft and circulate it, as the journalists had not circulated any draft so far. In the third meeting the consensus among the media personalities, as articulated at the conclusion of the meeting, was that since each of their organizations has its own code of conduct, there was no need for another. I did not take an offence at the outcome, and I do not blame them either. They must have had their reasons for not consenting to a common code of conduct and possibly wanted to deal the problem through self-regulation. So I moved on.

In the meanwhile, people continued to write against me and my team in the media, especially when I tried to fast-track the process of passing SEBI orders and decided to make them public. I learnt to take such criticism (even if it was unfair) against me with a pinch of salt and stopped bothering about it.

However, the gain from those meetings was the personal rapport and good friendship I built with the journalists. We built stronger bridges of understanding on some of the important issues relating to the capital market. Post our meetings, some of the editorials and columns reflected a more balanced picture of SEBI-related matters. Further, whenever I personally spoke to an editor, quick action followed.

Capital markets are very sensitive and react quickly to news. Sometimes the reaction is strong and substantial, and betrays the fundamentals of the economy (or the company reported on). Market reactions to statements by policymakers and senior functionaries of regulatory bodies are instantaneous; these announcements could influence the direction of an entire segment of the market or the entire market itself. As the SEBI chairman, therefore, I had to be very cautious. I had learned the art of making statements and giving interviews to some extent, both as communications head (for four years) and chairman of LIC. I do not remember having put my foot in my mouth on any occasion. In fact, I tried to make candid statements, leaving little scope for misreporting. I was acutely aware that media persons appreciate humour only at personal meetings; on the beat they are always hungry for exclusive stories, and humour provides fodder to them to spice up their stories. Also, I learned that there is nothing called 'off the record'; never make a statement if you do not want a story to be weaved around it.

I remember one situation that could have become embarrassing. Chidambaram was inaugurating BSE's SME trading platform, IndoNext, and he gave his opinion on a current issue to reporters who actually wanted my response. I avoided speaking because my view on the matter was contrarian. Subsequently, Chidambaram came to my office to address SEBI officers, and when I went down to see him off, the media were there again. They tried to extract a statement from me again on the issue, and I said, 'The minister has already given his view and what do you want me to say?' and moved on. My tone, probably, was the culprit, and my reply was interpreted as my holding a different view from the finance minister's on the matter. Next morning a prominent financial daily carried a front-page headline with photographs of both of us, indicating that we were loggerheads on the issue. Fortunately, the minister took it in his stride and there was no need for me to explain matters to him.

There were several occasions when I had to respond to statements made by other policymakers or regulatory body heads so that the stock market did not react adversely to those statements. Here, my rapport with the media heads was useful, as I could convey to them personally the correct perspective, in addition to my issuing a statement on the subject. And, most of the time, these editors took care to ensure the appropriateness of the news. Even though I was friendly with the media and gave interviews liberally, I consciously wanted to be in the news only when it was necessary and unavoidable.

12

RAISING THE BAR OF TRANSPARENCY: WHAT HAPPENS IN SEBI SHOULD (NOT) STAY

Only in SEBI

One fine day I got a note from the legal department seeking my decision on a request received from a party asking for a copy of a quasi-judicial order passed by SEBI. Even though the applicant seeking the copy of the order was not directly associated with the case, the party had a vicarious relationship to it. The department, as also the ED (legal), recommended that the copy of the order should not be given. Their supporting argument was that the order was meant only for the entity involved in the case and no one else. I was greatly surprised to read the contents of the note.

I had a talk with ED (legal) to understand the rationale of the negative response of the department and her own. She said the quasi-judicial order was a privileged communication between the concerned entity and SEBI, and how could someone else have access to it, and that too from SEBI itself? My immediate reaction was, why not? I argued that the orders passed by SEBI were quasi-judicial and appealable before the SAT, High Courts (then) and the Supreme Court, in that order. I also said the orders of SAT, High Courts and Supreme Court are made public, and their copies could be obtained on payment of a specified fee. Once an order of SEBI is challenged before SAT, it becomes public in any case. Further, it was my belief that SEBI had the responsibility of regulating the capital markets, which necessitates both prescriptive and preventive measures. Public knowledge of cognizance by SEBI of a conduct of a market participant should enlighten others not to indulge in similar activities that are not in conformity with the ground rules prescribed by the regulator.

This had so far not been the case, I was informed.

However, I then held the opinion—and continue to do so even now—that all rulings and judgements by SEBI should be made public, and anyone and everyone should be able to access them. I decided that all SEBI and SAT orders should be put up on the SEBI website. My decision was a dramatic turnaround from the earlier stance of SEBI.

There was serious resentment in the organization, particularly in the legal department, at my direction of putting the orders on the website. This was the pre-RTI era, and government institutions were just not used to the culture of sharing information about their functioning and processes with the common public. They were prone to secrecy. The general masses were not conscious of their right to information from government departments and regulators. Even when information was shared, it was with a significant delay. Since the status quo was challenged and was likely to send ripples through the organization and even externally, I had to be persuasive in my approach. I patiently heard everybody's arguments against my decision and tried to decipher the reasons for their discomfort. Deeper examination of their arguments revealed the main causes of their hesitation and resistance:

1. The quality of investigations was wanting in depth and specificity.

2. There were delays in carrying out the investigations, in the conduct of quasi-judicial proceedings, and even in passing the orders after proceedings were over.
3. The quality of orders passed, and their language, were far from satisfactory.

An attendant reason, albeit one that was less obvious, lay in the hazy rays of subjectivity evident in some orders. Public knowledge of all this was bound to attract serious criticism about the efficiency, efficacy and even objectivity of the people involved in the entire process.

I have mentioned in the beginning of the book my chance meeting with P. Chidambaram on a flight. He had told me two things, and one of them was about the quality of orders passed by SEBI. In my efforts to settle the dust of the storm caused by my direction to make public our orders, I saw an opportunity to: (a) improve the quality of investigations (b) improve the quality of orders (c) improve the timeline for taking regulatory actions and (d) enhance our objectivity in dealing with cases. I, therefore, had to take steps to prepare the organization, both psychologically and logistically, for this. I had several rounds of discussions with all concerned, and impressed upon them the points mentioned above. Even though building understanding among the staff was slow to begin with, it did happen, after a great deal of coordinated and concerted efforts. I agreed to a time frame of six months for commencement of making public our orders on our website. The officers would use this time to improve their processes, along with improving the quality, content and language of our orders, which eventually happened.

The orders on the website did evoke criticism in the media. Some of the criticism was directed at me personally, because in the initial phases most, if not all, of the orders were passed by me. Unfortunately, the SEBI officers who pass orders do not enjoy judicial immunity. Therefore the criticism was wholesome and the accusations sharp. There were moments when I wondered if my decision had been right. However, I was reconciled to the criticism because the underpinnings were: (a) I was objective in every case; if at all there was any shortcoming it could at worst be a genuine error of judgement. (b) I had to bring transparency in the functioning of the regulatory body and improve the perception of its objectivity.

Another challenge we faced was the objection by SAT to having its orders put on the SEBI website. I met the presiding officer of SAT to convince him of the need to put its orders on the website. After listening to me he was convinced about it. However, SAT decided to put its orders on its own website, and SEBI was provided a link to the SAT website.

Committees

While pushing the legal department to make all SEBI orders public to enhance transparency, I got thinking about many other aspects of SEBI, which I felt were opaque. One of the areas that caught my attention was the manner in which we enacted or amended regulations.

The process went something like this: The idea for amendment of a regulation or enactment of a new regulation would be initiated internally. Then a select committee, comprising industry bigwigs and reputed personalities, including legal eagles, would be appointed to give its recommendation on the clauses required, as also on how to implement the new regulation. Finally, these recommendations would be converted into draft regulations, guidelines or directions, and placed before the SEBI board. On approval by the board, it would take effect of a subordinate legislation. But everything, from the idea to the finalization of a new law, happened only internally, or at best within a closed group, and there was no obvious interface with the actual stakeholders of the capital market.

To the stakeholders, this appeared no different from a black box–like functioning. The new law would then be thrust down their throats. No wonder there was often deep resistance to accepting new regulations, even if they were for the benefit of the market and its participants. This approach portrayed SEBI as a 'know-it-all' kind of big brother rather than a well-wisher and a protector of market participants. There were also allegations that some of the committee members were profiting from the exclusive information they had about the proposed changes in the regulations and making selective leaks to the news media.

I decided to make a couple of changes to this process. First, I directed that every committee would be completely neutral, i.e., free from all external as well as SEBI influence. Second, the public would have an opportunity to give their inputs on the recommendations of the expert committee, and their inputs would be duly considered before the recommendations were put to the SEBI board for approval. To bring this into effect, I decided that the expert committees would exclude all those who have any possibility of creating unnecessary influence. Even the SEBI chairman and WTMs would be kept away from these committees. Only one or two middle- to senior-level SEBI officers would be available to the committee, to organize the logistics and to assist coordination between the committee and SEBI board.

Once the committee report was out, it would be put on the SEBI website for thirty days for consultation and feedback from market participants and the public at large. The feedback received would then be considered before drafting the regulations to be put up to the board.

The process would not end here.

These draft regulations would again be put on the website for fifteen days for the second round of feedback. Once the feedback was received, the draft regulations would be presented before the board for consideration, along with the feedback from the public and the details about how this feedback had been dealt with. The draft regulations and feedback would be discussed together at the board meeting before approval of the final regulation. Even approved regulations would be put up on the website for some days before their implementation, to ensure that all investors and market participants are aware of the new regulations coming in. Thus, all-in-all, there were to be three rounds of public feedback before finalization and implementation of any new regulation or amendment of an existing one!

It is indeed a matter of pride for me personally, and for the team, that SEBI was the first ever regulator in India to follow this consultative and iterative process of taking public feedback before passing new regulations. This actually set a whole new benchmark for other public institutions and regulators, like RBI and IRDA, who too started following a similar process.

SEBI's transparent process of framing regulations brought some immediate advantages. This two-way communication before the passing of a regulation was widely praised in the media. Acceptance of our regulations increased and their implementation became easier. The shock and surprise elements disappeared. Earlier, even after policy changes, people of influence would many a time disrupt their implementation under the pretext that the changes were brought in without any consultation with the affected parties. Now, since SEBI was providing three rounds of opportunity for people to raise their concerns, nobody could challenge us later. This advantage is best explained through an incident I vividly recollect.

It was sometime in 2003 that SEBI, to enhance the corporate governance standards of the listed companies, appointed a committee under the chairmanship of Narayana Murthy, with a number of corporate chieftains as members. The changes recommended by the committee were many. They included disclosures, observance of accounting standard and boardroom practices, etc. The recommendations, which went through the consultation processes of the new corporate governance rules in the shape of the amended clause 49 of the listing agreement, was put up on the SEBI website. The media picked up and flashed them in a noticeable manner. After the final amendment, when clause 49 of the listing agreement was put up on the website before its implementation, I got a call from the office of Ratan Tata, chairman of Tata Sons, informing me that Ratan Tata, Keshub Mahindra and Nusli Wadia wanted to meet me urgently. These gentlemen need no introduction. A suitable appointment was granted, and when they met me they expressed their displeasure at one of the clauses of the revised corporate governance guidelines. They wanted the clause to be altered. I pointed out to them that the final clause 49 of the listing agreement, before being put on the SEBI website, had gone through two rounds of consultation, as per our policy. Additionally, the Tata's group senior executive was on the committee and no objection had been raised. However, upon their insistence, and considering the fact that the three of them represented a quarter of the industrial sector, I agreed to reconsider the clause, given the possibility of amending the finalized rules.

The fact that we followed such a detailed and inclusive process before bringing in changes was a matter of pride for us.

SEBI's Own Citizen's Charter: SEBI Benchmark 2003

In continuing with my drive to increase transparency at SEBI, the next cause I took up was to make ourselves answerable to the public in whatever areas we dealt with them. A couple of things came to my notice in this area in the early days of my SEBI tenure. First, SEBI officers were taking a long time to grant approvals and, more importantly, there was no certainty about how long approvals would take. Second, I figured that the bitter public grievance about SEBI was not that it took a long time to act, but that the public didn't know how much time it would take for us to act, even if it was going to take long. So it was decided that we would list out all the areas that required interaction with the public at large, including approvals, and commit to timelines for the work to be done. This would then be put up on the website to make it binding on all the officers.

I asked all the officers to list down all the areas in which they were required to provide SEBI approval or consent or grant any kind of 'no objection'. These activities included IPO clearance, grant of licence—including renewal thereof—to brokers and mutual funds, resolution of investor complaints, adjudication proceedings, answering queries, and so on. I also asked them to assign the time required to complete each of those activities. This was met with some resistance internally, and understandably so because this would require the staff to be efficient and accountable for delays. However, instead of dictating a date for this process, I became persuasive. I had to assure the staff that I was fine with their keeping a margin and providing a slightly higher time limit, so long as they could abide by those timelines. Only after a lot of discussion and persuasion did our officers commit to timelines for all their activities involving external parties. These timelines were then put on the website, where they still continue to hold an important place.

Evidently, the public became more comfortable in dealing with SEBI. This change brought a huge amount of transparency in SEBI's functioning. Also, SEBI officers were on alert, and in general their efficiency went up multifold.

Charity Begins at Home

If I was going to be so demanding on my officers in terms of letting their work be open to media and public scrutiny, and making them answerable for service standards, I thought I should provide them adequate support from my end too. If I dreamt of making them and the public involved in the

SEBI processes, I had to start with my employees and make them part of the SEBI vision first. So I started conducting open house sessions, where all employees, right from the junior-most staff to the senior-most officials, were invited. Any officer could meet me on prior appointment to discuss anything, including his personal problems, and these appointments were given within twenty-four hours if I was at our headquarters. We shared SEBI's vision (in fact, divisional heads themselves were involved in its design), explained where we planned to take the organization, and encouraged everyone present to provide their views and concerns. Very soon, employees started feeling more involved in the affairs of the organization, got greater clarity on their roles, and their ownership of the organization and its policies strengthened substantially.

Further, I committed to decide on matters placed before me within forty-eight hours, if I was at the headquarters, and within forty-eight hours of my return to HQ if I was not.

Similarly, I made conscious efforts to be a lot more approachable to external people. If anyone wanted to meet me, appointments were given, usually within a week, and I invariably stuck to the time of appointment. All these steps made everyone (inside and outside the organization) sit up and appreciate that SEBI was proactively concerned about enhancing transparency.

New World Order

To understand the magnitude of the impact of these steps to improve transparency, imagine what would be the reaction of private sector companies if they were told to come under the purview of RTI? Such was the jaw-dropping change brought in at SEBI—making our orders public, taking public comments before passing/amending regulations, committing to timelines for services, sharing the organizational vision and progress with the team and, finally, meeting anyone who wanted to meet us. These are standards that few organizations, public or private, had in those days.

The argument that SEBI is a public authority and should be accountable to the public has gained momentum only in the last decade or so with the emergence of the new economy, and through the democratization of technology and globalization.

I think we changed the century-old psychological mindset, freed SEBI from the shackles of an old-world style of black box–like functioning, and prepared it to embrace the open new world order. This is not to forget that we were suitably facilitated by the emergence of a technological revolution in the form of the Internet.

When the RTI Act was passed in 2005 (post my exit from SEBI) many public institutions dreaded it, but not SEBI. I had already prepared it for such 'obscene levels of transparency', as someone from the organization had remarked, in a lighter vein.

The underpinning of my thought processes was to build an open, inclusive and transparent model of decision making; a 'reasoned' transparency and not a 'fishbowl' model of transparency. I strongly believe that transparency promotes accountability, enhances legitimacy and builds public trust. Transparency was one of the ways in which I wanted to rebuild public trust and credibility in the efficacy of the regime and enhance the standards of operational performance.

Transparency of Listed Companies

A new era under the SEBI Act

In the new regime under the SEBI Act, where companies no longer needed to obtain approval from the government to raise capital through IPOs and were free to decide the price, quantity, dividend/interest rate and other terms and conditions, there was a sudden jump in the number of IPOs in the year 2003. India had decidedly moved away from a 'merit-based' regime to a 'disclosure-based' regime. This became true for other public issues too—FPS, Offers for Sale (OFS), debt, etc. The only constraint was that companies had to function within the ambit of the SEBI guidelines for Disclosure and Investor Protection (DIP).

Initially, SEBI issued the DIP guidelines as originally mandated. Subsequently, the SEBI Act was amended to authorize SEBI to issue regulations for issues and disclosures. Currently, the regulations go by the names, SEBI Issue of Capital and Disclosure Regulations and SEBI Listing Obligations and Disclosure Regulations.

The DIP guidelines focused only on laying down standard disclosure norms for companies wanting to go public. This was to help the public make informed investment decisions. The pricing of an issue, its quantity, etc., was left to the company to decide, and investors could pick and choose where they wanted to invest. It ended the dominance of the CCI in the process of companies raising capital, and brought to play the market forces of demand and supply. Globally too, this was the trend. The DIP Guidelines of 1992 kept getting refined through various circulars before evolving into the DIP Guidelines of 2000—which was in force when I joined SEBI. The final, full-fledged regulations were issued in 2009.

Challenges in a Disclosure-based System

While a disclosure-based regime for public issues was a leap towards a free market economy, there was huge scope for improvement. I wanted to take the markets to a level where investors could discern, without exception, a good issue from a bad one.

Information enables efficacious analysis of a company's performance and perspectives. Such analysis unfolds the true risks; for example, inadequate transparency may obscure a company's borrowing level and its eventual exposure to bankruptcy. Similarly, financing of investments via holding companies ingrains in the company the potential for evaporation of some of the benefits of the investments. The investors, and even the customers, of a company seek transparency, which is enabled by full disclosure of accurate and candid information, in a form simple to understand and interpret. Inadequacy of transparency leads to erosion of trust. Transparency and trust are the two important requirements for building sustainable confidence among the stakeholders and for the growth of an enterprise itself.

This boiled down to ensuring that information about companies going for a public issue is available in detail, is consistent and yet presented in terms as simple as is possible (improved disclosure standards). Such information must be accurately calculated (improved accounting standards) in the offer document/prospectus. It was also important that this information was made available to all—to the general masses, HNIs, institutional investors, research analysts, advisors, etc., at the same time, and also updated regularly. All this would create a level playing field among potential investors and enable them to reward a good issue and stay away from the bad ones. And this is what I now began to look at closely—improving corporate disclosure and accounting standards.

After the collapse of Enron, the world realized that disclosure norms, even in the US, were not stringent enough as compared with those in the Indian markets. In India, the ownership of financial reports was specified, with the MD and whole-time director required to sign up. We wanted to strengthen the disclosure norms further, and on various counts. We decided that: 1) the identity of promoters be published in the prospectus, with their photos, ID numbers, etc. At the time, there was no concept of director identification number (DIN), which was later brought in when SEBI introduced MAPIN, 2) accounting norms be made on par with International Accounting Standards for listed companies, though the Companies Act, 1956, allowed more lenient accounting norms and 3) corporate governance for listed companies be strengthened.

To study what could be further improved in the above parameters while making public issues, I set up two committees— the Disclosure Standards Committee and the Accounting Standards Committee, both under the chairmanship of Y.H. Malegam, a leading chartered accountant, then head at Billimoria & Co., and later to become chairman of Deloitte Haskins. He was also a director on the RBI board and later also became chairman of the National Accounting Standard Committee. The committees compared the disclosure and accounting standards across the capital markets of the world with that of India and came up with many suggestions, which were, more or less, all incorporated to strengthen and streamline the disclosure and accounting requirements. The Narayana Murthy committee on corporate governance helped us comprehensively revamp our corporate governance norms through the famous clause 49 of the listing agreement notified by SEBI. The chapter on corporate governance talks about it in detail.

Improvements in Disclosure and Accounting Standards

Some of the important additional disclosures in an offer document/prospectus at the time of public issue, as well as disclosures on an ongoing basis for listed companies that we introduced to help investors, were as follows.

Additional Financial Disclosures and changes in Accounting Standards

I still recollect, during my tenure, Maruti Udyog making an offer for sale to the public at Rs 230 a share, a price twenty-three times the face value (FV) of the share, which was Rs 10. It was perceived to be expensive at Rs 230. So the company split the FV of their shares to Rs 5 and priced the public offer at Rs 115, once again twenty-three times the revised face value. Nothing had changed. The fundamentals of the company remained the same, the premium ratio was same, and the overall risk remained the same. However, purely because 115 as an absolute number was lower than 230, investors perceived the offer price to be reasonable. It gave them an opportunity to participate in the issue. This financial engineering before an IPO was felt to be misleading if it was done only with a view to getting the issue subscribed. Thus, in FY 2004–05, we restricted companies from splitting the face value of their shares before a public issue. This was an extremely critical change that SEBI brought about, ensuring that the information in the prospectus is not misleading.

In fact, during my tenure, the Institute of Chartered Accountants of India (ICAI) announced new accounting standards for Indian companies in accordance with international accounting standards only after consultation with SEBI, albeit on my persuasion. Accordingly, on an ongoing basis, listed companies were required to make disclosures regarding audit/limited-review, qualifications in audited/limited-review, financial results published by them, and the impact of this qualification on their profit and loss. The unaudited quarterly results were also subjected to limited review (earlier only half-yearly results required limited review), and it was made compulsory for a company to publish its consolidated financial results along with the standalone annual financial results.

The committee observed a trend where a large number of shell (investment) companies were created by corporate houses as a front for various irregular activities. Thus, it was made mandatory for the annual accounts of a listed company to contain the details of loans made by the company to its subsidiaries, associates and related companies, providing also their names, loan amount, terms of repayment, interest rate, loan amount at year-end, the maximum amount of loan granted during the year, end use of such amounts, etc. Relevant disclosures were required in the annual accounts of the subsidiary/associate/related companies too (even if they were not listed).

In addition, while raising capital, companies were made to provide in the offer document the detailed track record of their past financial performance, and new accounting parameters such as net tangible assets, details of appraisal of projects by FIs/SCBs under certain conditions, etc.

Making management more accountable

This was done through various steps, such as asking companies (going for a public issue) to provide management discussion on and analysis of the management's view on the performance of the company in the prospectus, asking for the promoter's PAN number/voter identity number/driving licence number in the prospectus, asking companies to commit to a minimum number of allottees for the public issue to materialize, etc.

For already listed companies, some restrictions (though not mandatory) were put on the term of their independent directors. The board of directors was expected to adopt a formal code of conduct, and regular CEO/CFO certifications and additional disclosures on related-party transactions and use of funds raised from the public were made mandatory in annual reports. The audit committee was made more accountable, and insiders and promoters were required to disclose their holdings periodically, etc.

Other additional disclosures

Some of the other disclosure-related measures that were brought in at the time were: (a) the order of the offer document/ prospectus was suitably changed to make it more readable, (b) the listed companies were required to publish the status of investor complaints along with their quarterly results, (c) brokers were required to disclose to the public all bulk deals in excess of 0.5 per cent of the number of equity shares of the company listed on the stock exchanges, (d) merchant bankers were restricted from dealing in shares of the relevant company for fifteen days after the close of an offer, and if already holding some shares in the companies, were required to disclose the same in the offer document.

In order to facilitate electronic filing of certain documents/statements by the listed companies and their immediate disclosure to market participants, SEBI introduced the electronic data information filing and retrieval (EDIFAR) system, similar to EDGAR in the US. EDIFAR, along with the guidelines for adequate disclosures to be published by companies on their website when they were raising capital, was to ensure timely and simultaneous sharing of information with all interested parties.

The corporate point of view

Certain steps were made easier for companies going in for public issue too. Earlier, the price band or floor price of public issues was required to be disclosed in the red herring prospectus, which was issued about a month before the issue bid opening. We relaxed the requirement of disclosing this price to at least one day prior to the bid opening. This way, companies had sufficient time to judge market sentiment to decide on an appropriate price for their issue. For FPO/OFS, this saved the companies from manipulation of their share prices, as the time between the announcing of floor price/price band and opening of the bid reduced drastically. Further, the details required in the pre-issue advertisement were reduced to the minimum (but important information had to be retained) to reduce the costs companies incurred on them, and to improve the readability of the advertisements.

Criticism

As usual, I followed a transparent process of gathering feedback from the public before effecting the changes and, expectedly, they met with resistance. There was a lot of criticism and comments, the most common being that the offer document/ prospectus would become too big with all the extra disclosures. The listed companies also argued that many suggestions, like quarterly limited review, need for management discussion, updates on investor complaints, provision of identity proofs of promoters, certification from CEO/CFO, were more in the nature of corporate governance issues, which were better left to the companies to deal with, and that SEBI need not interfere. The chairman and managing director (CMD) of an unlisted company went to the extent of saying that the 'tyranny of quarterly results' was perhaps enough of a deterrent to keep companies away from seeking a stock market listing. However, I made it clear that the revised disclosure and accounting norms had to be followed as specified by SEBI, and that there was no going back.

All Is Well

After having fought hard to bring about the changes in the disclosure norms, I felt a sense of triumph when, sometime during the latter part of my tenure, Prof. Florencio Lopez-de-Silanes (then head of the prestigious Yale University's International Institute for Corporate Governance and named among the 100 global leaders of tomorrow in 2002 by the World Economic Forum) in his research granted full marks to India for its disclosure norms.[1] There was similar feedback from several global organizations, as in our disclosure and accounting norms we stood shoulder to shoulder with most of the developed markets, such as the US, UK, Japan and Singapore.

I would also like to quote from an Economist Intelligence Unit study done in 2003: 'Top of the Country class, as might be expected is Singapore followed by Hong Kong and, somewhat surprisingly, India where overall disclosure standards have improved dramatically, accounting differences between local and US standards have been minimized and the number of companies with a majority of independent directors has risen significantly.'

I am also satisfied with the fact that most of the disclosure requirements we brought in still continue to be in force. However, the cherry on the cake would have to be the appreciation I received when I attended an event in China as SEBI chairman. Someone who was following the developments in the Indian market remarked in front of the entire audience, 'Bajpai, why don't you recommend this (a similar overhaul of disclosure and accounting norms) to the Chinese regulator too?'

Well, on this front, we were ahead of China, and someone there wanted them to emulate our steps!

Surrogate Advance Ruling: No Action Letter

One day, the chairman of a medium-sized company called on me with an appointment. He appeared distressed. When asked what the matter was, he narrated his tale of woe. It appeared that the company wanted to undertake some structural changes but the regulatory prescriptions were not very clear. His general counsel (GC) had visited SEBI, met the officer supervising compliance in the matter and sought his advice. But SEBI had been noncommittal.

The GC, on returning from SEBI, advised his company to seek legal opinion. The company decided to obtain the best possible opinion and approached a retired Chief Justice of India. Following the legal advice obtained, the company went ahead with the next step. However, on its action being reported, SEBI took cognizance of it and issued a show cause notice accusing the company of flouting the regulations. The chairman was a law-abiding citizen and wanted to follow the rules and regulations in letter and spirit, but despite his best intentions he was under the enforcement proceedings.

I've always believed that the majority of investors, intermediaries and firms are law abiding and genuinely seek to do the right things in full conformity with the applicable laws. However, oftentimes such people are unaware about how to comply with the law or are unclear about the applicability of some of the provisions. Thus, before undertaking any step that might provoke adversity, such people land up at the lawyers' doors to seek an expert opinion. This entails costs, yet the seeker remains exposed to regulatory onslaught because SEBI may hold a different opinion from the lawyer's. Thus in spite of their best intentions and after burning a hole in their pockets, genuine opinion seekers might sometimes find themselves pulled up by SEBI. If law-abiding citizens had doubts about our regulations, that had to be solved to help them, and also to build trust among the public in the fairness of the regime.

Finding a Solution

The income tax department had (and continues to have) something called Authority for Advance Rulings (AAR). I thought of creating something similar for SEBI too—to give advance rulings on SEBI-related matters at a reasonable cost to genuine opinion seekers, so that they do not have to run from pillar to post. For example, if a company is looking for a potential takeover and is confused about a provision relating to open offers, instead of going to a lawyer or other experts, it could directly approach SEBI and take guidance on the specific issue. However, since this had no precedence in SEBI, even I had to seek some advice.

The highest law officer of India is the Attorney General of India (AGI), who advises the Indian government on legal matters and also acts as its advocate in the Supreme Court. I wrote to him seeking his advice on what I wanted to do. We were advised to approach the Solicitor General of India. The ED (legal affairs) of SEBI met him to discuss the matter personally.

'The SEBI Act 1992 does not empower SEBI to give an advance ruling,' Harish Salve, solicitor general told the SEBI ED. Amendment of the SEBI Act would have been a long-winded exercise. The issue remained open. I was simply not prepared to take no for an answer. I decided to meet Salve myself. 'Please find a way out. I want to help the law-abiding stakeholders. If SEBI guides them well they will be its ambassadors (in ensuring compliance),' I told Salve on meeting him. He said he would think about it and get back to me.

And get back he did with this excellent idea: if a stakeholder wrote to SEBI seeking advice, SEBI should give its opinion in writing. If, in the future, for whatever reason, the dispute lands up in court (i.e., if a third person files a case against the stakeholder who had relied on SEBI's opinion), SEBI would stick to its stand and continue to back the stakeholder. It would not take a stand contrary to its specific opinion given on the matter. We designed the process exactly along these lines.

This letter from SEBI came to be called as the 'no action letter', meaning SEBI is declaring an opinion on the matter and it will stand by it. However, this may not necessarily be the correct interpretation of the law, as only courts have the right to interpret the law and give rulings.

The Fine-tuning

Once the process was broadly agreed on, the challenge now was to make it simple and easy. SEBI had to limit the advance rulings to genuine cases only, and also not allow anyone to misuse it. The worry was that if SEBI entertained everyone it would be flooded with queries and the legal department would be doing 'no action letter' related work only! Also, lawyers and intermediaries could take advice from SEBI, pass it on to their clients and charge them a full fee for it.

To rule out these possibilities, the following rules were designed: First, only a person/company who is going to be directly affected could seek advice from SEBI by approaching it directly and not through any intermediary. This way, the lawyers, intermediaries, investment bankers, brokers and advisors were kept at bay. Though the guidance provided would be useful for interpretation of the law in similar circumstances in other cases, it was made clear that the 'no action letter' cannot be treated as a precedent and that SEBI is not bound by it in other cases.

To prevent a flood of queries, we made the rule that SEBI's advice would be given only on a specific issue or specific instance of lack of clarity and in a particular scenario, on payment of a fee of Rs 25,000. The advice would not be given for multiple scenarios. This meant the party seeking advice would have to exactly describe the issue and scenario for which advice was being sought. They could not give multiple scenarios in a single request. If they wanted advice for multiple scenarios they would have to apply as many times as there were scenarios. Applying multiple times was not allowed, and if permitted, in rare cases, would cost Rs 25,000 for each advice. SEBI's turnaround time for each advice was kept as a maximum of ninety days. That was necessary, as the legal department had to consult many departments, consolidate their views and then respond to the stakeholder.

The Response to the Solution

The advance ruling scheme took off really well, with eight to ten queries every month. This was just the right number to manage, and took care of the genuine opinion seekers. Overall, the market participants seemed happy with it. However, no change in the world has ever come about without a few hiccups.

For example, in spite of the best intentions of SEBI, there have been some stray instances where parties lost cases before SAT after having relied on SEBI's opinion. The parties later publicly expressed their displeasure with SEBI. Then some of the lawyers whose business was eaten up were aggrieved by the whole arrangement. I was aware of the rent-seeking by some of the capital market intermediaries, in particular the investment bankers, who would obtain informal opinion from SEBI officers, advise their clients and charge them for it. This practice was open to breeding unethical activity, and even corruption, so the providing of informal opinion by SEBI officers has been banned. The market participants, though, seemed extremely happy with the 'no action letter' service, and this was validated by the fact that the arrangement, under the name of SEBI (Informal Guidance) Scheme, 2003, continues till date.

13

THE OTHER 'DABBAWALAHS':
THE STOCK MARKET BLACK ECONOMY

Byculla, a south Mumbai neighbourhood, is known for its crowded and narrow lanes filled with honking cars fighting for space, its rows and rows of vegetable sellers, delicious street-side non-vegetarian food and its non-descript, medium-sized residential and commercial buildings. One morning in July 2003, a group of four or five men struggled their way through the Byculla chaos to reach an old, worn-out, shabbily painted, medium-sized building. They forced themselves inside the building and entered the door bearing the name plate 'Bansal Sharevest Securities Pvt. Ltd'. Once these men revealed their identities as SEBI officers, there was commotion inside the office. Some people tried to escape through the back door, some threw documents outside the window, some simply sat at their desks in fear, and some rushed to making distress calls. The SEBI officers managed to calm them down and began their work of search and seizure of the premises. The interior of the office, with its sophisticated equipment and gadgets, was an antithesis of the dilapidated exterior of the building that housed the office. The other offices of Bansal Sharevest in Bhuj, Kolkata, Mathura and Bengaluru were also simultaneously raided by SEBI officers.

This was the first-ever raid conducted by SEBI. It was only a few months back, in December 2002, that SEBI had been given the authority to conduct search and seizure. What prompted SEBI to use this power within six months itself was the growing menace of 'dabba traders'. Over the previous months, SEBI had received various complaints against these illegal traders, and information that Bansal Sharevest was the most prominent player among them. SEBI had decided to crack the whip on them. From the raid on Bansal Sharevest, SEBI uncovered information on other dabba traders too. One of them was Sunil Kayan, whose premises in Kolkata were raided the next month, in August 2003. But before getting into these details, we must first describe what exactly dabba trading is.

The Dabba Method of Trading

This is how a usual share purchase in the share market looked like: An investor wanting to buy shares for, say Rs 100, would instruct his broker to execute the purchase on his behalf. The broker would either take the amount of Rs 100 upfront from the investor or, if he has sufficient margin money from the investor with him, would purchase shares for Rs 100 on the investor's behalf from the exchange by paying that amount himself.

Each trade involved some cost to the investor; a percentage of the transaction amount had to be paid as broker fee, exchange fee, SEBI turnover fee, stamp duty and, from October 2004 onwards, a percentage of the transaction amount would go to the income tax department as STT too. As it stood then, for a transaction amount of Rs 100, the total cost would amount to about Rs 101, the fees and other payments amounting to about 1 per cent of the transaction amount. This would be paid by the investor to his broker (even if the amount of Rs 100 was not paid upfront, some amount had to be kept by the investor with the broker as margin money). A similar cost would be incurred when the investor decided to sell his shares. The sale/purchase transactions would be recorded on a system, with proper trails and paper documentation. Obviously, settlement of a trade in the stock market is guaranteed, and even if one of the parties defaults, the buyer would invariably get his shares and the seller his money.

The Dabba Trader's Way

But there were certain brokers and investors with misplaced adventurism who preferred to trade the dabba trading way. As the name suggests, dabba trading is nothing but hoax trading or fake transactions.

Continuing from the above example, if an investor wanted to bet on shares for Rs 100, in dabba trading the trades would not be formally executed at all! The broker would, on behalf of his customer, execute the trade off the market. This meant the investor would simply bet on that scrip at a particular price point. If the price point rose the customer would gain and get the difference between quoted price and the price point, and if the price fell, he would lose and shell out the difference. In our example, if the price of the scrip fell to Rs 90 (on a pre-decided date, the reference price being Rs 100), the broker or investor would settle the position by paying or receiving Rs 10. All these transactions were done in cash. There was no actual share purchase or sale and no actual payment to the exchanges (either of the transaction amount or the margin money). In fact, the broker/investor did not even need Rs 100 with them to bet on trades. An investor could very well have Rs 10 or nothing in his pocket, and still bet on shares for Rs 100. Dabba trading was simply betting on stock movements. If the anticipated movement went in your favour, you gained money, and if it did not you lost money. Since it was not a transaction, there was absolutely no transaction cost.

To avoid confusion between the betting parties, a price point would be officially fixed by trading a small amount of shares in the formal market at that price (say, 1 share would be purchased through the formal route at Rs 100 to fix that as the reference price, while the total bet could involve ten shares, 1,000 shares or more). Thus there would be many small single transactions made by the dabba brokers and investors. There could be many buyers and sellers, and the trades would square off on a mutually agreed date. Whatever deals happened were on the basis of mere trust. Most of the time, the investors were willing participants in the dabba trade. Sometimes the broker did the dabba trading without the knowledge of the investor and even on his own behalf. At times brokers would speculate on a stock themselves by creating false client accounts to show that some genuine work was happening at their terminals.

So, what were the effects of this dabba trading?

Impact of Dabba Trading

The brokers/investors saved on the various statutory dues, such as broker fee, exchange fee, SEBI turnover fee, stamp duty, STT, etc., by doing their trades off the market instead of on the exchanges, which would attract all the above statutory dues, to the extent of about 1 per cent. They also did not pay the share purchase price or margin money to the broker or exchange, and avoided the blocking of their capital with the exchange. In formal trading, the entire share purchase price, or at least some margin money, was always blocked for safety. Thus, this *dabba* trading was akin to a full-fledged parallel black economy of the stock market. Lakhs of crores of rupees were being betted, but hardly any of it was happening through the exchanges, and many authorities (the exchanges, SEBI, the revenue department etc.) were being deprived of thousands of crores of rupees in revenue. Also, exchanges were deprived of the share purchase prices or margin safety. In addition, if the brokers/investors made any gains, they would not be paying capital gains tax on their dabba trades, causing a further loss of revenue to the country's exchequer. Black money hoarders would use their unaccounted wealth to trade in the stock markets through these dabba trading channels and further the black money economy.

Second, this dabba trading was akin to pure gambling, which is prohibited in India. Brokers and investors often make trade bets, risking crores of rupees without having the adequate amount with them for backing their bets, as anyway the bets were off market and there were no margins in reserve. So even if a bet was won, the losing broker or investor from whom the money was to be collected would vanish. In the end, investors' money would be at big risk, and there was no exchange guarantee and margin safety to protect them as the trades were not happening through the exchanges. The risk was even more in cases where brokers indulged in dabba trades without informing their clients. Some dabba traders would, however, hedge their net positions daily through official derivatives trades, but those were exceptions rather than the rule. All in all, this had the simmering characteristics of a low-lying systemic risk. And any area of activity that has contagion tendencies could become a systemic risk. Since dabba trading was becoming widespread, their volumes were growing and many gullible investors were getting drawn in. It had the propensity to become a contagion, which could eventually spread to the capital market in many ways: (a) with the growing dabba trades, the derivatives positions of some of the dabba traders were rapidly rising; the resulting unwinding or failure of large numbers of such hedged brokers to settle could be a risk; (b) a large number of aggrieved investors, gullible though they might have been, would rock the sentiment in the market and in Parliament, as it happened when the chit funds scam blew up; (c) large failures of dabba trades would affect sentiments in the capital market, and if they happened around the dates of derivatives settlement, it was bound to impact the market and become a low-lying possibility of a market-wide failure later. After all, these transactions were ostensibly done as stock exchange transactions. And how could the regulator permit this illegal activity?

Generally, dabba trading happened in centres where the smaller regional stock exchanges (RSEs) were present. RSE governing boards were not strictly monitoring the norms of trading and surveillance. Brokers in their zones often constituted a kind of financial mafia whom the governing boards had to obey. They had to ignore the illegalities committed right in or outside the stock exchange premises. Shockingly, some brokers had even convinced themselves that they were helping people through dabba trades.

When asked questioned about his activities, Sunil Kalyan, a Kolkata-based dabba trader, made the following statement in a leading daily, 'Whatever I am doing is a gainful economic activity for a lot of individuals. Investors who come to my office do it willingly. There is no truth in your statement that they have been cheated in the process.'[1]

It was estimated that the average turnover from dabba trades amounted to Rs 2,000 crore daily; whereas formal trades were in the range of Rs 4,000 crore to Rs 8,000 crore in turnover at the time. So dabba trades constituted about a third of overall market trades. That was a huge informal market. Some sections of the media even estimated the turnover from dabba trading at Rs 6,000 crore a day—that is, equal to or more than the formal markets. Ahmedabad Stock Exchange was particularly notorious for the dabba trading that happened outside its premises. Illegal trading volumes accounted for a high share of stock market transactions, and here, dabba trades happened fearlessly right outside the main exchange.

Investors seldom complained, as they did not have adequate knowledge about the markets or about their right to complain, and could be easily hoodwinked by the brokers with some fake story of money loss. Some investors wishing to complain were threatened by the brokers. And sometimes, investors themselves were involved in the speculation or gambling.

As far as documentation was concerned, some brokers tampered with their software to generate fake trails and paper documents. Believe it or not, there were special software providers for dabba trading. Using their software a broker could punch an order for ten shares on the exchange, but the actual order that would get executed would only be for one share. The numbers punched would automatically be divided or the zeros just vanish. So on paper one would see ten share purchase orders being executed, whereas in reality only one share was traded through the formal route (this was required to establish the reference price, as mentioned above). The balance nine shares could very well have taken the off market trade route. This software could convert 100, 1,000 or other big numbers to 1, 5, or other smaller numbers. In many cases the documents showed a trade properly executed on an exchange. It was very difficult to catch such speculators unless one probed deeper, as all the paperwork suggested a proper trade.

Inside a Typical Dabba Trader's Office

Once instances of dabba trading came to the notice of SEBI, it was decided to crackdown on the traders. A full-fledged search and seizure was planned. SEBI probed further, established proofs, unearthed the names of the brokers indulging in this illegal trading and finally formed a team of four or five officers to start the surprise raids on these brokers, among whom Bansal Sharevest was the first, and probably the most prominent one. Since these unofficial trades were also an illegal activity, in general, we sought the help of the respective state governments by writing to the concerned chief ministers for their support in curbing them. Many of these unscrupulous brokers (including Bansal Sharevest), not surprisingly, had political backing, and even had some politicians, amongst other influential persons, as their clients. But concern about the consequences of our action was not on our minds when we raided such brokers. SEBI had a job at hand, so we went ahead and did it, taking some risk of a possible backlash from the affected parties.

Every raid had to be planned with utmost precision and secrecy to avoid any information leakage. Since raids could turn hostile, help was taken from the police to accompany the SEBI officers on the raids and to facilitate forcible entry into the brokers' premises. The local magistrate was taken into confidence for formal judicial permission only the previous night (of the planned raid) as we did not want any third party to know about our plans, in case the whole purpose of the raid was defeated. At the end of the raid on Bansal Sharevest, computers and note books were seized and the employees and promoters taken for questioning. One raid led to the names of many other dabba traders, and over time, many illegal traders were nabbed; others shut down overnight on hearing of SEBI's operations against their lot.

Unfortunately, SEBI does not have the powers of a criminal court, and it could only do one of three civil actions against the culprits—issue them a warning, impose a monetary penalty, cancel their license and/or debar the traders from the market. In the end, we imposed the highest penalties possible under the SEBI Act 1992, debarring the involved persons from the market and cancelling the licences of the brokers involved in dabba trading.

Human ingenuity is limitless. The temptation to profit in an underhand way by exploiting opportunities is universal. Daredevils and evil minds marshal their ingenuity to translate their temptation into activities like dabba trading. Regulatory alacrity and fast judicial deliverance can certainly curb, if not entirely prevent, such misdemeanours from becoming widespread and posing a risk to the system. Whereas the regulatory alacrity was adequate, the criminal justice system in the country could not respond with equal urgency. Many criminal cases filed by SEBI have not been heard for years. So where is the question of ultimate action in these matters? I hope that one day the dynamics of criminal justice systems will get wings and the Indian judicial system a sense of urgency.

Surgical Strike Against P-notes

September 1992 was a landmark month for the Indian securities markets. That was the month when, for the first time, the Indian government allowed foreign institutional investors (FIIs) such as foreign mutual funds, pension funds, investment trusts, asset management companies, institutional portfolio managers, nominee companies and overseas corporate bodies to invest in tradeable securities in the primary and secondary Indian markets. The FIIs were required to be registered with SEBI. The registration process basically required FIIs to disclose certain details and also take permission from RBI to open and operate a bank account in India. Within a matter of six months, eighteen FIIs were registered with SEBI, and a net amount of roughly Rs 600 crore entered the Indian capital market through these FIIs, indicating its popularity. This was a major step towards the globalization of Indian markets.

Foreign individual investors, however, could not invest in the Indian securities markets directly, and the only way for them to participate in it was through FIIs. For example, an individual investor would give money to a fund manager, which is a registered FII, and this FII, in turn, would invest on that investor's behalf in the Indian market. The FII would hold the securities on behalf of the investor and give the investor a receipt to that effect. This receipt came to be called as a participatory note, or P-note, whose underlying asset was securities.

Now, while the identity of FIIs was completely known, the Indian authorities did not know the identities of the holders of the P-notes. As the Indian economy grew and inflows from FIIs became larger, there was increased investment in the Indian securities markets through P-notes. Soon these P-notes became a popular mode of investing in India for both individuals and institutions not wishing to disclose their identities, for whatever reason. FIIs kept coming in, so initially nobody seemed to mind the P-notes, until they began to be misused by investors (allegedly politicians, bureaucrats, businessmen, and the like; and, in extreme situations, even terror financiers) to route their unaccounted wealth back to India, taking advantage of hidden identity that P-notes allowed. Most of the money going into P-notes came from tax havens like the Cayman Islands, Mauritius, Panama, etc. SEBI or RBI had little control over these P-notes and had no idea whom they were being issued to by the FIIs.

The twist in the tale was that the P-note, which was treated as a security overseas, could be the underlying asset of another P-note. Many 'P-notes over P-notes' were being issued, creating many layers. Tracking the identity of the original investor, the last layer of ownership of the P-notes, became very difficult. Further, if sale or purchase was undertaken through Euro-clear (European clearing house), tracking became impossible, as Euro-clear is like an ocean, and fishing out the ultimate investors from it could be like looking for a needle in a haystack.

By the time I joined SEBI, net FII inflows in India had grown to around Rs 9,000 crore in the year 2001–02. The first time P-notes came under tremendous fire was in the aftermath of Scam 2001 where, as the December 2002 report of JPC pointed out, the P-note holders had rigged many stocks, hiding behind the veil of the instrument. There was a lot of pressure on SEBI to take some action against P-notes—either to ban them or to increase the disclosure requirements for them. The official stand taken by SEBI in 2001 was that in the matter of P-notes being issued outside India, SEBI did not have the jurisdiction to control them. The underlying issue was participation of individual investors from overseas. Since the broader framework, for reasons of efficacious superintendence, did not permit direct participation by certain overseas investors—which has since been allowed, albeit in a gradual and restricted way—banning P-notes would have deprived the country of sizeable money flows. After all, significant numbers of the entities investing in P-notes were believed to be genuine investors of credibility and respect, and were welcomed in all jurisdictions. Hence, my focus was on ensuring transparency. I took the decision that SEBI had every power to ensure that the entities registered in India, i.e., the FIIs who obtain SEBI registration, could be mandated to make disclosures about the beneficial owners of P-notes. This was the first time that a conscious forward-looking decision was taken to ring-fence our markets from elements sitting outside India and committing financial crimes in our markets. In fact, I would say that this was a precursor to the now famous FATCA, where other countries are required to give KYC information to the US regulator about entities from their countries operating in the US.

Therefore, as a first step, in Feburary 2004 we made it mandatory that P-notes could only be issued to and transferred between entities regulated in their home countries, and FIIs were required to disclose the names of the P-note holders periodically. Further, only one layer of P-note with underlying asset as P-note could be issued, to facilitate tracking of the ultimate investor. Earlier there could be layer upon layer of P-notes, as mentioned above.

However, even after this rule there were many reports in the media of widespread misuse of P-notes without SEBI's knowledge. Somewhere during the first quarter of 2004, *Outlook* magazine had published an article raising apprehensions that a substantial part of inflows into investments by FIIs in India comprised funds clandestinely taken out from India to tax havens like the Cayman Islands, Mauritius and Panama for reinvestment back to India. The objective was to bring the earlier unaccounted wealth into a formal securities market channel via the P-notes and FIIs. There were accusations that this round-tripping of money had intensified because of the upcoming general elections of May 2004. The money routing through tax havens also fetched tax benefits for the ultimate investor.

We decided to probe further into the P-note menace.

SEBI's Own Surgical Strike against P-notes

When we studied the data on FIIs and P-notes in detail, we found that investment in India through FIIs and P-notes was the highest via Mauritius, as it has a double tax avoidance treaty with India. Also, Mauritius being an offshore centre, it levied only 10 per cent tax on gains. At SEBI, we now wanted to know who were behind these P-notes, whether the rules of issuance, transfer and disclosure of P-notes made by us were being followed strictly, and whether the media accusations were true.

I have mentioned earlier that I was actively involved in building SEBI's relationships with global regulators. We had, in December 2002, signed a bilateral agreement with FSC Mauritius for sharing of information between the two countries. We decided to make use of this agreement to get transaction data on the P-notes being issued by FIIs in Mauritius. This was the first time something like this was being sought by an Indian regulator from a foreign country, so we wanted to maintain utmost confidentiality about the whole matter, lest it should lead to any unnecessary speculations in the Indian markets.

So, in secret, a team of two officers from SEBI was sent to Mauritius to investigate the FIIs and the P-notes they issued. Confidentiality was maintained to such an extent that nobody besides a very small select group of officers in SEBI and the finance ministry knew about this. Even the officers' flight tickets to Mauritius were not booked by the admin department of SEBI to avoid any possibility of information leakage. They were given my direct (unlisted) number, and were to call only me directly in case of any problems.

The two officers stayed in Mauritius for three days and studied the data. A preliminary perusal of the books of the Mauritius Offshore Business Activities Authority (MOBAA) indicated that Citibank (registered as an FII in India and investing in the Indian markets) had a Mauritius unit through which it was issuing P-notes. The crux of the issue was that these P-note issuances had not been disclosed to SEBI by Citibank. As per SEBI requirements, every FII was required to disclose this. Then there were other FIIs too holding P-notes which had not been disclosed to SEBI. However, Citibank was the more prominent one.

The SEBI team wanted further details on all FIIs and P-notes from Mauritius, and wanted to bring back the data with them as proof to establish a concrete case against the defaulting FIIs. That was when the Mauritius authorities showed reluctance to part with any further information or to give us any data copies. After all, confidentiality was an integral part of MOBAA's operations. So the matter had to be escalated, and finally, after many back and forth calls at the highest levels, MOBAA agreed to provide the details of any one entity that we chose. We chose Citibank, they being the largest seller of P-notes.

When the data on Citibank Mauritius operations came in, it got further established, with proof, that Citibank had not disclosed information about their P-notes as per SEBI requirements. The matter was now referred for adjudication.

Adjudication against Citi

SEBI began adjudication proceedings against Citi and issued a show cause notice to them to explain their actions. Simultaneously, a fraud report against Citibank was prepared and sent to the government, to keep them in the loop. Citibank was (and is) no small organization. It is an international bank with a battery of lawyers and significant clout, even with the government. Their lawyers would come and lobby SEBI, trying to convince the SEBI officers across hierarchies as to why they had not violated any rules. On top of it, there was pressure from various quarters including big players in the financial markets who asked us to reconsider our stand against Citi. But we stuck to our guns and said that since there was a violation, it had to be handled suitably. Finally, the Citibank accepted SEBI's stand.

The adjudicating officer imposed the highest penalty until date on Citibank. All of this was happening in utmost secrecy, and the media was given no whiff of it as investor sentiment in and about India at the time was all positive, and splashing this Citibank case in the media could have created a negative atmosphere in the market. Even the fraud report against Citi sent to the government was prepared by the officers at my residence, taken directly to the airport from there by a trusted aide and handed over personally in the finance ministry in Delhi to avoid any transitory leakage. Even Citibank did not contest SEBI's decision, and consented to the penalty for fear that the information might be brought out in public. That would result in brand erosion for the bank. It paid the penalty quietly.

Important Takeaways from the Citi Episode

This Citi drama (investigation, adjudication and final penalty) went on for a few months. The journey was a long one but there were three important takeaways from it, from the SEBI point of view.

First, this was the first time that the new revised powers of SEBI were used to impose a fine, and this was the highest fine charged till date. The SEBI investigation was conducted without any governmental interference, even though the government was kept in the loop. Even when there was pressure from certain quarters in the government to change our stand against Citi, we stuck to our decision.

Second, charging the highest penalty apart, a stern message was sent to the investing community that India or Indian regulators cannot be treated lightly, as just any another regulator. Before this Citi saga, foreign players had a condescending attitude towards SEBI, trying to preach to us about how SEBI needed to improve, how there was a gap between international practices and SEBI practices, and the like. But the Citi episode sent them the message that we were a no-nonsense regulator, equal to any other in the world. In fact, SEBI's global image went up a few notches, and our internal confidence deepened significantly.

Third, the whole Citi saga had a lasting impact on the Mauritius authorities too. The Mauritius Financial Services Commission chairman met me personally and assured me that in future the Mauritian authorities would be careful about preventing money laundering through its channels. And, post this Citi issue, they ordered inspection of all their entities operating in Mauritius.

Increased SEBI Confidence

The requirement of disclosures regarding P-note holders was really deepened after the Citi episode. The number of layers with P-notes as underlying security was restricted to just one, whereas there had been many layers earlier. One was allowed to provide liquidity and assignability of the P-note. We also showed that SEBI could walk the talk and suitably punish the guilty, even if it was a big conglomerate like Citibank. In addition, SEBI turned down the exemptions sought by ICICI Bank and TCS for allowing P-notes for their IPOs in mid-2004. This was particularly tricky, since big names like JM Morgan Stanley, DSP Merrill Lynch and JP Morgan were handling the TCS IPO.

Going forward, we kept a close watch on illegal P-note transactions (the ones not approved by SEBI) and wherever they looked suspect, relevant information from the concerned brokers was called for. The erring brokers were fined suitably. The broking community felt the pinch, and one broker made this comment in the media: 'SEBI has become extremely strict and only recently it had hounded two foreign brokerage houses to reveal the identity of their PN clients. We hear that SEBI has even slapped heavy penalties on two brokerage arms of global investment houses.' Earlier SEBI would not look beyond Indian shores, and the mindset was that if something was happening outside India, it was not within our scope or reach. The Citi episode entirely changed the SEBI mindset to not just 'we must know' what's come into India from outside, but also to 'we can know' what's coming into India from outside. This was the beginning of the tightening of norms for foreign money inflows into India and the beginning of an era of India being in the driver's seat regarding foreign money inflows.

Since then, the journey of P-notes in India has been shaky and full of ups and downs, depending on the economic situation and investor sentiment. In 2007, a rule was made that FIIs could not issue any further P-notes and that the existing P-notes have to be wound up in eighteen months' time. This decision was taken against the backdrop of a surge in capital flows and excess liquidity in the capital markets. However, in 2008 this restriction was removed altogether in the wake of the global financial crisis, amid fears of capital outflows. Though from 2011 onwards, the disclosure requirements for P-notes have only increased, and as a result participation through P-notes in India has decreased drastically, P-note issuance is far from over. Meanwhile, the debate in India still continues, as to whether P-notes should be banned completely, should be put under very strict disclosure norms (when India might risk losing out on foreign money) or continued with reasonable disclosure norms (risking entry of black money into the market). Recently, further issuance of P-notes has been prohibited.

But whatever be the final decision, India now has much better control of its foreign inflows, the seeds of which were sown in 2004.

14

HANDLING SYSTEMIC ISSUES: INSPIRING CORPORATE GOVERNANCE STANDARDS

Failure of governance in companies has caused significant distress to stakeholders across geographies. It has even threatened the stability of the entire capital market in the UK, United States and other European countries. In India, corporate governance standards were a step behind those of the mature economies.

Before my joining SEBI, the corporate governance framework outlined by SEBI, as a part of clause 49 of the Listing Agreement (now converted into regulations) was based on the recommendations of the Kumaramangalam Birla committee set up in early 1999. Much water had flown under the bridge since. The connivance of promoters and corporations in Scam 2001 spoke of the deficit in governance standards in India. By 2003, the Indian economy had taken a leap. Its high GDP growth was led by the vibrancy of the corporate sector; there was a 30 per cent quarter-on-quarter growth in lending, companies were growing in size and the Sensex and Nifty were booming. The urge to preside over a larger empire and profit from the market exuberance led entrepreneurs and even professional managers into practices that showed up the prevalent corporate governance standards as being wholly inadequate. The systemic risk was looming large over the Indian capital market, and this warranted proactive steps to revisit the governance standards that had been laid down to de-risk the system.

The two committees chaired by Y.H. Malegaon on improving disclosure and accounting standards had also highlighted the urgency with which the overall governance framework—boardroom practices in particular—had to be addressed. It was decided to appoint a committee under the chairmanship of Narayana Murthy, chairman of Infosys, with very prominent professionals from various industries, including the capital market, as its members. I had deliberately chosen Narayana Murthy to head the committee because the governance standards of Infosys were highly acclaimed, even by the market, and the stock of Infosys was trading at much higher Price Earning (PE) multiples than those of other large IT companies. This was market validation of the quality of the governance practices of the company led by Murthy. The committee began its work rather quickly, and in right earnest.

In the meantime, the department of company affairs (now ministry of corporate affairs) had appointed a committee under the chairmanship of Naresh Chandra, a former Cabinet secretary. To begin with, the mandate of that committee was to improve the accounting and financial reporting standards across the corporate spectrum, irrespective of whether a company was listed or unlisted. There was always a kind of tug of war between SEBI and the department of company affairs as to who has the jurisdiction over corporate governance. Whereas SEBI maintained that it has an absolute right to lay down governance standards for listed companies, DCA felt it was at the helm of the total spectrum and decided to extend the terms of reference of its committee to include corporate governance. The disagreement as to this jurisdiction continues even to this day. However, I didn't want to fall into the trap of a turf war and was determined to achieve the objective of improving the governance standards. To quell the turf war, the DCA was allowed a nominee on the board of SEBI, replacing the nominee of the ministry of law.

One fine morning I got a call from the finance secretary to say that the minister was unhappy at my appointing the Narayana Murthy committee when he had already appointed the Naresh Chandra committee. I made light of it, being very friendly with him, and told him not to worry; I would explain it to the minister. A couple of days into the conversation I happened to visit Delhi. After the items on the agenda for the meeting I went for had been discussed, I mentioned to the minister what the finance secretary had told me. Cool as he always looked during meetings, the expression on his face showed that he expected an explanation. I said, 'Sir you may not be able to improve the governance standards through legislation because of the pressure of economic agents (through legislators) on the matter of approval of amendments to the Companies Act that may be proposed. The overhang of systemic risk on account of corporate governance needs to be fixed. Let me do it through subordinate legislation.' The minister, an action-oriented political executive, seemed pleased with my answer and the conversation ended there.

The role of the Naresh Chandra committee was, however, not changed. A month or so later, I got a call to appear before that committee. The suggestion was not only ridiculous, but atrocious. It was not a Parliamentary committee, and I was an independent regulator by legislation and could be summoned only by Parliament or its committees. I offered to send one of my senior officers to provide the committee all the information it would like to have from us. However, the committee was insistent that I appear before them. Here was an impasse now, and battle lines were likely to be drawn.

I had come to the regulatory body from a managerial background; I have been trained to navigate rough weathers and move ahead rather than dig my heels in on status. In any case, I didn't want to pick up, or aid, a conflict. So in one of my conversations with one of the members of that committee, we agreed that I and Naresh Chandra, chairman of that committee, would meet at a mutually convenient place and time in Delhi to clear the impasse. The meeting was fixed and Chandra came to see me in my hotel room. We spent nearly an hour together discussing a variety of issues concerning the management of companies and the related regulatory framework. In that trail of discussions, the subject of corporate governance also came up very briefly. Naresh Chandra being a very senior, nice and friendly person who had served as a diplomat (India's Ambassador to the US), we ended the conversation on a very pleasant note of remaining in touch on a personal level, more so to sort out issues, if any, to avoid any kind of disharmony between us.

The Naresh Chandra committee submitted its recommendations, which were part of the new bill that was introduced in Parliament to replace the Companies Act 1956. My prophecy came true. The pressure of economic agents was so built that the bill had to be withdrawn. In the meantime, the Narayana Murthy committee submitted its report; SEBI considered it and the new clause 49 was notified. The changes brought about as a consequence of the recommendations of the Narayana Murthy committee were wide and varied. In fact, there was a near total overhaul of the governance framework. The major changes have been listed below. However, in quite a few areas, including limiting the tenure of independent directors, the suggestions could not be made obligatory because, as per the hierarchy of laws, what cannot be done by legislation cannot be done by subordinate legislation; and the proposed legislation incorporating those clauses was withdrawn.

The major changes in the new clause 49 of the listing agreement, which laid down the direction for governance of listed firms, were as under.

Obligatory:

1. Amendments to provisions relating to independent directors with a view to reducing the overhang of promoter and executive directors, and also treatment of nominee directors
2. Strengthening the responsibilities of the audit committee and financial literacy of members
3. Improving the quality of disclosures, more particularly in the matter of related party transactions
4. Ensuring utilization of the proceeds from public/rights/ preferential issues for the purpose for which they had been raised
5. Adoption of formal code of conduct by the board
6. CEO and CFO certification of financial statements
7. Enhancing disclosures to shareholders
8. Assessment and disclosures of business risks
9. Compensation to non-executive directors

Voluntary:

1. Adoption of whistle blower policy
2. Limiting the term of independent directors
3. Instituting training of board members
4. Evaluation of performance of board members and committees
5. Moving to a regime where financial statements are not qualified

A new regime of corporate governance, transparency and global accounting standards was ushered in.

The Companies Act 1956 could be replaced only in 2013, which brought about further changes in the areas of corporate governance, incorporating quite a few of the guidelines issued following the Narayana Murthy committee recommendations.

The moral of the story is, if there is a bulldozer on your path, do not try to take it head on, side-step it, find another path and navigate along it, even if you have to travel a few miles on rough land.

15

ARMING THE GUARDS: BUILDING A SOPHISTICATED INTEGRATED MARKET SURVEILLANCE SYSTEM (IMSS)

Malpractices like *benami* transactions, price rigging, circular and fraudulent trading, and various other forms of market abuse were rampant in the early 2000s. The key reasons for failure in the detection of such transactions included the absence of relevant data, lack of a common repository of identities of market participants and non-availability of analytical tools. In fact, the scattered data that was collected made any analysis difficult and stale. The regulator's inadequacy in deciphering the emerging risks in the various components of the market was obvious.

During my visit to the United States and the UK, I learnt that their regulatory bodies have a system of collecting data electronically (mainly) from one or two sources, collating them and building scenarios to anticipate the onset of events that would need to be de-risked.

I returned determined to create an integrated market surveillance system (IMSS) at SEBI; simply put, integrated data feeds from intermediaries, exchanges and banks into a common repository for all segments of the market—cash and derivatives, mutual funds, and the rest. The feeds could be voice, text, or numbers, or all of these. I aimed for the system to be scalable to assimilate the data relating to commodities, forex and interest rate derivatives transactions too; after all, the intermediaries are common to all of them and money is fungible. Such a system, with the help of analytics, should then be able to signal unusual patterns in trading or unusual behaviour among market participants.

It was decided to create a database of participants, called MAPIN. Integration of the MAPIN database into the surveillance system described above could make it possible for SEBI to quickly, if not instantly, identify the operators behind unusual market movements. The unusual patterns and movements could then be examined by the surveillance staff to decipher what risks could possibly emerge. We could then build elimination, containment or management measures. It would also be possible to pass on the data with evidences and audit trails to the enforcement department for further action if misconduct was detected. All this was a tall task and needed imagination, understanding, and the capability to create a very robust and modern IT system.

However, SEBI had already taken up its ambitious project to issue unique IDs to all market participants. In parallel, work on setting up IMSS for both the cash and derivatives markets began. The growing size and complexity of the market was considered in the process. I commissioned a study under a USAID programme as a part of the Financial Institutions Reform and Expansion (FIRE) project under World Bank to help design an apt structure for such a sophisticated surveillance system. The idea was to plan a state-of-the-art technology-based system capable of generating automatic alerts for price rigging, artificial volumes, insider trading, etc., by accessing and analysing quickly data from multiple sources like exchanges, clearing houses, depositories, EDIFAR, listed companies and market participants.

The surveillance system of National Association of Securities Dealers (NASD), the regulatory wing of NASDAQ, was very potent and versatile. So we asked them if they would like to undertake the project for SEBI. NASD quoted an exorbitant price—US\$ 80 million. Since I wanted a system even better than theirs, I had a chat with the FM, Jaswant Singh. He was very supportive of the idea and offered to fund the costs. He was very keen on building an efficient capital market. He said he would approach Parliament for approval of a special allocation for us, if need be. While thanking him for the offer I told him I would try to bring down the costs to the extent possible and fund the exercise from SEBI's own resources. I would approach the government for funds only if we ran out of money. He was very happy with SEBI's resolve to improve its surveillance mechanism.

The result was a roadmap for our IMSS, a very efficacious tool of surveillance. It was envisaged to be a research and regulatory analysis platform. The process for the proposed IMSS was initiated by appointing a high-level technical committee comprising eminent IT experts: Prof. Phatak of IIT Mumbai as chairman, Prof. Sarda of IIT Mumbai, Prof. Gulati, director, RBI Institute of Technology, and Prof. Sadagopan, director, Indian Institute of Sciences, Bengaluru, to study the requirements, suggest an IT architecture, decide the eligibility criteria, and prepare the basis for drafting of tender documents, evaluation of bids and specification of contractual terms. I briefed the committee as to the aspirations of SEBI so that they could design the architecture appropriately. Some of the committee members visited Australia, the US and Norway to study the advanced surveillance systems in those countries. The committee then met me again to understand what exactly I was looking to achieve from the IMSS. Having got the hang of it, they created a document for 'expression of interest', including the eligibility criteria for bidders for the project. It transpired that the terms were so wide and the requirements so deep that not a single IT company felt qualified to undertake the project by itself. So they joined hands with other IT companies for the building and project execution.

The tender documents were issued to four parties, including NASD. Bids were received and the contract awarded under the supervision of this committee. Eventually, after a stiff competition amongst companies to win the project, it went to SMARTS of Australia, which would do the project in collaboration with HCL of India for a price of about Rs 25 crore. Since the project was novel and an improvement over the best at the time in the world, all the interested bidders considered it as an exercise in building their own capabilities. With this unique project under their belt, they could scout for many such projects globally. This system was deployed in the year following my retirement.

During the period when the system was being set up, we implemented an interim enhanced surveillance mechanism in June 2003. For this, a group of top executives from the two major stock exchanges, the depositories and SEBI met regularly every week. These meetings, which were attended by the WTMs and usually chaired by the chairman of SEBI, constituted a standing forum for exchange of information, views and perceptions related to market movements and assessment of emerging concerns, helping to bring about coordinated actions. During specific situations, like volatility in the market, these meetings were held more frequently. Between July 2003 and February 2005, about 100 surveillance meetings were held.

Improved Coordination

The foundation of any incisive surveillance system resides in its ability to act on the information received from various sources from beyond the walls of the regulator or stock exchange. Therefore we set up an SEBI-RBI group on integrated systems of alerts, which recommended suitable measures for coordinated actions. Based on the suggestions of the group, the required data items were identified and adequate alerts put in place in February

2004. Similarly, an effort was made to put in place information sharing and coordination between the stock markets. We formalized a mechanism for coordination between the two major stock exchanges (NSE and BSE) in a variety of areas such as surveillance, investigations, scrip suspension, application of circuit filters and rumour verification. Under this arrangement, exchanges shared relevant information and also met periodically to discuss relevant issues.

Greater Accountability of Surveillance Cells of Stock Exchanges

It was important that the exchanges too take steps to improve their own surveillance capabilities. SEBI, therefore, advised the exchanges to develop and implement an online market monitoring and surveillance system on the basis of the recommended parameters. Since then, exchanges have implemented such surveillance systems in different forms, customizing them to suit their own trading practices and procedures, though basic alerts have remained similar at all exchanges.

The entire process helped SEBI bring about effective surveillance of the market; this is proved by the fact that no large-scale misconduct has taken place in the capital markets since 2002.

Mentoring Money Managers—Mutual Funds

In one of our public meetings early in my tenure, a senior citizen, apparently financially literate, narrated his tale of woe. He said, 'The so-called experts in investment management have messed up my investments in mutual funds (MFs) and I have lost a sizeable part of my small little fortune.' Pain was writ large on his face. I was moved. I noted the details of his complaint, and on return to the office got the entire case examined in depth. The analysis showed there was scope for improving the mutual fund industry significantly, and of preventing mismanagement.

It has evolved over a period of time that savers who do not have (a) adequate skills, (b) enough time and/or (c) desire a diversified investment portfolio, entrust their surpluses to experts called (i) wealth managers and (ii) mutual funds. These managers are expected to understand the needs and aspirations of investors, and to use their skills and deliver optimal returns within the overarching frame of security and liquidity.

The establishment of Unit Trust of India in 1964 was one of the significant developments in the Indian capital market. It opened up a new route of investment to ordinary investors. Even though it has a chequered history, the UTI had, over time, established a reputation for itself, acquired a size of consequence and done a fairly good job of handling investors' money. Following the agenda of liberalization, policymakers decided to open the mutual fund industry to other operators. To begin with, financial institutions like LIC, GIC and public sector banks were allowed to float mutual funds. Slowly and steadily, organizations in the private sector joined in.

Notification of the SEBI (Mutual Funds) Regulations, 1993, brought about a restructuring of the mutual fund industry. Apart from permitting the entry of private sector mutual funds into the industry, the regulations mandated an arm's length relationship between the fund sponsor, trustees, custodian and asset management company, which are the four constituents of Indian mutual funds.

Mutual funds in India operate on a three-layered structure. Right at the top is the sponsor of a trust. The trust launches MF schemes and owns the funds on behalf of investors. The trust also floats an asset management company, which, for a commission, manages the assets on behalf of the MF. In the initial euphoria of mopping up a large amount of surpluses and in the absence of a dedicated, empowered and incisive regulator, mutual funds floated schemes that even offered guaranteed rates of return. The cyclicality and vagaries of the market were a challenge to delivering the promised returns. Investors were chasing mutual funds to get them to fulfil their contractual obligations. The sponsors were compelled to fund the gap to meet their commitment to offer a promised return under their contracts with investors. I distinctly remember LIC having funded something like Rs 65 crore to meet its commitment of a fixed rate of return to investors in LIC MF. Due to the directives of SEBI, nine mutual funds in the public sector had to contribute about Rs 2,500 crore to assured return schemes to meet their shortfall in payment of promised returns to their unit holders. Later, the government had to pay assured returns in the case of the schemes of UTI when the Net Asset Value (NAV) fell along with an overall fall in the markets.

With the establishment of SEBI as the sole capital market regulator, control and superintendence of mutual funds fell within its jurisdiction. UTI was eventually brought under its purview. The rise in Indian equity indices and the exuberance and hubris in the capital market prodded common investors in 1998, 1999 and 2000 to again join the procession in search of profits from the potential possibility of further market rises. Even in 2017–18 too, a similar grand march by investors is fuelling the rise of MF Assets Under Management (AUMs) rather speedily.

Following Scam 2001, the Sensex and Nifty tanked. As in the case of equity, investors in mutual fund equity schemes too lost their shirts. The distressed balance sheets of corporations and the rise in bank Non-Performing Assets (NPAs) nearabout the same time led to substantial losses even for debt and balance funds. Whereas a significant part of the misery of the investors could be attributed to the fall in the capital market, inefficiency and even indiscretion on the part of mutual fund managers was equally responsible. Some of the fund managers, in connivance with people like Ketan Parekh, had put investor money into dubious securities, both equity and debt. Stories of unethical behaviour by fund managers—front-running, circular trading and pay-off—were in circulation. The role of the board of directors of MFs and Asset Management Companies (AMCs) were discovered to be deficient.

The unfortunate saga of that senior citizen, as also of large numbers of other investors, questioned the quality of management of the mutual fund industry. There was need for a comprehensive overhaul of the regulatory direction and practices in the market. I commissioned the services of the concerned ED at SEBI, a capable, industrious, proactive senior executive of quiet demeanour, to spearhead the reforms, which he very ably and conscientiously did.

Professionalization of the MF Industry

Thousands of intermediaries—distributors of mutual fund products—operated in an informal manner. The level of professionalism was low; there were no mandatory qualifications for the intermediaries and there was poor adherence to the code of conduct. Risk management processes were hazy, and the accountability of CEOs and fund managers vague.

Distributors

To begin with, SEBI mandated that all intermediaries selling and marketing mutual fund products should get registered with the Association of Mutual Funds of India (AMFI), which was subject to passing a certification examination. Adherence to the guidelines of SEBI and AMFI and continuous professional development were made essential for the continued registration of MF intermediaries. However, an exception to the rule of passing the examination was made in the case of senior citizens who had acquired significant experience in distributing mutual funds. The focus of the SEBI (Mutual Funds) Regulations relating to intermediaries was in areas relating to advertisements, sales literature and market conduct. MFs were also mandated to monitor compliance among their intermediaries and keep a strict vigil on their activities to ensure they did not sell mutual funds schemes in an unethical way. The intermediaries were advised to observe a code of ethics. The sharing of distribution commission received by them with investors was prohibited so that investors would pick funds for their merits rather than for the lure of kickbacks from the intermediaries.

Improving Risk Management Practices, Strengthening the MF Executive's Role

One of the key reasons for the malpractices, the operational mess and customer dissatisfaction in the mutual fund industry was non-observance of even the minimum standards of risk management by MFs and AMCs. A study of the current practices, as also of best practices across geographies, was carried out. Based on that study, a broad frame was prescribed, incorporating standards of due diligence and risk management across MF activities like fund management, operations, customer service, marketing and distribution, disaster recovery and business continuity. In fact, SEBI issued a comprehensive risk management manual to be followed scrupulously by the industry.

I was convinced that the role of chief executives and fund managers had to be strengthened first to improve the functioning of mutual funds and strengthen their risk management practices. After seeking feedback from MF CEOs and fund managers, SEBI redefined their roles in the SEBI (Mutual Funds) Regulations. The CEOs and fund managers were empowered as well as made accountable for ensuring strict compliance with all provisions of the regulations and investing in the best interests of their mutual fund unit holders. SEBI strived to ensure that they could do this without the stress of external influence or pressure.

Valuation norms were revised to bring about uniformity in the calculation of NAVs by mutual funds.

While the reforms were introduced to protect the interests of investors, the systems and procedures within mutual fund companies were simplified by amending the SEBI regulations to reduce their cost of compliance.

Role of MF and AMC Boards

I held separate meetings with the boards of directors of mutual funds, trusts and AMCs. Exclusive meetings with the chairmen of the mutual funds, trusts and AMCs too were arranged. Their role as trustees of public monies was the focus. They were briefed about the inadequacies in the functioning of the boards. Whereas good feedback and responses were received, the message directly delivered to these honourable men and women was loud and clear. In addition, the composition of the board, the structure of the board meetings, and the roles of independent directors and the chairman were clearly defined. The boards of AMCs and MFs (trustees) were advised to review the performance of their schemes on a periodical basis and compare them with the benchmark indices at all their meetings.

The MF trustees were directed to meet on bimonthly basis to review performance and compliance-related issues. Earlier, they were only meeting on quarterly basis.

Disclosure standards were strengthened to bring about transparency in the operations of mutual funds.

This led to significant improvements in the way the boards of MFs and AMCs functioned.

Supporting MF Product Diversity

The philosophy of widening the product basket was extended to mutual funds too. SEBI encouraged the launch of 'fund of funds' (FoFs), which allowed investors to invest in multiple funds through a single window. An FoF is a mutual fund scheme that invests in schemes of other mutual funds instead of directly investing in securities. Such FoFs may invest in equity- or debt-oriented funds, liquid schemes or sector-specific schemes. MFs were also permitted to invest in foreign debt securities from countries with fully convertible currencies. Initially, RBI allocated a limit of US$ 1 billion for the entire Indian mutual fund industry, which was later enhanced to US$ 2 billion during my tenure itself. Only investment in short- or long-dated debt instruments with the highest rating (foreign currency credit rating) from accredited credit rating agencies was permitted. The venture capital (VC) regulations were also revamped, based on the recommendations of the Ashok Lahiri committee (appointed by me) to add robustness to alternate investment schemes (AIS). Monitoring of mutual fund compliance was reinforced with a dedicated team at SEBI under the supervision of an ED.

The mutual fund regulatory framework has been strengthened further from time to time. Mis-selling continues, although it is declining steadily. But barring a few isolated instances of front-running and other misconducts by some of the fund managers, the industry has been able to deliver on its promises to its investors. In fact, the rise in mutual fund portfolios—through systematic investment plans (SIPS) in particular—talks volumes about the growing confidence of investors in the mutual fund industry. Possibly it was the comprehensive overhaul of the regulatory framework, including risk management, during 2002–05 that has played a role in building that trust. However, the adage, 'discretion is the better part of valour', is to be ever kept in mind. A sharp watch by the regulator over the MF entire chain—distributors, MFs and AMCs—continues.

16

OVERHAULING THE MARKET MACRO-STRUCTURE: MINIMIZING STRUCTURAL RISK

Identity vs Privacy: MAPIN

In the initial days of stock-taking of arrears, I was aghast to discover that many of the market misconducts were being investigated endlessly and remained inconclusive for years afterwards. Whereas there were allegations of lethargy, inefficiency, incompetence, subjectivity and even corruption against SEBI, there was a cogent explanation for all this. It lay in the difficulty in identifying the real culprit behind market manipulations. I wondered why. After all, the market intermediaries obtained a certified copy of their customers' PAN card, driving license, ration card or voter ID before undertaking transactions on behalf of them. However, given the multiplicity of identity cards and the absence of a unified database, it was difficult to pinpoint the culprit, who used different identifications for different transactions. The situation was compounded by the fact that the same person often had multiple PAN cards, driving licenses, ration cards and voter IDs. In fact, the Attorney General of India, defending the GoI order insisting that the AADHAR number be provided for income tax returns filed by individual assesses, had told the Supreme Court in April 2017 that people had multiple PAN cards.

Fortunately, I had the benefit of my programmed visits to the USA and UK. During my trip to US, I visited many facilities, including NASDAQ and New York Stock Exchange, and met top officials of the Securities and Exchange Commission, Commodities Futures Commission, Chicago Board of Trade, Security Industry Association and Institutional Investors Institute. I was overwhelmed by the passion of the US authorities, in particular, for data. They were strongly data-driven. Impossibly difficult insider trading cases were cracked by the enforcement agencies. In one case, they linked the insider information bearer with the trader, who had been his classmate. In another case, a neighbour of a rogue trader was picked up from among details of millions of citizens through the analysis of quality data fetched from a variety of sources. This was possible because (a) every person in the US has a unique identity, (b) there is availability of rich data from various sources, like credit cards, banks accounts, club memberships, residence mapping and college enrolments, and (c) all the information or data could be linked to the unique identity. Data analytics by itself cannot unfold stories of misconduct or patterns of market behaviour in the absence of a unique identity for citizens.

Information management and its analysis are critical for reasons beyond catching a wrongdoer. One can discern patterns in individual and group behaviour, and market trends, sub-trends and market propensities. The analytics can then help the regulatory agencies find out if the trends, patterns and behaviours are building market-wide risks—operational, systemic or structural. They can also detect the kinks being created for unscrupulous traders to misuse, to gain fraudulently from the market. Efficacy of markets cannot be ensured without proactively taking preventive steps. Our dream was to architect a very efficacious capital market. The key to that ambition lay in there being a unique identity for market participants—the brokers, directors of companies, investors, and so on—and the comprehensiveness of data about them.

Timely information is critical for the market. It is information-time (info-time) management rather than just information management that drives capital markets. A day-old newspaper is considered stale. However, in the case of capital markets, even minute-old information may be obsolete. In algorithmic and high-frequency trading, even a millisecond makes a difference. Eventually, everybody gets the same information, but it is important who gets it first. My thought processes were centred on info-time management.

Most of the representatives of institutional investors and high-net-worth individual investors I met complained about front-running in the Indian capital market, and also about the absence of a unique identity for market participants. Even multilateral agencies in their reports on the state of development of the Indian capital market had remarked about the absence of a unique identity for market participants in India. In any case, this was a serious structural deficiency, and therefore an unmitigated risk. I came back determined to do something about this inadequacy in the Indian market.

The Indian capital market was then struggling with the menace of 'benami transactions' in demat accounts. 'Benami' literally translates into 'without name', but in the case of the capital market, it is an adjective that is used when financial instruments, transactions or accounts, etc., are not in the real name of their owner. Benami accounts were run by the money and intent of another person, and a person with many such accounts was able to wield sufficient power to rig prices, create share price fluctuations and control the movement of stock; in general, they were able to disrupt the natural flow of the market.

Benami transactions also assisted the routing of unaccounted money into the stock market. There were also cases of cartels being formed with the aim of achieving the same objectives, but without the use of benami accounts. Either way, SEBI was caught unawares and was blamed for being lax in handling the unusual price movements and the tremendous volatility in certain shares over the eighteen-month period up to February 2001 (when the scam finally broke). SEBI found itself terribly short of tools to use as appropriate evidence to bust the cartels or benami accounts, as the case may be. There was no scientific way to detect patterns of trading, circular trading, price rigging and insider trading to pinpoint the guilty individuals (who in any case are notoriously tough to catch) and corporations. Analysts were of the opinion that SEBI's market intelligence was very poor, and indeed it was. Even during IPOs, shares reserved for retail applicants were being cornered by certain entities who made multiple applications in the names of fictitious/benami applicants. IPOs were made by companies that would vanish overnight, and locating their promoters in the absence of a unique identity would then be like looking for a needle in a haystack.

The documents required to open a demat account or to make a transaction in the market were basically identity proofs. They could be anything, ranging from driving license, PAN card and passport to electricity bill, bank account and others. Different identities for the same person were provided for different accounts opened by the person. SEBI was already staring at huge permutations and combinations of documents that could be used by a single individual to open multiple accounts. In no way could these documents be linked either. Even in such a scenario, someone trying to open thousands of accounts could still be caught with some basic due diligence on the part of DPs, but then our investigations clearly suggested that some of the DPs themselves were facilitating the opening of multiple accounts by falsifying documents or staging a cover-up. Apparently, some of the DPs were virtually serving family interests and conniving with the criminals! Business groups were also not far behind.

Hundreds of companies were created against the same address (and sometimes with different addresses); they constituted a network, but had no evident link to each other. In this maze, the efficacy of the market was perennially under threat.

As SEBI was constructing a market-wide integrated surveillance system, it was necessary to map the market activities of every person or entity against a unique number across exchanges and products. This was needed not only for the secondary market but also for the primary market where multiple applications by the same person for new share issues were a routine affair. These persons would use different names by using their names, surnames and initials in different permutations and combinations. In fact, SEBI wrote forcefully to the ministry of finance that if a unique identity for market participants was not implemented, it would result in scams involving multiple applications and multiple demat accounts. (Later, our warning proved true, as such an irregularity was discovered in 2006–09 in IPOs).

A unique ID would also support the ministry of corporate affairs' (MCA) goal of creating director IDs. This was essential because promoters and directors of companies used to disappear after raising IPO money. MCA and SEBI were already struggling with taking cognizance of the 'vanishing companies', as they were called. Many companies had fictitious directors, and rampant impersonation was also suspected. Creating an irreplaceable unique identity was the only solution.

Creating a Unique Identity—the First Step

As an idea it was exciting, but while designing it as an implementable plan, we were taken aback when we realized what a mammoth project it was going to be. The very first step, of course, was to choose an irreplaceable unique feature for all market participants. We had to then reduce every individual's key details into a number, and insist on quoting that unique identity number (UIN) everywhere in the markets. Beyond the basic details, the data should include the names of an individual's school and college, his or her qualifications, data about their immediate family and associates (like promoters, directors, employees, subsidiaries). The market participants' movements could then be easily tracked.

Another unique ID

The first problem lay in the word 'unique' itself. Ironically, Indians already had so many so-called unique IDs, like the PAN card, passport, voter ID, driving license and ration card. All these IDs could have been options for us, but the details taken for their issue were not exhaustive, and it was not very difficult to create many of any of these IDs for the same individual. In fact, identity numbers that rely only on demographic fields (like name, address, gender, age) and personal reference checks (like details of relatives, qualifications, school and college details) are only surrogates of identity and vulnerable to forgery, falsification, theft, loss and other corruptions. All these details—and more— were needed to completely ensure that the uniqueness of an ID is not compromised ever. So another ID had to be created, one that was truly unique.

USP of our unique ID

An truly unique selling point was essential for people to buy the idea of another ID. We began our extensive research to find out the best practices available for creating such a unique identity. As a first step, a study of overseas stock markets, like those of the US, UK, Hong Kong, Canada, Australia, Brazil and continental Europe was taken up. The USAID-FIRE programme, which was assisting SEBI, extended support too in terms of providing guidance.

Most of these markets had a system of using a unique identifier for their participants. But these were based on demographic fields and personal reference checks. In the United States and the United Kingdom, the social security (SS) number is used. In their case, the SS could be relied on, as the breeder document for it (the document which is submitted to create such identity proofs) was the birth certificate, which was also reliable. India surely could not rely on the passport, driving license, and other IDs of government issue. So our aim was to eliminate dependence on unreliable breeder and identity documents, and on operators, (say a DP) expecting them to be trustworthy. There was a need to leverage technology in a way that obviates dependence on error-prone documents and people-based processes.

This was the rationale applied by the US authorities after the horrendous 11 September 2001 terrorist attacks. They created a whole new security department and invested heavily in fingerprint, face and iris detection technologies for keeping a tab on immigrants, suspected elements and past cheats. This was biometric technology, now well known.

All this research was mind-boggling at a time when penetration of mobile phones was low. Facebook, Twitter and other social media did not exist, and most of the corporate world in India was still struggling with technology. However, I was convinced that if we were to create a truly unique identity, it had to be through something unique about an individual's body itself. Trying to achieve this in any other way would be to fool oneself, compromising on the whole idea and risking yet another scam in the markets. It felt a little too big an aim to achieve, but it could only be this way. The popular biometric options available were fingerprint, face and iris recognition. Fingerprint recognition was clearly the preferred choice, for multiple reasons. There are ten fingers compared with one face and two eyes, and reading fingers is easier than reading the face or eyes. Fingerprint recognition was cheap, and the technology more commonly available than for the other two. Also, the former had established itself as a truly unique biometric source over the years and had a successful history in solving criminal cases.

How many fingerprints?

At that time the market had a total of about 70 lakh investors and a few thousands of other participants. 'Other participants' included brokers, approximately 10,000 (around 40 per cent corporate), sub-brokers, around 13,000, listed companies, around 9,000, and other intermediaries (MFs, underwriters, portfolio managers, merchant bankers, debenture trustees, FIIs, VCs, etc.) numbering approximately 2,000. In addition, we were contemplating bringing in the relatives and associates of various participants under the radar too, and their number would be another 50 lakh. This would make our system almost comparable with the US VISIT and US Visa system—the largest biometric databases of the time! An elimination process began, to figure out which parties to exclude. Barring investors, everyone else was an involuntary element in the wheel running the market. It did not make sense to exclude any particular section or put any threshold limit for individual investors or their relatives Besides, the investor's numbers were hardly in the thousands (even including their relatives and associates), and were manageable. The real decision making was to happen in the case of investors. The annual turnover of the markets at the time was in the region of Rs 16 lakh crore from roughly 20 crore and 38 crore annual transactions on BSE and NSE, respectively. An average transaction size was about Rs 25,000 on BSE and Rs 30,000 on NSE. Since SEBI's inception, this number had peaked to Rs 1,00,000 only. It was really low at the time because of the market disturbances caused by Scam 2001. In any case, we were not looking to cover investors whose trading was sporadic and who visit the markets once in a while, and whose single transaction value was below the market average. So there was some direction in excluding retail investors who invest less than Rs 1,00,000 in a single transaction. The number then reduced to 40 lakh investors (including relatives and associates), which was still big. For some time we toyed with the idea of increasing the threshold limit further, but then, the numbers did not reduce drastically. So the limit of Rs 1,00,000 for a single transaction was fixed. However, we were clear that we would cover all corporate investors and all investors requiring margin trading facility, irrespective of the amount involved. Anyone needing a margin trading facility was using an important market instrument and we needed to know more about them. Similarly, body corporates investing even a small amount was important information.

Who was going to implement it?

After all the research, discussion and deliberations, we had finally mustered the courage to take up the task. The next step was to find executers who believed in the dream and were willing to help us implement it. Broadly speaking, we had to procure technology for fingerprint recognition, storage and matching, open centres all over the country, hire people and ensure safety of the data. The important criteria SEBI was looking for in a partner were trust, reach and sound technological capability. Ideally, multiple options should have been considered before zeroing in on one partner, but this time NSDL had been on the back of our mind for quite some time. NSDL—the first and largest depository in India—was then serving around 50 lakh demat accounts. The total value of securities held by it in demat format was close to Rs 40,000 crore. It was already a familiar and respected name among market participants and had extensive reach across India. For us, it meant increased credibility and comfort for the people who would participate in this exercise. Backed by NSE, NSDL had proved to be a game-changer in establishing demat technology a few years ago. They were used to challenging existing norms. It was not easy to rope them in for the task, but C.B. Bhave, then MD and CEO (later to become SEBI chairman) was a forward thinker, and when I broached the idea and told him about the dimensions of the project, he exhibited tremendous enthusiasm and confidence to undertake it. NSDL did not have its own branches to do countrywide MAPIN capture. They had to rope in other intermediaries like Karvy, who were into data management on a large scale. Also, since the IT Act had been enacted only in 2003, the practice of the law was not developed, and there was a lack of clarity about who would own the data and how data security would be managed. The technology development capabilities required for a project like MAPIN were inadequate in 2003.

And who was going to pay for it?

Rs 120 crore. When I first heard that figure, it struck me like a lightning. That was the turnover of many medium-sized companies of those times. A government organization undertaking such an exercise would itself raise eyebrows. We decided to fund this out of the MAPIN fees that we would charge. The fee for each unique ID was kept as Rs 300, by no means a small amount more than a decade ago.

The sum of it all

To provide a perspective, this is what we were trying to achieve. We were going to create another unique ID for close to 40 lakh Indians using biometric technology. This number was not very far from the numbers handled by the largest biometric systems of those times across the globe. It was the first time that such a biometric-based ID was going to be used for people investing in a stock market anywhere in the world. And finally, it was going to cost the country a whopping Rs 120 crore! While there were no questions raised about the cost of the project, there was immense opposition to fingerprinting from the larger stakeholder quarters, nationally known persons and opinion makers. 'A militant threatening of privacy,' was just one description of the project.

The Launch

On 25 November 2003, we officially launched the MAPIN Database (MAPIN, a name given by the SEBI team, was the acronym for Market Participant and Investor). The first unique identification number and identity card was allotted to me by the managing director of NSDL. In the first phase, we made the ID mandatory for over 70,000 market intermediaries (mainly stock brokers, depositories, DPs, exchanges and their members, underwriters, RTAs, mutual funds and portfolio managers), including their associated/related persons, and got them to complete the process by 31 March 2004. Over the next eighteen months, other market participants, like sub-brokers, investors (body corporate or otherwise), FIIs, listed companies and persons related/associated to these entities were also required to complete the process by different deadlines.

The definition of related/associated persons covered promoters, directors, proprietors, partners, sponsors, asset managers (as the case may be), certain key employees and other people exercising control over participants. In the case of natural persons, related/associated persons included spouse, parents, children and siblings (dependent or otherwise). The data captured for each and every UIN consisted of the name of the person (with proof), father's/husband's name, mother's name, PAN, TIN, address (with proof), telephone (office/resident), qualifications (with proof), training information (with proof), fingerprints of forefinger and thumb of both hands taken by the service provider on the computer, and photograph taken by the service provider on the computer. Individuals had to personally visit the designated Point of Services (POSes) in their region with the necessary documents. Fifteen POSes were opened across nine major cities—Ahmedabad, Bengaluru, Chennai, Kochi, Mumbai, Kolkata, Delhi, Jaipur and Hyderabad, with Mumbai alone having five POSes. Five service providers were delegated the task, with NSDL overseeing the progress.

After a reasonable build-up of the MAPIN database, each participant would be given a unique, traceable identity. Further, investors would be able to get basic information about an intermediary and whether he is facing disciplinary action by simply checking against his MAPIN on the website. The intermediary, in turn, would be able to verify the client's identity by using the client's MAPIN. We were on our way to making MAPIN a reality. Or, were we?

The Initial Struggle

As one can see, creation of this central database was in no way simple or easy. The resistance we faced with MAPIN was not only expected but also a classic case of angst among people when they are forced out of their comfort zone. Some of the well-known, respected professionals, independent directors and industrialists wrote nasty letters to SEBI and scathing articles in newspapers and magazines.

Are we criminals?

The exercise offended many, as until then fingerprints were taken only when one bought property or from potential suspects in a crime! So all this felt a little strange to everyone. People were even scared that they would be followed everywhere, their privacy invaded even outside the stock market. The intermediaries were particularly miffed that they required to obtain MAPIN for their family members who were in no way connected with the markets. PILs were filed against the exercise, and in March 2004, just a few days before the first project deadline, Delhi High Court temporarily exempted relatives of intermediaries who had no dealings in the capital market from obtaining MAPIN. The court also held that the data being collected was extremely confidential (especially something like digitally stored fingerprints) and there was a huge risk of such information being misused if it fell into the wrong hands.

India did not have any particular law for storage and protection of such digital data. The involvement of NSDL greatly helped in soothing people's wariness. NSDL had verbally announced that fifty persons were caught attempting to obtain duplicate MAPIN numbers, and when confronted, their explanation seemed not very convincing. However, we did not want to be diverted by trivialities, in the interest of the project's progress. So we just made sure duplicate IDs were not issued, and moved on.

The cost

Questions were raised by the media and market participants regarding the utility of this exercise compared to its cost. Intermediaries who were body corporate were miffed at having to obtain MAPIN for all their employees, as employee turnover was usually very high, and each time an employee left they were required to inform SEBI within twenty-four hours and obtain a new number for the replacement employee, shelling out Rs 300 every time there was a replacement. MAPIN was not employment-specific, in the sense that if MAPIN is obtained by a person while at a certain job, the same ID can continue to be his at any other employment too, and even if he decides to work independently. MAPIN was unique to an individual and not linked with any company (though any change in the underlying data, like address, employment, etc., had to be intimated to SEBI). Still, in the case of intermediaries, there would always be some fresh recruits without MAPIN, and the onus of obtaining it each time and bearing the costs would be on the intermediaries.

There were many investors outside the nine cities where we had MAPIN centres, and they had to spend time and money to travel to a different city to get their IDs. This was often cited as an excuse by many groups requesting extension of the deadline for MAPIN.

Harassment

We had a tough time explaining the long-term benefits of the altogether new unique ID, which was in addition to the already existing PAN, voter ID, etc. Some people were trying to create a perception that SEBI and the government were harassing the investor community instead of ensuring better coordination among their agencies. At a time when the government was seeking greater investment, in particular from foreigners, another arm of the government was now demanding that even citizen-investors seek a licence to invest their own hard-earned money in a public limited company on a public market—this was the general view.

In all this hoopla, the first deadline of 31 March 2004 for all intermediaries and their associates/related parties to obtain their UIN was far from being met. Only about 30 per cent of the targeted intermediaries had completed the process. We stuck to our ground for what we felt was the right thing to do, but extended the deadline to 30 June 2004, amidst a lot of representations from market participants asking for more time.

Change of government

As if the present challenges to MAPIN were not enough, another potential, existential threat to MAPIN were the general elections in May 2004, which was before our extended deadline. If the government changed, it could mean starting things right from scratch or even scrapping the whole exercise. It had come to my knowledge that certain aggrieved sections had already started talks with some of the Opposition parties to convince them to scrap the entire exercise if they come to power.

In the first luncheon meeting of business house chiefs with the prime minister, a well-known business leader of the time, known to resist everything new, raised hell over MAPIN. He even went to the extent of telling the PM, 'Are we criminals that we have to give our fingerprints!'

The lunch having concluded, the FM, fumed about MAPIN to me. It took me a while to calm him down and explain why it was essential for the Indian securities market. Being a sensible, knowledgeable and involved political executive, he understood the matter and asked me to send a note to him, which I promptly did. I was told the note was sent to the PM and that no further information or explanation was required. The MAPIN process continued smoothly.

Give and take

Our struggles, however, were far from over. Even the deadline of June 2004 was not met, and was extended further to August 2004. Among the many complaints against MAPIN was that SEBI had made no attempt to track the wealthy investors who had been hiding behind multiple layers of sub-accounts of FIIs. We then gradually fixed a timeline for sub-brokers, investors, listed companies, FIIs and their sub-accounts to obtain MAPIN by December 2004. This deadline applied to everyone but the retail investor, for whom the last date for compliance was March 2005. When retail investors were brought into the ambit of MAPIN, the mutual fund industry was particularly agitated. They were worried that investor sentiment in the semi-urban and rural areas, where they were particularly focused on penetrating, would be severely affected. A delegation from the mutual fund industry met me to ask for an extension of the deadline by at least another three months. But I stuck to my guns and asked them to stick to the schedule for complying with the requirements.

Even though, following a High Court directive, we revoked the requirement of MAPIN for associates and related parties of listed companies and body corporates (i.e. investors, intermediaries, sub-brokers and FIIs), MAPIN was required for promoters, directors and body corporates. Similarly, for certain intermediaries, key employees were still covered under MAPIN. All circulars and instructions regarding the process to be followed, along with the list of POSes and their contact numbers, were updated on our websites in a timely manner. We tried to provide all support to applicants if it looked like the deadline was not going to be met. To handle last-minute demands, we authorized centres, particularly in the last few days before the deadline, to procure additional scanners. These centres had also been asked to enter into individual agreements with either brokers or mutual funds to further sub-let the process to them, thereby reducing their own work burden. All this had to be done without compromising on the quality of fingerprints collected. Many irregularities were also thwarted by us; we put up warnings about them on our website and at POSes. For example, we advised participants against dealing with some fraudulent middlemen who were creating false panic about MAPIN and were seeking to get the mandate to issue MAPIN identities for some money.

Handling opposition

To sum it up, the implementation of this scheme was in no way straightforward. Multiple reminders were sent to ensure that deadlines were adhered to. Still, we were always way behind our target, even though deadlines were not extended after a point. My tenure was about to come to an end in a few months. That too was probably holding back people from accepting MAPIN completely, under the hope that the new regime might provide them some relief. Considering the size of the exercise, it was a steep learning curve for all of us. But our focus, even in the midst of all the opposition, was on the final vision of a truly world-class capital market. Not for once did we doubt our intent or vision, and were willing to see this project to the end, even with all the accusations and conflicts thrown our way.

One of the key accusations was that we could have done better by creating a consensus among the market participants before taking this up. My simple rationale was, consensus is very difficult to achieve for unconventional projects, particularly if the target group is large and varied. This was a bitter medicine that had to be administered. If we had seen it through, everyone might have realized its benefits. But . . .

And so it happened that I left office on 18 February 2005. At that point, many intermediaries, sub-brokers, listed companies, investors (particularly body corporates and those requiring margin trading facility) had already completed the exercise in adherence to the 31 December 2004 deadline and had started using their UINs for trading. A large chunk of investors, particularly retail (for trades of Rs 1 lakh and above) was left to be issued UINs, as their deadline was 31 March 2005. However, immediately after my exit, the deadline for obtaining UIN was extended till December 2005 and a committee was appointed to re-examine MAPIN altogether. The committee's terms of reference did not include examination of the need for MAPIN; it had only been asked to suggest the category of market participants that would need it. However, many saw the appointment of the committee as the beginning of the end of MAPIN.

In June 2005, on the committee's suggestion, the biometric angle in MAPIN was scrapped and further registrations discontinued. The need for UIN was recognized, but a new system was suggested for it. This system required additional information from participants, to be obtained in a more cost-efficient manner (the major cost was to be borne by SEBI itself). The new system also emphasized collection of information on relatives and associates, which we had relaxed after its initial introduction. The suggestions were not immediately implemented and MAPIN lost momentum, until (as we have seen before) certain incidents forced SEBI to think about it again but it did not take this forward and the matter was buried forever.

Maybe for good reasons. One of the reasons could have been the national controversy over issue of AADHAR cards playing on the minds of the policymakers.

Vindication

In January 2006, two back-to-back incidents of multiple demat-related misconducts of largish magnitude were discovered in the IPOs of Infrastructure Development Finance Company (IDFC) and Yes Bank which were issued in July 2005. The modus operandi and the people involved were the same in both the cases. A few investors were found to be controlling multiple benami demat accounts, to the extent of 15,000 to 20,000 accounts! Using these they had cornered a large volume of shares meant for other retail investors (it was reported that they cornered 8 per cent of the retail allotment) putting paid to fair market opportunity. These shares were then transferred to their financiers in off-market transactions just before the IPOs were listed. The financiers sold off these shares immediately after the IPO listed, making disproportionate gains. Something suspicious was detected, but only in October 2005, almost three months after the IPOs, and that too since there was an IT raid on one of the financiers. The culprits were identified only by January 2006, six months after the damage had been done. Many more skeletons tumbled out as many earlier IPOs—like those of Jet Airways, Suzlon Energy, NTPC, TCS, etc.—were discovered to have been rigged in the same manner. The reported gains to the operators were to the extent of more than Rs 75 crore.

It had exactly played out the way we had feared—there were DPs involved, multiple addresses, the same person investing under different permutations and combinations of names, etc. The matter was taken up very seriously by the finance ministry, and the identified culprits were suitably fined. But how do you compensate the retail investors for their loss of opportunity?

There were disgorgement orders, which were upheld by the Supreme Court. Some of the disgorged money was given to the investors who had been cheated. Had MAPIN been successfully implemented even after my exit, the opening of multiple demat accounts would not have been possible in the first place. Further, any kind of rigging using related accounts would have been detected in time and prevented. This would have been better than a delayed cure. I felt vindicated when a section of the media started emphasizing the need for something like MAPIN. These two incidents prompted SEBI to rethink their decision to scrap MAPIN. Once again, in 2006, talks about MAPIN started gaining momentum. However, by the end of 2006, only PAN was made mandatory for market participants and acted as the unique number, going forward, which continues to this day. MAPIN, as originally conceived, was buried, with its own RIP. SEBI does not have a unique ID for its participants even today.

My final closure with regard to MAPIN came when UIDAI was established in January 2009 after the Planning Commission of India issued a notification. If one reads the rationale behind UIDAI, it is more or less the same that we had for MAPIN, except that for UIDAI they were thinking country-level, and we thought market-level. UIDAI has all three biometrics— face, iris and fingerprint recognition underlying its unique ID. Post 2005, many other government schemes and projects have used biometric systems successfully. Some of them are E-shakti, NREGA in Bihar, the Coastal ID card project of RTI, Orissa's UNWFR programme, Andhra Pradesh's iris-based ration card enrolment, the Employees State Insurance Scheme of India (ESIC) and RSBY.

When a rocket is launched, it consumes maximum energy during the first few minutes of take-off, when it has to leave behind its inertia and fly. I feel MAPIN was such a launch pad for something as mammoth as UIDAI. It is likely that it led the government to believe that something like this was possible and immensely advantageous. An unimaginable, intangible and scary proposition transformed into something more tangible and achievable. It also removed the taboo among people about providing their biometric data. It provided a platform on which other such exercises could be built. As cliched as it may sound, MAPIN was ahead of its times. I rest my case. Regulators need the courage of conviction to fight resistance. A deficiency can be menacingly disquieting and dangerously threaten the efficacy of the stock market. And a structural deficiency in India's securities market subsists. Hopefully, AADHAR will completely fill it one day, as it has since been mandated by SEBI as compulsory for securities market transactions.

17

FROM BOON TO BANE: REGIONAL STOCK EXCHANGES

Manek Chowk, a notable city square in old Ahmedabad, is usually on the must-visit list of tourists to the city. It is known for its street food, historical architecture and old-world charm. Old-timers in the city will tell you about the significance of one of the structures that once represented the glorious days of the chowk. The sturdy, ninety-three-year-old two-storeyed heritage building of Victorian architecture is the house of Ahmedabad Stock Exchange (ASE). Till about twenty years ago, this building symbolized the spirit of Gujarati entrepreneurship, which is today globally acclaimed.

There was a time when the building bustled with enthusiastic traders and representatives of brokers signalling bids with their fingers, shouting out numbers and company names, trying to outdo one another on the floor of the exchange. ASE, the second oldest exchange in India (the first being the BSE, established in 1875), came into being in 1894. In fact, Manek Chowk was to Ahmedabad what Dalal Street is to Mumbai. ASE is one among the many regional stock exchanges (RSEs) in the country, which slowly and steadily became irrelevant with the emergence of a digital India. The deserted ASE building still reminds the older generation of its vibrancy and serves as a place for some good, nostalgic indulgence.

Very few young Indians would know that not very long ago India actually had twenty-three stock exchanges recording thousands of secondary market transactions each day. These exchanges were spread across the length and breadth of the country. There was even an exchange called Magadh Stock Exchange in Patna. Apparently, the name was chosen in a historical context, after emperor Ashoka's prosperous kingdom of Magadh, the capital of which was located in present-day Patna, earlier called Pataliputra. In the early 1900s, Meerut Stock Exchange was also incorporated. However, it wasn't given permanent recognition, and folded up.

The primary reason for the creation of these stock exchanges was to facilitate localization of capital-raising and secondary market transactions, and to ensure liquidity of scrips and larger investor participation. The open outcry method of trading required the physical presence of a trader, which made it difficult for people across the country to trade on a daily basis on the stock exchange in Mumbai (then Bombay). In places like Calcutta, which is very far from Mumbai, entrepreneurs and investors found it cumbersome and time-consuming to trade on the BSE. Until an exchange platform was made available locally, a investor would call up a broker at BSE, collect information, place his order, receive confirmation of the execution of his order several days afterwards, and settle months later. The same cycle of trading was repeated day after day by those who wanted to benefit from the institution of the stock exchange. The flow of information was never in real time. There was total dependence on third parties for obtaining information and for execution of trades. The communication bottlenecks led to disputes, and even misconducts. Raising capital, as also buying and selling in the secondary market, had become an exercise in dependence and delay. The person in command of the information and trading activity always had the upper hand.

The Securities Contracts (Regulation) Act, 1956 (SCRA), which governed recognition of stock exchanges, did not permit exchanges to open branches at different locations. Localization of market or the trading platform then became an eminent necessity. The journey began with the opening of stock exchanges in industrial and commercial hubs like Ahmedabad, Calcutta (Kolkata) and Madras (Chennai). The government, with a view to promoting economic development, saw the need for wider participation of investors from across the country to channelize their savings into the equity market—that is, capital formation, and bring about a higher multiplier impact. Further, to encourage the balanced economic development of the many states of India, the government felt that regional stock exchanges at vantage geographical locations may help. Hence the government encouraged, supported and provided incentives for the rise of regional stock exchanges. Eventually, almost every state had a stock exchange, and that is how the number swelled to twenty-three.

The growth and sustenance of RSEs was facilitated in the decades of 80s and 90s by (a) the government-ordained obligation of every company that raised risk capital or equity from the public to list on at least one national exchange BSE/NSE and one RSE, and (b) to help enterprises that were smaller and operating regionally, and which could not get a foothold in the national exchanges to list. Over a period of time, RSEs became an important pillar of the economy and served the purpose of their creation substantially. In effect, they were a boon.

The rise of NSE as a silent, technology-driven (without a physical trading floor), anonymous, price-time-priority trading platform tarred the road of the downhill journey for RSEs. The conduct of the traders and brokers at RSEs, their mismanagement, and the members' misconduct and misbehaviour in their dealings led to the slow but steady shift of trades to NSE. The volumes of trade were like the flood waters, receding fast and eventually reaching a situation where transactions on most of the RSEs dried up completely, like seasonal rivers in the summer.

Even the volume of business at the one-time supreme, broker-managed, arrogant BSE contracted to less than 30 per cent of NSE volumes.

It has been my belief that underutilized or over-leveraged infrastructure clouds a system. Structurally, even for India's geographical and demographic size, twenty-three stock exchanges were one too many. The absence of, and negligible or subdued trading activity on these exchanges had become a serious structural risk to the Indian capital market, and there was an urgent need for de-risking the situation. While brooding over the root causes of major market misconduct by a large number of entities in 2000–01, I found that the underutilized terminals of RSEs were being used to create circular trades and false transaction volumes in a variety of scrips. Gullible investors had lost their shirts in the milieu of hype about the scrips and manipulation of their prices through bogus transactions. The inadequacy of risk management in Calcutta Stock Exchange, and the failure of settlement of transactions of just Rs 120 crore eventually led to the collapse of its index from 6000 to 2600. It brought widespread misery to innocent investors, sub-brokers and even brokers. Scam 2001 was a national tragedy and became a stormy political issue. The RSEs, which once proved a boon to the country, now turned into a bane for the Indian capital market.

What brought me to centrestage, both as LIC chairman and, in particular, as SEBI chairman was this major market misconduct led by Ketan Parekh and his associates with the connivance of promoters and fund managers. Promoters funded Ketan Parekh entities, facilitated share placements with institutions like UTI, MFs, and FIIs, and cashed out substantial holdings in their companies. The bubble had burst with the settlement crisis in Calcutta Stock Exchange. LIC of India and NSE, where I was non-executive chairman at the time, had providentially escaped and emerged unscathed. As chairman of SEBI, I had the burden of the responsibility of sweeping out the mess.

To me it was an utter shock that the third largest stock exchange of its time had defaulted on settlement of a mere Rs 120 crore when it had an annual turnover of more than Rs 3.5 lakh crore in 2000-2001, just before the scam broke. What about the credibility of the exchange? The best way to restore our own credibility at SEBI, I realized, was to ensure settlement of transactions on that trading platform. We had to make sure that the responsibility for that devolved squarely on the exchanges. We had to comprehensively re-engineer the market macro-structure.

My attempt was to de-risk all the perceived structural risks stemming from under-utilization and mismanagement of the infrastructure of RSEs. I came up with the following solutions.

1. To create a financially potent clearing corporation (CC)/ settlement guarantee fund (SGF) for the settlement system to transit from delivery-vs-payment (DVP) to central counter party (CCP)
2. Contract the settlement cycle quickly to shrink open positions in between settlements
3. Reorchestrate the risk management framework, bringing in a margining system that was dynamic and upfront; bring in real-time monitoring of positions and automate disablement of terminals on margins running out
4. Weed out undesirable elements from the management of the exchanges, and
5. Provide very effective oversight of exchange operations, including through surprise inspections

In 1997, SEBI had advised all stock exchanges to set up a clearing house (CH) /clearing corporation (CC) or settlement guarantee fund (SGF) to ensure that there was no delay or default in settlements on account of failure of any member to honour his commitment. This fund/corporation would basically collect funds and securities from members (brokers), and use them to settle transactions.

In the case of SGF, the counterparty in any trade consists of the members themselves, and only in case of default does the SGF undertake to complete the settlement without the normal process of trading being affected. In the case of a CC, all trades are settled through the corporation, which becomes the counterparty for all trades, besides guaranteeing settlement of all trades. The end objective of both the CC and SGF was same. The exchanges were given an option to set up either of the two. If any exchange wanted to expand its terminals to centres outside its city, it was compulsorily required have a clearing corporation or settlement guarantee fund in place first. Since these facilities are for the safety of the exchange members, a contribution to the corpus of SGF/CC was required to be made by them. It was made clear that this contribution should not be passed on to the investors by the members. The contribution had to be calculated based on various factors, such as trade volumes, delivery percentage, maximum settlement liability of members, history of defaults at the exchange, capital adequacy of the members, and the degree of surveillance and safety measures—i.e., imposition of mark-to-market margins, trade restrictions and the like, implemented by the exchange. This contribution was to be revised periodically, based on changes in the above-listed parameters.

By 2003, only NSE had a CC, and BSE and CSE had SGFs. But, as Scam 2001 suggests, the financial muscle of CSE's SGF was deficient, as it could not even make good a Rs 120-crore gap. The rules were neither mandatory nor specific. Every exchange was doing as it pleased. Most of the RSEs did not have the safety pillar of a CC or SGF at all. I strongly felt that if this had been mandatory and had been followed in true spirit, it would have prevented overexposure of the members during the build-up of the scam. Secondly, even in case of default, it would have helped bridge the gap from the CC or SGF.

In a landmark regulation, we made it compulsory for all exchanges to have one of the two. BSE objected to it, as they did not have a CC, and creating a financially potent SGF (based on the new parameters) implied that brokers now had to shell out more money. The deposit money of brokers was the only money they had, and that was being used for building construction, maintenance, etc. A deadline was set for the exchanges to establish their CCs/SGFs of adequate financial strength. Most of the exchanges found the CC a very difficult proposition, even though NSE had one. The BSE and RSEs were unwilling to use NSE's CC. Just to prevent political games, I did provide one or two extensions in the time limit for exchanges to get their CC or SGF in place. Brokers started pleading with me not to make the SGF compulsory, and when I did not seem to relent they asked for more time. To be fair to myself, I did give them further extensions, initially one month, and then three months, but no more. After that the option for exchanges was to either get a CC or SGF or shut down.

Around the same time that these regulations were being brought in, something else was happening. Abolition of *badla*, which was the backbone of trading at the Calcutta, Delhi, Ahmedabad, Kanpur and Ludhiana stock exchanges and a few others, dealt a serious setback to trading at the RSEs. The introduction of uniform trading cycles and the transition from account period settlement to rolling settlement at all exchanges had diminished opportunities for arbitrage transactions. The introduction of compulsory rolling settlements in T+2, the proposed demutualization of exchanges and the mandating of SGF/CC further sealed the fate of the RSEs, reducing their share of trading to just 5 per cent of the country's total within just a year.

However, the body blow was caused by the requirement of compulsory SGF/CC, which meant additional funds from the already cash-starved RSEs and their brokers. None of the RSEs could comply with any of these requirements, and there was no reason whatsoever left for investors to use their facilities. The exchanges had no volumes, no investor protection norms, and their transaction costs were high.

The ultimate reason for the fading away of trading at the RSEs was that all the major operators at RSEs had, in the meantime, acquired memberships in either NSE or BSE, or both, while others became sub-brokers of members of NSE or BSE. Most of them switched over completely to these national exchanges.

It was clear to me that RSEs now had to either raise their standards or shut down. But how do you initiate the shutting down of exchanges, some of which had been around for 100 years? The fact that Scam 2001 had an RSE at its centre would have worked in our favour to shut them down, but still, to shake the present establishment meant going against various people, some even powerful and influential, who would go all out to maintain the status quo. It had to be done gradually, and I got my team ready to do detailed research and prepare a robust fact-based argument.

The socio-economic fabric of India with its robust democratic order does not permit decisions to be implemented immediately, even if they make perfect sense. Multiple stakeholders have to be taken into confidence. This I realized first-hand when brokers from various RSEs made representations to me directly and through various influential persons, including politicians and forums, about how they would still try to revive their exchanges. For some it was a matter of pride, for some an emotional matter, and for yet some others it was the sheer benefits they were deriving from the exchanges.

Balanced regional development—it was being suggested in all seriousness—would be difficult without the existence of active RSEs to help mobilize capital for projects in the backward states. I felt the RSEs were only giving an opportunity to small number of ambitious people to project themselves as presidents, vice-presidents and office-bearers of these exchanges. Even when the RSEs had no trading activity whatsoever, they regularly elected their governing boards and office-bearers. They had become outfits of rent-seeking.

The whole matter was being made into a political issue. I remember an instance when I had superseded the board of CSE for serious irregularities there. In the absence of availability of a competent person to handle the exchange, I was toying with the idea of closing it down. I got a call from the chief secretary of the West Bengal government who told me that the chief minister, Buddhadeb Bhattacharjee, who was trying to bring the economy of the state out of a serious down-cycle, perceives the shutting down of the exchange as a huge setback for the state. He was requesting me not to close down the exchange. When I expressed my difficulty in finding a suitable person to be administrator in the absence of a board for effective management of the exchange, the government of West Bengal offered to recommend a suitable person. Eventually, Tushar Kanti Das, an IAS officer who had just retired as additional chief secretary of West Bengal, was recommended and appointed.

We made it clear to RSEs that they would either comply with the new rules or give over control to SEBI to decide their future. Serious regulatory concerns about the RSEs had led SEBI to take recourse to the extreme measure of superseding the governing boards of four exchanges—Pune, Bhubaneswar, Baroda, Calcutta—and even to withdraw recognition in the case of one RSE. CSE had a unique problem because of West Bengal's long history of left rule—they had 120 employees and 120 subordinate staff. So effectively, each staff had a sub-staff. Anecdotal references suggested that every time a new president was elected, he would employ a coterie of three or four—a driver, a man to fetch him paan, another to carry his bag and to do his personal errands and one to work as the office boy. Each president brought his own people, and they all became permanent employees. And in

Kolkata you could not sack anyone. So over the years 120 staff had accumulated!

Additionally, RSEs had spent a cumulative Rs 200 crore on upgradation of their infrastructure, and they did not want this investment to go to waste. So we decided to combine the resources available and gave them one last chance to survive, through the Inter Connect Stock Exchange, ICSE. But ICSE did not take off. The finance minister, in his budget speech on 8 July 2004, had announced the intention of the government to set up a trading platform for small and medium enterprises (SMEs) to raise capital—both debt and equity—as well as to provide liquidity to such securities. To operationalize the announcement, SEBI took the initiative to encourage the BSE and the smaller stock exchanges to set up this trading platform. Accordingly, BSE-IndoNext was set up as a separate trading platform under the BOLT trading system of the BSE. It was a joint initiative of the BSE and the Federation of Indian Stock Exchanges (FISE), of which eighteen RSEs were members. The BSE-IndoNext market was intended to be an SME-specific market. The government amended Section 13 of the SCRA to facilitate trading by the trading members of RSEs on this market. This move was widely debated and criticized by the media as a futile exercise. BSE-IndoNext (more details in a separate chapter) did not survive beyond a couple of years.

By February 2005, when I left office, RSEs had zero trading, and NSE and BSE had taken over the entire market in the ratio of 2:1. Trading at RSEs had stopped because SEBI directions did not permit transactions in the absence of a CC/SGF, which these exchanges could not establish. Thus structural risk was completely de-risked, even though the RSEs were not shut down before I handed over charge as head of SEBI.

Later, a committee was set up to study the future of RSEs. It suggested means by which RSEs could shut down voluntarily, failing which SEBI would take strict action against indisciplined exchanges. Some efforts were still made by the likes of Delhi, Ahmedabad and Calcutta exchanges to revive, but nothing concrete resulted. Finally, by mid-2012, the order was brought in, and one by one, within the next four years, most of the RSEs were derecognized.

18

ELIMINATING CONFLICT OF INTERESTS: DEMUTUALIZATION AND CORPORATIZATION OF EXCHANGES (MAKING EXCHANGES INDEPENDENT AND PROFESSIONAL)

Whenever I travelled outside India and met FIIs, they had one standard grouse. Which was that whenever they placed an order with their Indian brokers, the brokers would first do front-running (execute orders in their personal capacity) and only then execute the FII orders. Usually, this resulted in the purchase price of the scrip going up by 1–5 per cent for the FIIs. For the large volumes that FIIs dealt in, this margin could make a difference of crores of rupees.

Then, during Scam 2001, the president of BSE, a broker himself, was accused of acquiring information from the surveillance department of the exchange and allegedly using it before it was revealed to the public. He had to resign amidst these allegations, and investigations were launched against him. However, sufficient evidence was not found to implicate him. Finally, during Scam 2001, Calcutta Stock Exchange defaulted on a payment of Rs 120 crore. It is widely believed that the brokers at the exchange did not adhere to the prescribed clearing, settlement and margin trading norms.[1]

The common thread in the above three incidents was that while various rules existed for brokers trading on exchanges (be it prohibition of front-running, insider trading, T+5 settlement or rules for clearing and settlement systems) they were blatantly flouted by the brokers. One did not have to be a genius to figure out that brokers were able to get away with flouting the rules largely because the exchanges, though functioning as a Self Regulatory Organization (SRO), were being run by the broker-members, and had ineffective independent representation.

Origins of Broker-Exchange Links

Stock trading in India was informally begun by twenty-two enterprising traders in the mid-nineteenth century under a banyan tree at Horniman Circle in the Fort area of Mumbai. In 1875, this informal group organized themselves formally as an Association of Persons (AoP), with all the traders as its broker-members, mainly to trade among themselves. They created Bombay Stock Exchange (BSE), the oldest stock exchange in the country. Like BSE, historically, stock exchanges all over the world were 'mutual' organizations owned and run by member-brokers for their common benefit. Consequently, all these entities became broker-clubs of sorts, where the right to trade on the exchange, the right to exercise oversight on the market for trading and the right to manage and govern the exchange were all vested with them. Over a period of time, it was observed—globally, and more so in India—that this triality of rights led to conflicts of interest, culminating in serious misconducts and disruptions of the market. These institutions were operating by the typical credo of 'of the broker, by the broker, for the broker'.

Ideally, the exchange should be an impartial body where buyers and sellers transact their business. Yet, because exchanges can't deal with millions of buyers and sellers, there have to be intermediaries between the buyers and sellers who can take care of the financial strength of the persons undertaking transactions. In the absence of technology, which is available today, it was not possible to check the financial strength of customers directly (globally), so a broker had to be involved to ensure that transactions were settled. The exchanges were expected to be neutral entities—just efficacious trading platforms—with no interest in transactions except for a small fee on them for use of its platform.

Was it too idealistic to expect this of broker-clubs?

Conflict of Interests

The defining moment for Indian stock markets came in the eighties, when as many as fourteen RSEs came up across the country on the back of progressive tax and economic reforms by the government. The growth in the volume of trades created a fertile ground for brokers to indulge in guilty pleasures, particularly when they could charge a commission as high as 2.5 per cent of the value of transactions. The blatant misuse by brokers of their powers was common practice, and took the following forms:

1. **Front-running**—This is when a broker buys or sells ahead of his clients. Brokers are the first in the market to know which shares are being bought or sold, especially by their own clients. They often use this information to buy or sell those same shares from their personal accounts first before executing their client orders, thus profiting unethically from inside information. For example, if a person comes to a broker and places an order to buy 1 lakh shares of ABC Ltd at Rs 100 apiece, the broker knows that this transaction will move up the price of ABC Ltd. So the broker sneaks in a personal order of a few shares for himself at Rs 100 each before placing the client's order. On placing the client's order, the price goes up to, say, Rs 110. The broker now sells

the shares he bought at Rs 100 for Rs 110, making a neat profit for no extra work. In fact, in some cases brokers would square up their position (which was disguised) by selling their clients the same shares they had bought for themselves ahead of the client's trade. A similar process would take place when a sell order was received.

Both malpractices were conveniently possible in the pre-technology era when the client had limited access to knowledge of market movements and the time of execution of a trade.

2. **Complete bypass of risk mechanisms:** Every exchange had specified risk mitigation mechanisms in terms of the maximum amount of trades allowed for a broker, based on the margins available. However, the brokers would often bypass these margins and trade beyond their mandated limits, putting the entire system at risk (example: the CSE settlement failure mentioned at the start of the chapter). There were also instances of brokers tampering with the surveillance mechanism to wrongfully tweak their margin requirement so that they could trade for higher values.

3. **Failure of settlement:** Since brokers were in the management, they would decide when settlements happened. So common was this practice that in an international conference where I was speaking on the progress of India to T+2, a foreign participant joked that in India the settlement cycle was 'T + Anything'. Earlier, there had been badla, which was to be closed every fifteen days, and if the brokers found they couldn't settle by providing security or cash, they would roll the trades over by another fortnight for settlement!

All the above infringements were overlooked because the brokers themselves were running the show and could play around with the rules as per their whims and fancies. And so the question arose globally, as it did in India too, as to whether stock exchanges should be allowed to be run by brokers.

Attempting to Bring Independence in the Operation of Exchanges

SEBI was established in 1988, but acquired statutory status in 1992 when the SEBI Act 1992 was passed. One of the earliest measures SEBI proposed was to put a leash on brokers and limit their clout as they were tampering with the efficacy of the market and working against the interests of the investors at large. The SEBI chairman of the time waged a war against brokers, more particularly with the strong BSE brokers, on many fronts, directly and indirectly. He made broker registration mandatory, exposing the operational loopholes that allowed brokers to not collect margins, uncovered their price-rigging racket and exposed their lacklustre response to investor complaints, etc.

Accordingly, SEBI then demanded a change in the composition of the board of directors of stock exchanges (which had only consisted of brokers till then) to bring greater representation from the public. It was even decided that the exchanges would have a chairman who is non-executive and independent. This did not go down well with the strong broker lobby, which scoffed at the idea. The chairman of an exchange who was described as an arch enemy of the broker community was unceremoniously replaced, and it was made sure that the next chairman was not aggressive enough to free the exchange from the broker-raj. In fact, it was a serious structural risk, and had in the past facilitated misconducts and scams. The market was crying out for its de-risking, and so, without further delay, I picked up the threads to deal with the menace.

Demutualization and Corporatization

The best way to end the broker-raj, I felt, was to demutualize the exchanges. I studied some of the key features of the exchanges before implementing this.

1. Before joining SEBI, I had been chairman of NSE, which had already established itself as the top stock exchange in the country, displacing BSE. (In the very first year of its operations, NSE became the largest exchange in the country). For FY 2002, NSE's share of total market volumes was about 60 per cent, and BSE's 33 per cent. This was when BSE was 125 years old and NSE not even ten. One major reason for NSE's success was that it was demutualized and corporatized from day one, and that gave confidence both to the broking community and the investors. It was registered as a 'for profit' company and had complete separation of exchange ownership and management from trading rights, which were granted to the members. Brokers stood one step below, as part of the consultative committee.

   NSE was initially (in the early nineties) meant to be only a debt-trading platform, but because of the misconducts of BSE and other RSEs, it was permitted to do equity trading too by SEBI, and the result is there for all to see. The strict Chinese wall between management and trading rights ensured that appropriate rules were framed, that brokers could not deviate from the rules as they pleased, and that the exchange had better control over the activities of the brokers. This professional approach enhanced its credibility and attracted more transactions on NSE as compared with BSE. So it proved that demutualization had the blessings of the investors.

2. Globally, the monopolistic nature of exchanges was being considered increasingly obsolete because of the Internet and generic technological progress, economic reforms, globalization, etc. Exchanges could no longer command dominance based on their geography alone. Investors had access to markets across the globe. For the first time, exchanges now had to fight for investor attention and focus on increasing their market share by being more professional

than other exchanges. Accordingly, the major global exchanges had started the demutualization process. Some of them were the Stockholm SE (1993), Amsterdam SE (1997), Australian SE (1998), Singapore SE (1999), Toronto SE (2000) and London SE (2001).

However, not every stock exchange followed the same management and ownership structure post-demutualization. For example, the Australian SE was converted into a company but the trading brokers continued to have a sizeable shareholding in it and a significant say in the management, quite unlike NSE, which did not give trading members any stake in the ownership or management. London SE too had an approach similar to that of the Australian SE. However, over the years, the institutional shareholding of London Stock Exchange has gone up and that of the brokers has gone down. The Toronto Stock Exchange converted into a company and completely separated its ownership and management functions from its operational function. Basically, each country followed its own method of demutualization.

3. One common feature among all demutualized stock exchanges was corporatization. Corporatization helped in segregating trading rights and ownership rights, which were earlier bundled under membership rights at the exchanges.

In India, there were in all twenty-three exchanges at the time. Three—BSE, ASE and Indore Stock Exchange—were AoPs and had to be both corporatized and demutualized. Eighteen of the stock exchanges—Bangalore, Bhubaneswar, Calcutta, Cochin, Coimbatore, Delhi, Guwahati, Hyderabad, Interconnected SE, Jaipur, Ludhiana, Madras, Magadh, Mangalore, Pune, Saurashtra-Kutch, Uttar Pradesh, and Vadodara—were already corporate entities and had only to be demutualized. Two stock exchanges, NSE and OTCEI, were already corporatized and demutualized. Except for NSE, all the exchanges were not-for-profit entities.

4. Finally, Scam 2001 and its many outcomes created an appetite
    for some drastic changes. The time was ripe to introduce
    demutualization and corporatization as no broker or vested
    interest could then afford to politicize matters in the face of
    seething public anger against them. Even the FM of the time,
    Yashwant Sinha, had emphasized the idea of demutualization
    of exchanges in his budget speech of February 2002.

SAT, in the Anand Rathi appeal (28 February 2002) case, made
this observation:

> By way of post script, I would like to state that it is high time
> that the stock exchanges are liberated from the control of the
> brokers. Stock exchanges should no longer be allowed to be run
> as exclusive clubs of the brokers, by the brokers, for the brokers.
> Perhaps a totally broker less management of the exchange would
> be the answer in this regard. I would suggest that the authorities
> may adopt appropriate measures to streamline the stock exchange
> management to impart more credibility to the institution to
> enhance the common investor's faith in the capital market.[2]

Bringing about Transformation

Within one month of my joining, i.e., in March 2002, I set up a
committee under the chairmanship of Justice M.H. Kania (former
Chief Justice of India) for careful examination of various legal,
accounting and tax issues and to study the many demutualized
exchanges across the world. He would then prepare a detailed
roadmap for implementation of demutualization and corporatization
of Indian exchanges. The report provided its observations and,
overall, recommended the concept. On the basis of its findings and
my own study, by January 2003 a notice was given to all exchanges
in the country, making demutualization and corporatization
compulsory. The following were the key implementation points:

1. All the exchanges were given six months (till June 2003) to frame a scheme for demutualization and corporatization to be approved by SEBI.

2. The broad guidelines for the scheme were as follows:

–   All exchanges had to be a company (limited by shares) under the Companies Act.

–   All existing members of the exchanges (brokers) would be provided shares of the new entity; the shares were tradable and could be sold by the member to any willing buyer; however, it was made clear that the shares could not be traded for money from the exchange itself.

–   Persons other than shareholders with trading rights (brokers), had to hold at least 51 per cent of the equity shares.

–   The board of the demutualized stock exchange would have equal representation of brokers, shareholders and the investing public, except in the case of NSE, where the present structure of the board was to be maintained (the NSE structure was already more stringent than what was being suggested by SEBI). Thus, the broker-shareholders of the demutualized exchange could have up to one-third representation on the board of the exchange.

–   Appointment of all the directors of the board (including the broker-directors) would be approved by SEBI and their tenure too decided by SEBI.

–   The chairman of the board had to be non-executive, and an independent person.

The exchanges did not come forward, on some pretext or the other. An ordinance was promulgated on 12 October 2004 mandating exchanges to demutualize within a specified time or else face derecognition. This required all recognized stock exchanges to submit within such time as may be specified by SEBI a scheme for corporatization and demutualization for approval by SEBI. From the perspective of the brokers there were two contentious issues in the ordinance. First, it provided that SEBI shall not approve any scheme that proposed issue of shares for a lawful consideration or provision of trading rights in lieu of the membership card of the members of a recognized stock exchange or payment of dividends to members out of any reserves or assets of that stock exchange. Second, SEBI, while approving the scheme, may (a) restrict the voting rights of the shareholders who are also stock brokers of the recognized stock exchange; (b) restrict the right of shareholders or a stock broker of the recognized stock exchange to appoint representatives on the governing board of the exchange; and (c) restrict the maximum number of representatives of stock brokers on a recognised stock exchange to be appointed on the governing board of the exchange, which shall not exceed one-fourth of the total strength of the governing board.

Even the closure option (derecognition) was not effectively available to the exchanges, as they were not-for-profit organizations, and in case of closure the property and assets would vest in another non-profit organization and not with the brokers. The premises, which had been made available to them by the government, would revert to the government. Thus it appeared to the broker-members that they could not take away a single paisa from the exchange, whether it was demutualized or derecognized. This was the bone of contention. They could get trading rights. They could also get ownership rights, subject to several limits and restrictions on shareholding and participation in management.

To complete the transformation, there were other nagging issues to be sorted out. Among them were the issue of valuation of the exchange and distribution of shares among the members. The members had different stands on this. Some wanted shareholding in BSE, others wanted to exit for money. For one, I made it clear that nobody could get cash from an exchange for opting to give up their shares in it because that would result in erosion of the financial strength of the exchange. 'You can do a one-to-one sale of your shares in BSE if you want to exit,' I told the members.

The Challenges

Despite the mandate, which had been made through an ordinance, none of the exchanges came forward with any scheme. Not one exchange! Most of the broker-members were worried that the deposits they had paid to the exchanges to become members would now convert to company reserves (once exchanges were converted into companies) and would become difficult to retrieve. RSEs were already on their death bed by now, and I was separately considering closing them down permanently.

By 2003, BSE was sharply sliding in terms of market volumes as compared to NSE. BSE members knew its existence was threatened, but they still were not open to any course correction. Demutualization, in all likelihood, would have helped BSE the most in recovering its lost glory, but surprisingly the biggest opposition to the scheme came from BSE. When I tried to reason with BSE members, they denied all allegations of front-running, manipulation, information leakage and bypassing of risk mechanisms. They used all kinds of political pressure to stall BSE's demutualization.

A Strategy to Convince BSE

However, I put my foot down and told them that whether they were up to mischief or not, having an exchange function as a mutual entity was not a good practice for its functioning even as an SRO, and this had to change. Still there was no positive response from BSE.

I assigned this task to M.S. Sahoo, who was then CGM at SEBI, and later became a WTM (he is currently chairman of the Insolvency and Bankruptcy Board). He had already successfully resolved the contentious thirteen-year issue of brokers fees. I asked him to dedicatedly look into the matter of BSE. It was only after months of struggle and the use of both carrot and stick (at one point of time, I had to forcefully change the complete board of BSE) that SEBI managed to finalize the scheme for demutualization and corporatization of BSE. Here I must appreciate the diligent, persuasive and farsighted work of Sahoo.

The transformation was to happen around the end of my tenure, in February 2005. That was when the issue of stamp duty on transfer of assets upon BSE changing from an AoP to a corporate entity came up. This was waived by smuggling in a provision in Budget 2005–06. By the time I left SEBI, waiver of stamp duty was to come into force (it happened only after the passing of the Budget sometime in May 2006), but the scheme was broadly drawn up. On my demitting office, the brokers got another opportunity to bargain with the new chairman. However, they did not succeed. SEBI approved the demutualization scheme submitted by BSE and notified it in an order on 20 August 2005. By that time, Sahoo had already negotiated the schemes of demutualization with other exchanges, and they all fell in line one after another following the BSE demutualization. SEBI approved the corporatization and demutualization schemes of nineteen exchanges in 2005.

The salient features of these schemes were:

i.   The stock exchanges, which were associations of persons (AoPs) were converted into for-profit companies limited by shares. The exchanges that were companies limited by guarantee were converted into or re-registered as companies limited by shares.

ii. The ownership and management rights were segregated from the trading rights associated with membership cards. As a result, it became unnecessary for a shareholder to be a trading member, and vice versa.

iii. The membership card-holders became the initial shareholders of the emerging exchange while obliging the exchange to ensure that the public, other than shareholders having trading rights, holds at least 51 per cent of its equity shares.

iv. No shareholder who is a trading member has voting rights (taken together with the voting rights of persons acting in concert) exceeding 5 per cent of the voting rights in an emerging (new and upcoming) exchange.

v. The membership card-holders, limited trading members and trading members of the derivatives segment became the trading members of the respective segments of the emerging exchanges initially.

vi. Not only would there be only one class of trading members with similar rights and privileges, but uniform standards were to be followed in terms of capital adequacy, deposits, fees, etc., while admitting any person as a trading member or accepting his surrender of membership.

vii. The governing board of the emerging exchanges was to be so constituted that representatives of trading members do not exceed one-fourth of the board's total strength and the remaining directors are appointed in the manner as may be specified by SEBI from time to time. The chief executive of the exchange is an ex-officio director on the governing board, and SEBI has the right to nominate directors, as and when deemed fit.

viii. The trading members clear and settle trades till the clearing and settlement functions are transferred to a recognized CC.

ix. The exchanges ensure that the assets and reserves transferred from the erstwhile exchange are utilized only for the operations of the stock exchange.

A GAME CHANGER'S MEMOIR

The two major elements of the process were: conversion of the exchange into a corporate entity; and divestment of 51 per cent equity to non-trading members. The exchanges completed their conversion in 2006-07 and their divestment in 2007-08.

It took another two years for BSE to fully implement this scheme, which it did by May 2007. The 51 per cent stake which was to be given to non-trading members was sold to twenty-one investors, some of them quite well known—LIC (5%), SBI (4–5%), Bank of India and Central Bank. BSE was then valued at close to US$ 1 billion (roughly Rs 4,000 crore). Thanks to BSE's demutualization in 2010, Deutsche Bank and the world-renowned investor, George Soros, bought a stake of roughly 4 per cent in BSE Ltd, showing faith in the Indian equity markets. And, finally, all this enabled BSE to get listed.

As far as the RSEs were concerned, their schemes for demutualization and corporatization were accepted too under the SEBI guidelines by the end of my tenure. However, trades on these RSEs had almost dried up, and a few years later they were officially shut down and derecognized by SEBI.

The Current Situation

BSE and NSE continue to be the leading equity stock exchanges in the country. Even in 2017 and 2018 BSE's share of total market volumes ranges between 15 per cent and 20 per cent, and NSE's between 80 per cent and 85 per cent, but the important thing to note is that BSE survived and did not meet the fate of the RSEs, which at one point looked like a distinct possibility. The majority of the shareholding of the two exchanges is held by independent parties and their management is professionally run. And, most importantly, there has been no major market misconduct since then.

The scheme had the foresight to provide for a demutualized exchange to list its securities. It was expected that at least BSE would list in a year or so. For various reasons, that didn't happen. In September 2016, in a historic development, BSE filed a prospectus with SEBI and has since got listed. It has joined the league of international listed exchanges like NYSE, London Stock Exchange, Deutsche Bourse, Hong Kong and Singapore exchanges. NSE had also filed its prospectus for listing, and one hopes that by the time this book is out, it too will be a listed exchange.

I can safely and proudly claim that among other things, our push to corporatize and demutualize the exchanges laid the solid ground for the survival of BSE, a scam-free fifteen years of equity markets and the landmark BSE IPO; and above all, de-risking of the most significant structural risk in the capital market.

Capacity Building: Educated Investor = Protected Investor

Structural reform of the Indian securities markets gathered momentous pace in February 2002. Between the years 2002 and 2017, there has been a sea change in the public perception of the securities markets because of the foundations laid.

The new generation of the investing population has some knowledge about the markets and a basic idea of what equities, insurance and other financial products are.

In those days, to throw terms like margins, T+2, futures/ options, derivatives, fundamental analysis, technical analysis, circuits, Sensex/Nifty, sectoral indices, macro-economic factors, IPOs, RHP, bid, listing gains, STT, etc., at the layman who wished to invest in the capital markets was like teaching the theory of relativity to a second grader. In most cases, the investor would respond to these terms with a blank expression on his face and run miles away the next time there was even remote mention of these terms. Those laymen who were a little more daring in spite of the flood of jargon unleashed on them and still wanted to invest in the stock markets had as their window to the markets the intermediaries (like brokers, sub-brokers) and non-broker financial advisors (merchant bankers, mutual fund distributors, investment advisors). Thus the common investor's knowledge of the markets was limited to the knowledge selectively fed to them by the above-mentioned market intermediaries and advisors.

In fact, at a public meeting in Hyderabad early in my tenure, a lady in the front row said with great anguish that she had lost a substantial amount of money in the capital market following its collapse after Scam 2001. She wanted SEBI to get her money back. When I asked her why and how she came to invest in equity, she was at a loss to answer me. She was not diffident but her silence was on account of her complete absence of knowledge and understanding of the market. She was frank enough to admit there was a kind of 'talk of the town' to 'invest in stock and make money', and she had joined the procession without ascertaining anything about the stocks she invested in, the promoters and managers of the company or the functioning of the stock exchange when she invested.

I was dumbfounded; not because I was unaware of the rampant financial illiteracy in the country but because of the mindlessness of even the sophisticated elite when it came to investing. I left the function with an impression that it was lack of informed decision making that was singularly responsible for the distress of many investors in the stock market. I concluded that education and capacity building were the answer, and resolved to take it forward resolutely.

To become a broker/sub-broker one had to pass an examination, but that was it. There was no way for brokers/sub-brokers to keep their knowledge updated and enhance their skills beyond just execution of transactions on the investor's behalf. While one still needed to pass certain exams to become a broker/sub-broker, there was no criteria by which anyone could call himself a financial advisor. And yet many people were referring to themselves as financial advisors. Yes, there were professionals like CAs, MBAs and CFAs running their financial advisory services, but they were very few compared with nearly a million who called themselves financial advisors. (The SEBI Act, 1992 enabled registration and regulation of investment advisers. Since they operate under the jurisdiction of many regulators, it took a very long to time sort out the manner in which they could be regulated. So the investors did not know whom to trust with their money. Besides, there were umpteen examples of brokers or advisors putting their personal interests ahead of the investors' and taking them for a ride. The recent scam had acted as a huge morale breaker for investors. In short, the common investor had very limited options to truly understand the markets and make informed investment decisions.

Capacity building, synonymous with institution building, has the twin objectives of empowerment and participation. In the case of a regulatory body, capacity building entails the processes of developing and strengthening skills and abilities, and building the resources of its participants to survive, adopt and thrive. Such capacity building cannot be limited only to human resources internal to the regulator, but has to be extended among the intermediaries, investors and other market participants. Inadequate capacity leads to ineffective regulation, erects kinks for easy misconduct and even frustrates the fundamental frame of a regulatory regime.

Helping Investors, the Internal Way

The various initiatives taken till then were all means to widen the basket of products, better regulate the market and protect investors. I wanted to help investors to grow their own capacity to take informed decisions and protect themselves. I wanted to educate them and make them financially literate. (A disclosure-based regulatory regime works only if the investors are capable of making use of the disclosures, that is, taking informed decisions based on the disclosed information and be responsible for their own decisions). In addition to helping them understand the market jargon, I wanted them to know their investment options, their rights with respect to brokers, exchanges and regulators, selection of intermediaries/advisors to deal with, complaint redressal mechanisms, long term vs short term investing, and risk vs benefits of various tools and techniques of investing.

I also wanted to extend and deepen the financial literacy education of the intermediaries and financial advisors in the market, and even of SEBI employees. Periodic certification and training for intermediaries, advisors and SEBI employees would not only benefit investors but build a human resource pool trained specially for the capital market. I wanted SEBI employees to be more knowledgeable and skilled than the population being regulated.

To bring this about, our broad idea was to create an institute to train potential investors and trainers on various capital market concepts and provide round-the-year training to securities market intermediaries, financial advisors and SEBI employees through certificate courses, seminars and workshops. The long-term vision was to introduce diploma courses in the institute and make it the de facto provider of human resource for the various needs of the constituents (intermediaries, advisors, manpower requirement of SEBI, investor educators) of the capital market, cater to the training needs of international regulators too, particularly from the Southeast Asian and African countries, and also promote research and development (R&D) in the securities market through this institute.

We set up a dedicated international committee to plan the structure, scope and the end-to-end establishment of the institute. Some of the distinguished members of the committee were Howard Davis, then director of the London School of Economics and Political Science and earlier chairman of Financial Authority, UK (FSA); David Fischer, then chairman of Capital International; Venu Srinivasan, chairman and managing director of TVS Motors; Pawan Kant Munjal, MD and CEO,

Hero Corporate Service and also president of CII at the time; Hemendra Kothari of DSP Merrill Lynch and T.N. Ninan, then editor of *Business Standard* and now chairman of board of directors there. The idea to include international members was to impart the best security market practices and training methods from all over the world to students of the institute. After all, this institute was envisioned to play a key role in building capacity, in creating a well-educated and trained force.

In addition to the institute, a separate academic council was created to prepare a curriculum to cater to the needs of various types of students (potential investors, brokers, professional advisors, or just students wishing to work in some capacity in capital market-related areas) of the institute. The council consisted of luminaries like Dr Pritam Singh, who had been the director of IIM Lucknow and was then director of the Management Development Institute, Gurgaon; Dr K.C. Mishra, then director, National Insurance Academy; C.B. Bhave, then managing director of NSDL (who later was SEBI chairman from 2008 to 2011); Ravi Narain, then managing director of NSE; R.K. Mishra, then ED at SEBI; M.S. Sahoo, then chief general manager at SEBI, later to hold the positions of WTM, SEBI, member of Competition Commission and now chairman, IBB.

Based on the discussions of these two committees, the institute was named National Institute of Securities Market (NISM) and was registered as a society and a trust. The courses were designed around six broad areas—financial literacy, corporate governance, certification for intermediaries and advisors (on broking, merchant banking, mutual fund distribution, investment advisory), regulatory studies and securities research.

Premises for NISM

I had big plans for the institute and started looking out for some land to build it from scratch in a grand way. I spoke to the chief minister of Maharashtra, Vilasrao Deshmukh, regarding acquisition of land for the project, and he was very cooperative. On his suggestion, I visited a 65-acre plot in Khandala and liked it. I told Deshmukh that SEBI was ready to acquire the land and he agreed to give it to us at a nominal price. Verbally everything was in place, but somehow he could not make the land available to us (well, getting land even for progressive purposes is never easy!). By this time my tenure came to an end, and it was left to my successor to take the institute forward. In the budget speech of 2005–06, the finance minister announced that he had authorized SEBI to set up NISM.

To their credit, my successors continued this initiative with equal enthusiasm. However, since land was not readily available, and wanting to start the educational activities of NISM rightaway (instead of waiting to build a new institute), SEBI acquired the Vashi premises of UTI Institute of Capital Markets (the education arm of Unit Trust of India), from SUUTI within a year of my leaving. Subsequently, the government transferred UTI Institute of Capital Markets to SEBI. SEBI continued to have both institutes, but found it difficult to merge them. Only in 2015 were they merged. That year NISM started its first enrolments and certifications.

NISM remained located in Mittal Court till 2009 before moving to Vashi in Navi Mumbai (the location of the erstwhile UTI institute) in December 2016. It later shifted to a dedicated campus in Patalganga (about 60 km from Mumbai) spread over 70 acres, costing close to Rs 300 crore. This place has residential in-house capacity for 5,000 people. The inauguration of the campus was done by the prime minister, Narendra Modi.

Today NISM is a one-of-its-kind institute; probably no securities market in the world has a campus of such a scale. It is a behemoth of a very modern institution, providing full-time and part-time post-graduate courses in the securities market and related subjects, with good placement records across banks, broking houses, equity research and other financial services companies. In addition, it annually awards about 1.5 lakh professionals with twenty different certifications, and has partnerships with various financial institutions for periodic seminars, workshops and continuous investor awareness programmes. It also acts as a training centre for Pension Fund Regulatory and Development Authority (PFRDA), National Housing Bank and RBI (for its functions related to the capital market). Sooner than later, NISM will be all set to become an independent university. It is a happy augury that the initial steps catapulted an idea into an enviable capacity-building institute that anyone associated with the industry can be proud of.

Securities Market Awareness Campaign

I realized there was a need to improve investor education at the prompting of Ramesh at SEBI. The big idea of having NISM and its execution started only after a couple of years of this. So before NISM was visualized, we had already started taking other steps towards increasing investor awareness about capital markets. In fact, these steps became a precursor for the eventual launch of NISM.

One big step was to start periodic investor awareness programmes (seminars and workshops) in every nook and corner of the country, and even overseas, with the support of various government and private agencies. We took into confidence agencies like Association of Merchant Bankers of India (AMBI), AMFI, brokers, business chambers and industry associations, corporations and entrepreneurs, depositories and depository participants, educational institutes, interested NGOs, investor associations, media, other professional organizations like ICAI, ICSI, Registrars Association of India (RAIN) and the stock exchanges to help us conduct the programmes throughout the country and even to advertise it to their respective members.

For funding this activity (in addition to funding by SEBI) we approached the ministry of finance, the stock exchanges, educators, the investor education and protection fund (of the department of company affairs), the Indo-US financial institutions reform and expansion project, corporations, SROs and other intermediaries and investor associations, and got their support. Once the funding and partner organizations were in place, I planned to launch the programme.

Since my vision for this nation-wide programme was grand, I wanted a big-bang inauguration with appropriate media coverage across the country so that no existing/potential investor missed the news that such a programme was on. What better way, I thought, to ensure media coverage than to invite the FM, Jaswant Singh, for the inauguration! So I approached him. He understood the whole matter and not only agreed to come for the inauguration but also came up with another great idea, 'Why don't you invite the PM?' he asked me.

I said, 'Fine, kindly invite him.' Obviously, inviting the PM would have ensured coverage as nothing else could. But Singh asked me to go and invite the PM myself. When I called on Atal Bihari Vajpayee to invite him, he said, in his characteristic style, yet with a pinch of humour: '*Mujhe ye satta bazaar ke chakkar mein kyu fasate ho?* (Why are you involving me in this stock market gambling?)' This was his way of conveying that the PM was not to be engaged in such trivialities.

I explained the significance of the whole programme to him. As a statesman deeply concerned about the people of India and their welfare, he was always looking for opportunities to take all possible decisions and steps to mitigate their miseries. He was pained at the outbreak of Scam 2001 and the financial loss it caused to millions of investors. He very willingly agreed to inaugurate the campaign and spent more than the budgeted time with the large number of participants at the function to instil in them a sense of confidence.

The Actual Campaign

On 17 January 2003, amidst much media fanfare and in the presence of the PM, FM, industry veterans and various industry associations, SEBI launched its 'Securities Market Awareness Programme' at Vigyan Bhavan, New Delhi. In the next few days itself, the campaign was extended to twelve states, with no less than the governors or chief ministers of the states launching the campaign.

To boost the project and keep the momentum going, we kept searching for newer avenues and ways to increase its reach to beyond where our partners could take us. Letters were sent to the MPs of both the Lok Sabha and Rajya Sabha requesting them to indicate the names of centres in their constituencies where SEBI could organize workshops for investor education. Accordingly, several workshops were held in the centres indicated by these MPs. Exchanges were requested to hold an 'open house' for investors once a month in their premises and invite the compliance officers of listed companies, mutual funds, stock brokers and other market intermediaries to not only address/ educate the investors but to also attend to their grievances. To make the campaign interesting, audio-visual techniques were used. Educative materials were distributed free of cost across the country and a dedicated investor website was created to handle investor complaints and provide reading material, FAQs, explain common terms and laws online.

We even started advertising in the newspapers, radio and television across cities. Our print advertisement strategy was extremely aggressive. We issued about 700 advertisements in forty-eight different newspapers in ten regional languages covering 100 cities. To keep costs down we did this in partnership with the various partner organizations in our campaign. All India Radio was kind enough to allot certain free radio slots to us from time to time.

I asked almost all the business news channels to air free informational and educative advertorials. I met the chief managing one of the channels and persuaded him to do this. Most of the channels aired investor education messages for several months. In fact, NDTV Profit, which was then headed by Shivnath Thukral, designed the concept of a half hour interview with the chairman of SEBI on various aspects of the securities market. I readily agreed, and six episodes were telecast by NDTV Profit during my tenure. I also suggested to the head of CNBC the holding of investor meets as a campaign, to which he agreed. To give a push to those meets, I inaugurated quite a few, commencing with the Bengaluru session. In fact, the Delhi meet was addressed by the FM, Chidambaram.

This was the first time in SEBI's history that a dedicated investor education programme on such a big scale was being conducted. By the end of my tenure, SEBI had covered twenty states and around 500 cities and towns with 2,000 workshops (at the rate of three or four workshops a day) reaching out to at least half a million people. This investor awareness programme continues successfully even today in various forms.

Taking the Campaign to the Grassroots

As part of the nation-wide securities awareness programme I specifically wanted to target the country's youth at the threshold of adulthood. The best way to do this, I thought, was to catch them young and make investing a part of any young adult's life, just like voting, driving, college or a job. Also, a young adult is more receptive to new ideas and is better tuned to learning from trial and error. Obviously, once they grew older their investing habits too might continue. So I wrote to the HRD ministry to introduce stock market fundamentals as a part of the curriculum at the high school level itself. However, nothing came of it at the time, and my tenure too came to an end.

I was extremely happy to know that recently, after a decade of my suggestion to introduce capital markets as a subject in schools, CBSE has introduced the subject of 'financial markets' for class X students from the academic year 2015–16 onwards. I am told U.K. Sinha, then chairman of SEBI, was behind this.

The Result of Our Efforts

I still remember a leading journalist's remarks in her article about our efforts at SEBI to create NISM: 'Why should an understaffed and overworked regulator (like SEBI) want to duplicate what can probably be done (i.e., training of securities market professionals) as effectively in any leading management institution in India?' However, each of the visions we drew up ten years back—for increasing investor awareness, training intermediaries and advisors and building the human resource capacity of the capital markets—has fructified sooner or later, and with good results. We laid the foundation for making investor awareness a priority for SEBI. Today it has seeped into SEBI's culture. We visualized an institute to fulfil the various training and human resource needs of the capital markets and started NISM; today it is on the verge of becoming a full-fledged university and is the biggest provider of manpower and training for the capital markets. Finally, we thought of imparting knowledge of the securities market to school children; and today the subject of capital markets is a part of the school curriculum.

Today India has about 3 crore individual investors in the stock market, which is three-fold the number that existed during my tenure. Over the same period, the number of unique investors in mutual funds has gone up to over 1 crore from a few lakh, and the cumulative AUM of mutual funds has increased to Rs 20 lakh crore from about Rs 1.54 lakh crore. Even the cumulative mutual fund AUM-to-GDP ratio in India went up from approximately 5 per cent during my tenure to closer to 14 per cent. I believe the investor awareness programme run by SEBI has aided all these improvements.

While there is definitely an increase in individual investor participation in the capital markets, we still have a long way to go when compared with many other countries. Only about 3 per cent of the population in India invests in the stock market, whereas in the US almost 40 per cent of the population buys equity and in China about 10 per cent. Even the cumulative mutual fund AUM-to-GDP ratio in India is much behind that of other economies (in US and UK this ratio is 90 per cent and 40 per cent, respectively). The global average for the percentage of equity and equity-related products in the total investment of individual wealth is 25, and in the US it is as high as 45. It is hoped that SEBI will continue its untiring efforts at building capacity, in turn helping to create a capital market that touches the life of every potential investor in the country.

19

SELF-REGULATION

Tackling ground-level issues

During the decade from 1991 to 2001, Indian stock exchanges witnessed stupendous growth. The yearly turnover on the exchanges increased from about Rs 1 lakh crore to around Rs 30 lakh crore—an increase of about 3,000 per cent. The number of investors rose from a few lakh to close to 50 lakh. The BSE Sensex grew from the 2000 levels to the 6000 levels, and the stock broker community doubled from 5,000 to 10,000. The mid-nineties were also a period of IPO boom in India. The funds raised from the primary market grew more than four times, from Rs 6,000 crore in 1991–92 to peak at Rs 27,000 crore 1994–95. The number of merchant bankers rose from 100 to 162 approximately. Investments through the mutual fund route too expanded remarkably during this decade, the number of mutual funds increasing five times, from a mere eight to forty. Their AUM went up three times, from around Rs 40,000 crore to around Rs 1,20,000 crore, and the number of mutual fund distributors grew manifold. Even portfolio managers increased in number, from about 28 to about 40. In short, the stock market expanded its reach, from catering to a small elite that traded on it to a mass of investors.

As the range of services and volume of transactions grew, and as the number of brokers, merchant bankers, mutual fund distributors, investment advisors and registrars also grew, it became increasingly difficult to detect the growing malpractices and compliance lapses; overall, investor grievances rose from a few thousand in 1991 to about 27 lakh in 2001.

The small SEBI team scattered across a few offices was wholly inadequate to the task of effectively monitoring and preventing disasters in the market. This structural deficiency was a serious risk.

Ground-level Issues

Take mutual funds, which are regulated by SEBI. A distributor of mutual funds often ended up balancing the conflicting roles of representing the interest of the manufacturer of the product and being an authentic guide to the investors of the product. Naturally, the distributor's bias would often be towards the manufacturer of the product, who is his paymaster, though riding on the business the distributor gets from the investor. This creates a ripe ground for mis-selling; the mutual fund distributor would naturally push the product that pays him the most, even though that may not be in the best interest of the investor. In effect, the distributor often ends up serving his own enlightened self-interest. This happened consistently.

The risks with merchant banking and investment advisory services were similar. Even though rules to mitigate all the potential risks in intermediation were laid down, the challenge of enforcing them at the grassroots level remained. Even stock exchanges, with brokers as their members who could influence the management, often walked the tightrope between their regulatory and operational functions.

Soon after joining SEBI, when I first studied the effectiveness of the market regulations, one thing became amply clear. SEBI, with its manpower of about 350 and offices only in select cities, was in no position to keep a direct tab on the ground-level activities of brokers, merchant bankers, mutual fund distributors, investment advisors and registrars et al., given the continental size of the market. Further, what happens on the ground is known in its purest form only to those people who are close to the ground of action. SEBI's sources for getting information were formatted and second-hand, and thus diluted. Even otherwise, a regulator sits atop a hill. He can comprehend the wider expanse, in what is described as a 'helicopter view', but cannot see clearly what activities are happening in every square foot at the ground level.

As far as creating an effective redressal mechanism was concerned, from the investors' point of view, complaining directly to SEBI for everything seemed a little intimidating and bureaucratic, demotivating them from making complaints at all. Even when SEBI did get complaints, its preoccupation with so many matters delayed quick action against the culprits. Investors needed the comfort of a quicker recourse for their troubles.

One potential, theoretical solution was to expand SEBI's infrastructure—its offices, technology and manpower—but the cost-benefit analysis did not make sense. SEBI may still not be fully in command of the situation. In short, it was nearly impossible for SEBI, with only a bird's eye view of the markets, to provide effective oversight and detect and prevent conflicts and misconducts. There had to be a better structural solution.

What is a Self Regulating Organization (SRO)

Globally, the regulation of capital markets has two tiers of regulation. The first tier consists of the statutory regulatory body, which governs the entire capital market, including the intermediaries (e.g. SEBI for India, SEC for US stock markets). The second tier consists of the organizations of intermediaries, typically in the form of SROs, who govern themselves under the broad direction, guidance and oversight of the first-tier regulatory body (SEBI).

An SRO, as the name suggests, is an organization which regulates itself. The simplest example of an SRO is a club house or gymkhana, where the club members elect a few of their own members to create rules and govern all the members. On the one hand, the rules need to take care of the comfort of the members (allow them access to facilities at all times); and on the other, the rules needed to restrict certain behaviour or practice (like banning access to facilities for members not dressed appropriately). Be it privileges or restrictions, in the end it is the members who regulate themselves, always working under the broad oversight of the Indian laws.

Another facet of the functioning of SROs is the training and education of their members. For example at a brokerage, dealers, broking staff and back-office staff are trained, because well-trained manpower is a prerequisite for providing efficient service to investors. Since SEBI could not directly engage in training and certifying lakhs of people, it was necessary to create an effective SRO mechanism as part of capacity building in the securities markets. However, as the institution of SRO was not shaping up, the idea of a capital market institute (NISM) was conceived for capacity building, which has since fructified, although after my exit.

I felt that every category of participant in the capital market—brokers, merchant bankers, mutual fund distributors, investment advisors and registrars—could organize itself into an SRO, regulating itself through its own members. Of course, this would be done under the superintendence of SEBI. There could be many benefits from this. These SROs, expert in their domain and more aware of the ground realities than anybody else, could design guidelines (supplementing SEBI's regulations) to enhance efficiencies in operations and to deter dishonest dealings and other malpractices among their community. Even if there were instances of corrupt practice and/or misdemeanour among its members, the SRO would notice them much earlier and more accurately than SEBI. The investors, too, would find it easier to register their complaints with a dedicated body like an SRO for quicker address of their grievances. In this way, SEBI's burden would be shared. An effective SRO self-disciplines the working of its segment, thus winning the confidence of investors. Section 11(2)(d) of the SEBI Act mandates SEBI to take measures for promoting and regulating SROs.

With this broad idea in mind, my team and I started our work on making SROs a reality. We peeped into the existing rules in other countries as well as into the very recent history of SEBI for reference.

Global and Indian SROs

Most of the developed countries had their own SROs for some or all of their financial intermediaries—brokers, security dealers (US, Canada, Japan, South Korea), merchant bankers (Japan, South Korea), mutual fund distributors (Canada, Japan, South Korea) and investment advisors (Canada, Japan, South Korea). A few other countries too, like Turkey, had SROs for regulating their securities-related transactions.

In addition, the world over, most exchanges operated as SROs and their operations were at arms length from their regulation. For example, NASD regulated NASDAQ, with no overlap between the regulatory and operational functions. Similarly, Toronto Stock Exchange in Canada was demutualized in the early 2000s, and its market regulation function was separated from its for-profit operations.

Similar patterns in the regulation of exchanges run across most of the developed market geographies. All the SROs focus on regulations completely independent of the day-to-day operations of the respective industry segment (brokers, merchant bankers, mutual fund distributors, investment advisors and registrars) they were regulating. Almost all of them operated through a governing board with an adequate number of independent members— usually expert professionals with proven track record and reputation. Almost all of them performed the following as part of their regulatory role—enforcement, inspection and disciplinary actions against their own members, dispute resolution between their members and investors, and investor education.

In India, historically, all stock exchanges, including the regional ones, functioned as SROs. Exchanges were regulated by their own member-brokers under the oversight of SEBI, and before SEBI was formed in 1992, under the oversight of the capital markets division of the ministry of finance. The exchanges were in a position to detect mischiefs like price manipulation and take quick action, such as suspension of trading in the related scrip, only because they functioned independently as SROs and regulated the companies listed on them. Though there were inadequacies and even delinquencies in their SRO functioning, their utility was not undermined. Hence, in the case of stock exchanges, in order to further strengthen their functioning as SROs, corporatization and demutualization were mandated.

Then there were AMFI, AMBI, BSE's Broker Forum, and RAIN, which already existed but as industry associations acting merely as an interface between their industry and regulator rather than as SROs. They were recognized by SEBI but did not work under any specific SEBI regulations.

Bringing the SRO to India

SRO regimes can be of various forms: cooperative, delegated, devolved, facilitated and tacit, but I was aiming at building a co-regulatory regime, where responsibilities could be shared between SEBI and the SROs. Whereas the SRO was to focus on mundane and ground-level operational areas, SEBI was to concentrate on the big-picture issues, effective superintendence of the SROs and coordination of the two frames of the regulatory structure. The idea was not for SEBI to abdicate or disengage from doing its part of the regulatory work.

However, I was acutely aware of the possibility of 'regulatory capture' or 'regulatory inflation' in addition to the possibility of ineffective or motivated regulation of the areas delegated to the SROs, as had happened in the case of stock exchanges. The envisaged SRO regulation and effective oversight were to mitigate those risks. In fact, I was aiming at building adjuncts to the regulatory regime—an alternative mechanism, which has reach and depth, to enhance the effectiveness of the modern regulatory state.

To create SROs in India, I spoke to the leadership of the existing associations of the many intermediaries, and almost all of them seemed very positive about the idea. However, there was serious resistance from AMFI. Since AMFI was a well-recognized industry association, I wanted it to become an SRO. After several rounds of intense discussions I finally told them that if AMFI did not want to become an SRO, I would think of some other body. Most of the MFs were not supportive of AMFI becoming an SRO. It's an irony that over a decade later, when SROs are now being approved by SEBI, AMFI has jumped the queue amongst the applicants. It had been unwilling to become an SRO initially.

We aggregated all our findings and learning and issued a discussion paper on SROs around mid-2003. The paper discussed relevant issues—whether the SROs should be for-profit or not, whether they should be industry-wise or not, should there be a single SRO for the capital market as an industry or not, who would be the decision-making authority in SROs, would there be sufficient representation of independent members in their decision-making body, whether SROs should be allowed to take disciplinary action against their members, and the extent of SEBI's control over SROs. The paper was posted on the SEBI website, and comments on its merits and de-merits called from the public and market intermediaries. As was the norm, two rounds of feedback were done before approval of the regulations by the SEBI board. Finally, on February 2004, the SEBI (SRO) Regulations, 2004, were notified.

In between all this, sometime in mid-2002, a few months after my joining SEBI, we had set up a committee under the chairmanship of Uday Kotak to outline AMBI's role. The committee recommended restructuring of AMBI as an SRO under the SEBI guidelines, in line with what we were thinking at SEBI. At the same time, Asian Development Bank was asked by the government of India to draw up a report on the reforms required in the domestic MF industry. However, the ADB report was contrary to what we believed at SEBI. The report advised against an SRO for the MF industry and instead advised SEBI to strengthen its own supervision of it. It cited the example of the failure of SROs in the UK as the basis of its recommendation, though the size and structure of UK market are completely at variance with ours. Convinced about our concept of an SRO, we nevertheless went ahead and introduced the SEBI (SRO) Regulations 2004, as mentioned above.

Highlights of the SRO Regulations

The key highlights of the 2004 regulation were the following:

The structure of the SRO was to be that of a non-profit company operating through a board of directors, with independent directors making the majority.

An SRO had the freedom to establish various committees— screening (for selection of members), disciplinary, arbitration, etc., provided that the majority of the members of each such committee were independent. SEBI would have the power to appoint board members, select the chairman of the board, revise the constitution of the board, if required, call for books of accounts, order independent audits on the SRO, take disciplinary action against it, etc. Besides forming rules along which the members would operate, SROs were also permitted to form their own rules for enforcement, inspection and disciplinary actions against their members and for dispute resolution between their members and their clients. Finally, any association (be it one of stock brokers, merchant bankers, mutual fund distributors, investment advisors and registrars etc.) desiring to be recognized as SROs could independently apply to SEBI for the recognition. Needless to say, everything was to be done with the approval of SEBI.

We were hoping that the associations, who had been quite excited about the SRO idea, would quickly come and register, but there was no immediate action from their side after our regulations were notified. As ill luck would have it, by the time we could push the associations to register as SROs, my tenure was nearing its end. However, post my exit, the SRO regulations went through their own slow journey.

20

THE MISSING MARKET
OF RETAIL DEBT

The name is bond . . . retail bond.

As of December 2015, India's outstanding bond market stood at around US$ 1,300 billion, roughly Rs 90 lakh crore. This makes India one of the top ten debt markets in the world. But ask an ordinary retail investor about bonds, and in all likelihood you will be met with a blank look. Bonds, pure debt products, are safer than equity as bonds are asset-backed, rated, and if listed become liquid with a penalty-free exit, and also provide reasonable yields, not as much as equity but more than fixed deposits. One would imagine a strong market for this product, especially among retail investors, who constantly struggle to choose their investment options between the two extremes of equity and fixed deposits.

The situation in India's debt market was bad around the time I had joined SEBI in 2002. Corporations had the option of either raising equity money, if eligible to do so and possible, or knock at the door of banks and other lending institutions like insurance companies. I decided to get the bond markets and the retail investors to know each other a little more so they could connect.

The Story of Bond Markets and the Left-out Retail Investor

Higher yielding government bonds were open only to institutional investors (mostly banks, insurance and pension funds) because of the rigid investor eligibility criteria and the high monetary value involved in buying them in pre-defined lot sizes.

Primary issuance of corporate debt paper by both private and public companies was through private placement with banks and insurance companies as the disclosure requirements for this were minimal. The few primary issuances that were listed, although in the wholesale market of NSE, were largely by NBFCs who found it difficult to raise funds in other ways. Needless to add, the ratings of some of these NBFCs were suspect, and an average investor was not sufficiently financially literate to evaluate a good NBFC from a bad one. Further, there was no liquidity in these bonds. Retail investors could not invest in corporate bonds because they did not offer options to choose from or have liquidity. In short, the debt market in India was marked by the dominance of government securities (over 95 per cent of the debt market) and PSU bonds. Then there were a few corporate bonds including those of banks.

A full-fledged retail debt market with corporate and government securities can lead to efficient mobilization of resources, financing of developmental activities, liquidity management, diversification of credit risk across the economy, market discipline, nurturing of the credit culture and above all, effectiveness of the financial system in bringing about more efficient capital allocation. The other obvious benefits are more avenues for stable and predictable income for investors and lower costs of borrowing for companies. In fact, a vibrant and liquid debt market is considered to be the backbone of the financial system all over the world, in particular for developing economies like India. This market was missing in India.

A New Idea

We wanted to create a separate trading platform on BSE and NSE for all types of debt instruments focused primarily on retail investors but with institutional participation. As it existed then, all government debt securities (in the primary and secondary markets) were subscribed to and traded through the negotiated dealing system (NDS) of RBI. All categories of bonds—government, public sector, private sector—were allowed to be traded in the wholesale debt market (WDM) of NSE. Retail investors had little access to any of these platforms. A more focused retail platform would facilitate provision of the right information (credit ratings, analysts' reports [even analysts would find it easy to track a focused retail debt market]) suited to retail players for their participation in the debt market with comfort. This separate, focused platform would also entice institutional investors to participate in it, which was important to ensure liquidity.

A segregated retail debt platform would also encourage issuers of bonds—government, public sector units and private companies—to come up with products more suited for retail investors and also open their existing debt products for them. This would also provide the issuer an additional (better and cheaper) avenue for raising debt capital. Greater participation of issuers and investors would build liquidity and fine pricing, with the result that the hitherto neglected retail debt market would flourish. In any case, the opaque pricing of debt papers would get tested by the transparency of a trading platform.

I studied the developed debt markets of the US, Europe, Japan, South Korea and some other economies. In many of these countries (particularly in the USA and South Korea), besides governments and PSUs, a large number of corporations preferred to tap the debt market in preference to private placements, public deposits, bank loans, and the like. Also, in many of these countries (especially in the USA) trade volumes in the secondary debt market were far higher than in the secondary equity market, largely thanks to super-active institutional participation. The higher liquidity in the debt market, due to institutional participation, provided a good ground for greater participation of retail investors too.

Now, in order to start the retail platform, there were two requirements: first, the technical and financial aspects of putting the platform in place; and second, to convince the government and the public sector units to custom-make debt securities, which could be directly subscribed to by individual investors, or to open their existing debt products to individual investors. We had to change the mindset of the private sector companies from raising debt funds only through private placement to agreeing to list their bonds. And finally, we had to educate the investors— retail and institutional—to participate in the debt market in large numbers. The most important aspect was to bring banks on the trading platform. They were the major investors in the debt market.

Convincing Government and the Corporate Sector

A committee was formed to prepare a report on creating a dedicated retail debt platform on the exchanges, to be presented to the government. It was easy to convince the government, since the idea did not seem to disturb any particular vested group or status quo (from the government's point of view at least). In fact, it would promote the government as retail-investor-friendly.

In the listing of corporate bonds, there was a chicken and egg situation. Because there was no liquidity in the debt market, companies stayed away from listing their bonds. And because companies stayed away from listing their bonds, investors had nothing to invest in the debt market. So we started the process of persuading the corporate sector to get their bonds listed. At the same time, we had plans to strategically market the retail platform to encourage the retail and institutional investors. I was confident that in due course, once the platform was created, corporations would warm up to the idea of getting their bonds listed. This, combined with our campaign, would draw investors to the retail debt market.

While these tasks were challenging, the most daunting one turned out to be creation of the platform itself. Another difficulty was the unexpected resistance from several quarters.

Creation of the Platform

Yield curve

Since NSE was already experienced in successfully running the WDM platform, we gave the task of building the retail platform to the exchange. While the technical aspects of the platform were being built by NSE, we hit a logjam when it came to the financial aspect. Since a platform focused on retail debt products was being created for the first time, there did not exist any precedent for the yield curve that could help retail investors benchmark the yield so that the price of new issuances could be made available on this platform by the government and by the public and private sector companies.

To solve this issue, another committee was appointed under Prof. Jayanth Varma of IIM(A), a former WTM at SEBI. Along with NSE, the committee created a dummy ten-year yield curve for retail bond products, which acted as a benchmark for any new issuance on the new retail debt platform. All this took tremendous time and effort, and the NSE-SEBI team deserves full credit for it.

The roadblock

As mentioned earlier, government debt securities accounted for over 95 per cent of the bond market and were predominantly traded through the RBI's platform, NDS. NDS allowed institutional members to electronically submit bids for the primary issuances of government securities when auctions were conducted, and to get the security allotment online and pay online. NDS also provided a clearing and settlement system (through a separate securities settlement system [SSS] of the Public Debt Office of the RBI) later to be taken over by Clearing Corporation of India for settlement of transactions in government securities conducted in the secondary market. In short, the end-to-end process of dealing in government securities in India, in both the primary and secondary markets, was controlled by RBI.

Now, the functioning of the new retail debt platform was to be independent of RBI's involvement and would be controlled by the exchanges. So, while creating the new debt platform, we needed RBI's inputs too, since the apex bank had experience in running a similar debt platform. It took some time to take RBI into confidence, and they finally agreed to help in setting up the new platform.

Finally a retail platform was developed by NSE from scratch with the help of RBI. Though NSE had experience in creating the technology system for the wholesale debt market earlier, they took quite some time to develop the new system. On our persuasion, the government and some corporations allowed a few of their bonds for direct trading by retail investors. The new retail debt platform was inaugurated on 16 January 2003 by Jaswant Singh from his office in New Delhi. It was a fully automated order-driven screen-based trading platform, which could be used by retail investors through more than 10,000 terminals (of BSE, NSE and OTCEI brokers) spread over 400 cities, just as in the equity market. It was decided to bring all types of government debt securities to the retail market in a phased manner. The platform followed the same T+2 settlement system as for equity markets. The minimum amount for investment was kept as Rs 1,000. Singh became the first user of the platform and bought government securities worth Rs 10,000. I followed suit and bought ICICI bonds worth Rs 10,000. The event was covered widely in the media and attended by several luminaries.

Well begun is half done, or so they say. Here we had begun well. A separate platform had been created, the government and the corporate sector had given their initial nod by listing a few of their debt securities on this platform, and the media had covered the launch event as a positive development. Now all I needed was to ensure liquidity. For this we had to draw in more corporations, which would in turn attract more retail investors. For this liquidity, I relied on participation by institutional investors. And here is where the 'well-begun, half done' theory fell apart.

The biggest institutional investors in government securities—the banks—decided to stay away from the debt platform. *Why?* Because RBI wouldn't allow them to trade on it. I wanted banks to shift a good chunk of their trading in government debt securities to this new platform to ensure liquidity on it. But RBI was not comfortable with the banks shifting trades to the new platform.

When I met the governor of RBI to discuss the issue, he said that they didn't trust the brokers (for something as important as government debt securities). Possibly the Scam 1992 fallouts, where institutions like NHB, SBI and even RBI received flak, were still haunting the apex bank. I responded to this saying that if that were the case, then I would provide the banks with broking licences for their proprietary trades so that they could trade on their own accounts and did not have to go through the brokers. The governor was okay with this, but wanted to wait and see what he could do.

At my request, the government amended the Securities Contracts (Regulations) Rules to allow banks to register as brokers for proprietary trades. By all accounts, this was a big amendment. Since I was so keen to develop the retail debt market, I wasted no time in making banks eligible to become brokers. However, banks still did not use the new retail debt platform. Since banks did not participate and help liquidity on the platform, our new platform remained illiquid even at the time I left SEBI.

Progress in this matter since the end of my tenure has been slow, although the retail debt platform we created still exists in a marginally modified form. Committees have been formed to suggest reforms in the debt market. Some steps have been taken too (RBI has allowed banks to become members of stock exchanges to trade in corporate bonds at least). The absolute value of the bond market has gone up, but the exposure of the retail investors to the bond market remains poor. The platform, Corporate Bond Market, was relaunched during U.K. Sinha's tenure as SEBI chairman, but it remains a non-starter. In the meantime, RBI has allowed individual investors and others to trade in government securities on NDS. However, both retail investors and liquidity continue to remain elusive.

The Indian financial market suffers from a serious structural gap post dissolution of development bank viz. IDBI, ICICI etc. into commercial banks. The responsibility of long term financing including of infra-structure projects has fallen squarely on shoulders of commercial banks in India, which have short term liabilities and long term assets on the balance sheet creates a mismatch. However, the announcement in the Union Budget of 2018–19 of raising a significant percentage of long term borrowing from the market and stabilization of the bankruptcy mechanism are bound to help in development of debt market.

21

SEGREGATING WEALTH CREATORS: BSE-INDONEXT

The RSE's last chance

Till the year 2003, it was compulsory for companies to list on the RSE closest to its registered office, irrespective of whether they were listed on a national exchange (BSE/NSE) or not. India is probably the only country that encouraged listing on multiple exchanges, one of them having to be a regional one. The primary reasons for this were lack of technology and balance in the economic development of regions in a federal structure. The prevalent 'open outcry' method of trading required the physical presence of a trader, and those who stayed in faraway Calcutta, for example, found it difficult to trade on BSE or elsewhere on a daily basis.

The Fall of RSEs

Scam 1992 had brought BSE, Kanpur and Calcutta exchanges under severe criticism for their lax regulations against market manipulations, poor margin maintenance, misuse of badla, faulty settlement systems, etc. This forced SEBI to rethink the various parameters of the functioning of the stock markets, particularly their use of technology for effective governance of markets, which has been discussed in the chapter on RSEs.

Survival of Companies Listed on RSEs

As already mentioned in the chapter on RSEs, trading at RSEs had become so bad that we wanted to move towards shutting the exchanges down completely. Since RSEs had been around for quite some time (some even 100 years old) and had many companies listed on them, this was easier said than done. We had to do something about those companies that were listed only on RSEs but were not traded at all and were only breeding structural risk.

Since the option of delisting through buyback of shares by the promoters was not available, we had to think of alternatives. One option was to get these companies listed on a national exchange like BSE, where they could fetch some trading interest nationally. However, BSE had stricter listing criteria than the RSEs, such as minimum paid-up capital size of Rs 10 crore or above, and NSE's criteria were still more stringent. So these companies were ineligible for listing on BSE and NSE. The Securities Laws (Amendment) Act, 2004, amended section 13 of the Securities Contracts (Regulation) Act, enabling trading of securities between members of different, recognized stock exchanges.

After a little bit of brainstorming, we arrived at an idea. We would have an independent exchange to list these companies, and this exchange would be a national exchange, thus providing some liquidity to these stocks. This exchange was called IndoNext. At the same time, the eligibility criteria at this exchange with respect to listing, filing and compliance would be comparatively lenient. SEBI took the initiative to encourage BSE and the smaller stock exchanges to set up this trading platform. Several regional exchanges and companies were extremely positive about IndoNext.

'While they are not traded on RSEs, the high entry barriers on the NSE/BSE prevent them from getting listed there. Small companies need to be nurtured, as many have the potential to grow into large corporations. IndoNext, which was conceived for such companies, is yet to take off. This platform needs to be reviewed urgently,' said Prithvi Haldea, MD of Prime Database.[1]

'We are waiting for Indonext to happen, we'll decide our course of action based on that,' said M.K. Anantha Kumar, ED, Bangalore Stock Exchange.[2]

'Indonext project differed "significantly" from earlier attempts to revive regional stock exchanges. Indonext sought to eliminate a conflict of interest among regional stockbrokers by disallowing participating exchanges to retain a separate trading platform. Members will be permitted to trade only on the Indonext platform,' said P.J. Mathew, ED of Madras Stock Exchange.[3]

Even BSE and Federation of Indian Stock Exchanges (FISE) (all regional stock exchanges created a body which is the federation and issued a joint statement) said, '. . . this (Indonext) was a major capital market initiative, as the formation of BSE-IndoNext would help investors throughout the country through enhanced liquidity in their shares of small- and medium-cap companies. It would also rejuvenate the vast network of about 7,000 members of RSEs, who cater to investors in far-flung areas of the country.'

Accordingly, in January 2005, BSE-IndoNext was set up as a separate exchange under the BOLT trading system of the BSE. It was a joint initiative of the BSE and FISE, of which eighteen RSEs were members. The government also amended section 13 of the SCRA to facilitate trading by the members of RSEs on this market. During the launch of IndoNext, Chidambaram, then finance minister, even commented, '10 years from today, we would be able to say that most of the companies that were launched on IndoNext would turn out to be national winners and one or two of them would be international winners.'[4]

IndoNext got off to an extremely positive start. About 7,500 SMEs (from the RSEs) got listed on this exchange, to begin with. In addition, BSE-IndoNext was also intended to be an SME-specific market to provide listing opportunities to unlisted and future SMEs. Within a month, daily turnover at the exchange reached the levels of Rs 80–100 crore, and market capitalization, Rs 31,000 crore. Some of the top stocks traded on it were Infotel, Amtek Auto, Atlas Copco, United Breweries and Mercator Lines. Many hitherto ignored scrips, like Amtek Auto, found new buyers, and their turnover increased by more than 100 per cent.

Simultaneously, we had also come up with the idea of Central Listing authority C LA, which was to set the minimum standards centrally for listing of new SMEs on this new exchange.

IndoNext Fails

However, some of the SMEs on the RSEs did not register on IndoNext, which failed on two counts. One, the promoters of these SMEs were themselves not very keen on running their business and were not interested in joining any national platform and getting noticed. The presence of their companies on a national platform would require them to become more transparent and share all company data, something they dreaded. This was because they wanted to acquire land on the sly and not be questioned about their activities, which was bound to happen on a national platform like IndoNext. So the companies continued to be poorly run, invoking no fresh investor interest.

Second, BSE itself was not very keen to support IndoNext as it already had thousands of companies listed on the main platform to take care of. So eventually, IndoNext ended up being no one's baby, and failed.

After about a decade of my attempt at trying to get IndoNext up, both BSE and NSE have launched their versions of SME exchanges. These exchanges are similar in concept to IndoNext, except that IndoNext was also meant for listing the SMEs already listed on the RSEs. Today's SME exchanges are meant for new SMEs wishing to utilize a dedicated platform for their listing. Unfortunately, those platforms too seem to have met a similar fate as IndoNext, their progress being not noteworthy at all.

Somewhere in mid-2012, SEBI mandated new norms requiring all exchanges to have a minimum net worth of Rs 100 crore and an annual turnover of at least Rs 1,000 crore within two years' time. At this time, BSE and NSE had annual turnovers of around Rs 7 lakh crore and Rs 30 lakh crore, respectively, but most other exchanges lagged far behind and had close to nil trade, resulting in their subsequent derecognition by SEBI. In the absence of a platform like IndoNext, the investors (even institutional investors like LIC) in the companies listed on the RSEs were stuck with nowhere to trade their investments, and had to effectively write them off.

Delisting of MNCs

There was another area where the issue of delisting had been a challenge—voluntary delisting of companies (especially MNCs) for business reasons. Beginning from the year 2000, at least twenty-six companies, mainly multinational, such as Philips, Cadburys, Reckitt Benckiser, had delisted themselves from the stock exchanges, while a good number proposed to do the same in the coming years. The Indian government had initially made a rule that MNCs could not operate in India only with a representative office; they had to create a subsidiary company. Converting into a company meant adherence to compliances, reporting and tax laws. It also helped the Indian capital markets if these companies wished to raise funds through the capital market route. Listing on the capital markets would obviously not be possible with just a representative office. Now some of the

MNCs, for various business considerations, wanted to move out of the Indian markets and needed to delist their shares.

While some companies tried to give a proper exit to their investors, some did not. In the absence of appropriate rules, there would often be a tussle between the investors (selling back their shares) and promoter-shareholders (buying back the shares) over the price being offered to the investors for their exit. Investors always wanted more, while the promoters would try to keep the valuations on the lower side.

During this period, SEBI was receiving many complaints from investors against MNCs and other companies which were delisting. This was the situation when I joined SEBI. We had to find a solution. SEBI could not create a *chakravyuh* in the Indian capital markets for MNCs or, for that matter, for any company, where you could get in (list your shares), but could not get out (delist your shares). The sign of a mature market is when companies can delist from as well as list on it with equal ease. At the same time, investors had to be compensated adequately.

Listing and delisting are two sides of the same coin. There was a substantial body of law that governed listing. Unfortunately, delisting did not find place in any statute, rules or regulations.

The earliest trace of provisions relating to delisting is found in a circular of the government issued on 28 June 1979, which permitted stock exchanges to delist securities if three conditions were fulfilled: losses incurred by the company seeking delisting during the preceding three years; the stock is infrequently traded; the stock still remains listed on at least one exchange. If a company did not fulfil any of these conditions, approval from government was required for delisting. In 1985, the exchanges were allowed to delist a company if the number of shareholders fell below 5 or the capital to Rs 10,000, and public shareholding below 50 per cent of the public offer. SEBI subsequently issued a detailed circular on 29 April 1998 to provide for voluntary and compulsory delisting. It issued the SEBI (Delisting of Securities)

Guidelines in 2003 under section 11 of the SEBI Act, which allowed a listed company to voluntarily delist its securities from a stock exchange after providing an exit opportunity to the holders of the securities at a price determined through reverse book building. An exit opportunity was not required if the security still remained listed on an exchange having nation-wide trading terminals.

Since no statutory provision for delisting existed, doubts were raised as to whether delisting was permissible at all under the laws. This was clarified by an amendment to the SCRA in 2004, which explicitly provided for delisting of securities. It provided that an exchange may delist securities, after recording reasons thereof, on any of the grounds as may be prescribed in the rules, after giving the company concerned an opportunity of hearing. Further, an exchange may, on a request by the company, delist any securities, subject to the conditions: (a) the securities of the company have been listed for a minimum period of three years; (b) the delisting of such securities has been approved by the shareholders by a special resolution through postal ballot, and the company, promoters and/or the directors of the company purchase the outstanding securities from those holders who wish to sell them at a price determined in accordance with regulations made under the SEBI Act. This process can be waived off by SEBI if the securities remain listed at least on NSE or BSE.

What seemed fair was that if you allowed investors to build a book while investing in IPOs, you allowed them to decide on the exit price too, obviously keeping adequate checks and balances in place to ensure that there was no price manipulation by either the investors or the promoters. By mid-2002, we came up with the idea of the 'reverse book-building' process. Its highlights were:

1. Just as in the normal book-building bid process, a floor price would be set by the company wishing to delist (it was

suggested that the floor price be based on the average of the past twenty-six weeks' traded price).

2. Thereafter the investors would bid on the price on an online, fully automated, screen-based bidding system (to ensure transparency).

3. Thereafter the shares would be bought back at the price at which the most number of bids were received (it was also mandatory that whenever promoter holding crossed 90 per cent, whatever the price at which the 90 per cent holding was crossed, the balance shareholders could be bought back at that price; if the promoter holding did not cross 90 per cent based on the bids received, the process had to be repeated)

4. The company could not buy back shares, that could be done by the promoters only

5. If the company felt the exit price was too high, it could call off the delisting process and start a fresh reverse bidding process

The minimum floor price ensured that the investors were assured of certain minimum share value. Thereafter they could bid at any higher price. However, since the shares would be bought back at the price at which the most bids were received, this eliminated the possibility of a few investors sabotaging the deal by bidding too high while also protecting the ignorant investors who may give away their shares too cheap or may not bid at all (because even if the promoter holding crossed 90 per cent, the balance of less than 10 per cent would get an exit at the same price as the others who helped the promoter holding cross the 90 per cent mark). In any case, companies had the option to call off the bid if they felt the price was too high (which they would not do unreasonably as it would only delay their delisting). It was a win-win for both exiting investors and the acquiring promoter-shareholders.

Even then there was opposition to this method from the Confederation of Indian Industry, who wanted the price to be either decided by the companies themselves or by a fixed formula (example, average of twenty-six weeks' or fifty-two weeks' traded price). Their argument was that investors form a small universe in the reverse book-building process (unlike in the normal bidding process where the universe is much larger) and may not be competent to decide a fair price. However, the alternative methods suggested by CII were highly biased towards industry. For example, in a depressed market, a twenty-six-week or fifty-two-week average may not be the best indicator of the underlying value. And companies could definitely not be left to unilaterally decide the price on their own. So we went ahead with the reverse book-building process in spite of the opposition.

In the end, the reverse book-building process was a success. By the time I left SEBI in February 2005, twelve companies had adopted the reverse book-building process, and out of them ten had accepted the price sought by a majority of the minority shareholders. As envisaged, the process became popular for its ease of implementation, and neither the companies nor investors had any complaints. The durability of the method can also be judged from the fact that it continues to be used even today for delisting of companies.

22

WEAVING DREAMS; CONSOLIDATION OF THE DERIVATIVES MARKET

The future of equity and commodity markets

National Spot Exchange Limited (NSEL) a market in trading in commodities downed its shutters in 2013 on the back of a market-wide scam, leaving behind around 15,000 investors in the lurch with cumulative unsettled payments of over Rs 5,000 crore. NSEL was the leading spot commodity exchange in the country, with an annual turnover of Rs 3 lakh crore and a market share of more than 95 per cent when it was shut down. Two years after the NSEL scam, the Forward Markets Commission (FMC), chief regulator of the commodities futures markets, was merged with SEBI on 28 September 2015 to ensure better and consolidated regulation of the derivatives market.

During my tenure as SEBI chief, we had vigorously highlighted the inadequacies of FMC to the government and had predicted a calamity if the regulatory deficiencies were not removed. Ironically, we had even insisted on merging FMC with SEBI in 2004, which finally happened in 2015!

Let me talk about the evolution of derivatives and its challenges and opportunities first. Derivatives have the propensities of an atom. Their appropriate harnessing can deliver enormous economic good. Unbridled and unruly creativity in their use and inefficacious regulatory oversight on them can cause Hiroshima and Nagasaki in the world of finance. The global meltdown of 2007–08 is being attributed substantially to the market ingenuity in manipulating derivatives, in this case Credit Default Swaps (CDS), one of its many forms. Financial derivatives, some of which Warren Buffet called weapons of mass destruction, have achieved in hours a scale of global destruction that overambitious operators in the real sector could not even dream of in centuries! The origin of the 2008 crisis was attributed to NINJA home loans. It was not the original home loans to the poor that were toxic, but the complex products that were mounted over them through greed-based financial engineering models, over-securitization and complex product innovations.

Derivatives contracts are a risk management tool in the hands of the hedger, but this is possible only when, on other side, someone is willing to buy that risk, i.e., a speculator. The low margin requirements for derivatives trade unfold leverage for excessive trading, which introduces multiple risks to the system. On the other hand, the derivatives market facilitates efficient price discovery. Since it is a weapon capable of mass destruction, it is allowed to be used only with care and caution.

The sixties witnessed a period of great decline in global markets; market after market was closed down as the rise in price of various commodities was attributed to speculation, a la forward trading. Finally, in 1969, the government of India banned trading in forward contracts in certain commodities through a notification issued under FCRA. Also, options trading in commodities was prohibited.

Liberalization of the economy and globalization of the Indian markets, which began in 1991, did propel a relook at the derivatives market from the scientific point of view of its usefulness. Since derivative instruments have a natural tendency to become speculative and an effective regulatory framework was not in place, stiff resistance was put up by the legislature in providing assent to amendments to the legislation facilitating trading of equity derivatives. Finally, in the year 2000, less than two years before I joined SEBI, the government permitted introduction of derivative instruments with shares as their underlying security. Derivatives trading can broadly be divided into four types—index futures, index options, single stock futures and single stock options. There are a few other small categories like sectoral index derivatives and interest rate derivatives.

When I took over at SEBI, the derivatives market was at a very nascent stage, with an annual turnover of about Rs 1 lakh crore for the financial year 2001–02 (98 per cent of it with NSE and only 2 per cent with BSE). By the end of my tenure, in the financial year 2004–05, the annual turnover had increased to around Rs 26 lakh crore (NSE still ruling with a 99 per cent share; BSE had a mere 1 per cent share), an increase of about 2500 per cent and its CAGR at around 200 per cent. NSE became the world's number one exchange in Single Stock Futures and number three exchange in Index Futures!

So what exactly did SEBI do to bring about this stupendous growth?

The whole idea behind reintroduction of financial derivatives in the beginning of the new millennium was to widen the investment options in the capital market and also to provide a cost-effective hedging option against market risk. To achieve these two basic objectives, the key requirement was to introduce stringent risk control measures, as it is very easy for derivatives trading to cross the line and become excessively speculative, putting the entire capital market at risk. Committees (L.C. Gupta committee and Varma committee) were set up for advice on implementing the derivatives markets in India, and various risk control mechanisms were suggested by them. Some of these measures were already introduced by the time I joined SEBI, and for some others, it fell on my tenure to carry the baton forward. The growth numbers shown above for the derivatives markets suggest that we quite lived up to the task. We introduced and suitably modified some key risk control measures to keep up with the times.

1. We laid down the eligibility criteria for scrips to be traded in the derivatives markets, such as liquidity, derived as a function of market capitalization and average daily traded volume of a scrip and the median quarter sigma order size of a scrip (another measure to ensure the stock is highly liquid). It was required for the stock to be among the top 500 in terms of market capitalization and average daily volumes, and have a median quarter sigma size over the last six months of Rs 1 lakh crore. The benchmark was slightly different from what was suggested half a decade ago by the L.C. Gupta committee, and this was to keep up with the changing market structure.

    All these criteria were to ensure that all scrips available for derivatives trading had sufficient depth and volume so as to avoid any potential speculation or mischievous trading.

2. New products were introduced by us. Interest rate derivatives were introduced, based on the notional ten-year government bonds yield curve, in NSE in June 2003; futures and options on sectoral indices were introduced in August 2003.

3. Mutual funds were allowed to participate in derivatives trading for the sole purpose of hedging and portfolio balancing, under strict guidelines; FIIs and NRIs were permitted to invest in exchange-traded derivative contracts.

4. Trade margin concepts were introduced in the cash market, and then applied suitably to the derivative markets too.

5. Stock lending and borrowing scheme: When derivatives were first introduced, it was decided that derivatives trading shall begin with cash settlement and then move on to physical settlement once the infrastructure was ready. To facilitate this

transition to physical settlement of trades, we upgraded the facility of the already existing stock lending and borrowing schemes. As the name suggests, the scheme allowed one to have stocks on rent by paying a certain fee, instead of having to buy the stocks. While earlier such transaction could take place only through a registered intermediary, we expanded the base by making all clearing corporations of the exchanges intermediaries so that one did not have to look specifically for a registered intermediary to take a stock on rent.

6. Surveillance: Finally, surveillance in the derivatives market was raised to levels higher than in the cash market—open positions in the derivatives market vis-à-vis the cash market were periodically scrutinized to see if there was any undue advantage being taken by some vested parties; a close tab was kept on the timing of information disclosure by corporations; a close eye also kept on any unusual volatility on the monthly expiration dates of the derivative instruments; periodic MIS were called for from the stock exchanges on their derivatives trading etc. We even initiated a world-class, high-end, comprehensive integrated market surveillance system (IMSS) across the cash and derivatives markets for timely detection of abusive market movements. IMSS was fully implemented in December 2006, nearly two years after I left.

Thus, during the years from 2002 to 2005 efficacious regulatory management, as well as promotion of the derivatives market—its deepening and widening—was architected.

The journey of growth and development of financial market derivative instruments has since been fast paced. Today, the Indian markets trade in almost all forms of derivative contracts—forwards, futures, options, swaps, etc., and rank amongst the top ten markets of the world in all areas of reckoning: volumes, clearing and settlement, risk management, product basket . . . and so on.

However, we soon realized there was structural risk in the scattered derivatives markets. The risks to a financial system with common intermediaries (brokers), fungibility of money and a lax regulatory environment were obvious.

The derivatives markets in equities, interest rates and forex were fairly well regulated. However, the regulation of commodity derivatives was still being evolved. Unification of regulation of the entire derivatives market was the only answer. This way, the commodity markets would also benefit from the regulatory skills SEBI had. Why reinvent the wheel?

FMC, regulator for the commodities futures market, was attached to the ministry of consumer affairs, food and public distribution (MCAFPD). And therein lay the problem.

First, there was no single regulator for the commodity markets as a whole. The cash market for commodities was not regulated by anyone really. It was supposed to be regulated by MCAFPD or the state governments. As far as FMC was concerned, it had been set up under a fifty-year-old law and was too outdated to effectively withstand the technology surge and changed context of the times. Some of the other troubles with FMC were,

- It was a kind of extended MCAFPD and had no operational or functional autonomy. How good really can a regulator that has no independent mind of its own be?
- One of the basic powers a regulator needs is approval of registration of various intermediaries (sub-brokers, clearing corporations, exchanges themselves, etc.) to effectively regulate them. FMC, shockingly, did not have these powers! Simply put, it had no real right to question or monitor the various entities (from brokers to exchanges) participating in commodity derivatives trades.
- The penal provisions were time-warped and stuck in the fifties; they needed a major revamp.

– Commodity derivatives exchanges were not demutualized or corporatized, clearly a major drawback.

Thus, the poorly regulated derivatives markets, instead of helping the cash and spot commodity markets, were used to manipulate the prices of commodities, leading to notional shortages, inflation, etc. At the launch of National Multi-Commodity Exchange in November 2002, the prime minister, Atal Bihari Vajpayee, had commented that he would like the regulatory system for commodities exchanges to be strengthened to create confidence among all stakeholders.[1]

At the time a senior journalist had also made this comment in one of her articles: 'The Forward Markets Commission (FMC), which is the commodity markets regulator, has not been upgraded and strengthened on the lines of the Securities and Exchange Board of India to handle its new responsibilities . . . It is important to remember that commodities trading, especially the futures and options markets were shut down for decades due to speculative excesses. Unless the FMC is upgraded in a hurry and focuses on development and supervision, history could well give us a repeat performance.'[2]

Now there were two solutions—either to strengthen the regulatory powers of FMC or merge FMC with SEBI. Considering the snail's pace at which legislations get enacted, the former was only wishful thinking. Besides, since the time it was decided to bring back commodity derivatives trading, there had been a lot of clamour to first strengthen FMC, but nothing much had happened. So, as a concerned financial market regulator, I felt it was best if FMC were merged with SEBI. After all, SEBI has to co-share the responsibility of ensuring the proper functioning of the financial markets. The spillover and risks to the capital market from manipulations in the commodity markets was discernible. The markets for derivatives, whether commodities, securities, currency or interest, are fungible from the investor perspective, and hence they are inter-linked. Positions can shift across markets, so also risks. After all, irrespective of the underlying instrument, a derivative is a financial product. That is why in the subsequent years, trading in currency derivatives was allowed on exchanges. Running a platform for derivatives and regulating the derivatives market are synergistic activities.

In fact, the FMC chief met me in 2004, asking for help to provide some teeth to the commission, and also to put effective risk management in place. Even though it was not easy, I promised to help. After all, it took SEBI itself ten years and Scam 2001 to cross political hurdles to become an empowered regulator and build an effective risk management framework. However, in my mind I was clear that the best option was to merge FMC with SEBI.

Merging FMC with SEBI

It was customary every year for the finance minister to call the SEBI chairman to discuss his proposals to be included in the budget. In the run-up to Budget 2004, I got a call from the FM's office, as usual, for my inputs. Among other things, I proposed merger of FMC with SEBI as one of the key recommendations. To the FM's credit, he was very receptive to the idea but wanted to understand the rationale for the suggestion a little deeply. So we ended up discussing the issue for about half an hour, and he finally saw merit in my proposal. It was indeed included in the FM's budget speech of 2004, and the proposed merger was approved by the Lok Sabha a good eleven years before it finally happened.

Why did it take so long?

After Budget 2004, there no significant movement from either of the ministries concerned about this proposal, and it was suspended in the midst of bureaucratic hurdles. After a good deal of time, the FM then spoke to the minister of agriculture, consumer affairs and public distribution (MoAC&P), a very senior and powerful politician in his own right, and it was agreed that SEBI would prepare a presentation for the agriculture ministry. The proposal was prepared by us, modified by the finance ministry and presented at the residence of the minister of MoAC&P by none other than the FM himself to the minister in the presence of MCAFPD bureaucrats, senior bureaucrats of the finance ministry, and me and my colleagues from SEBI. In the end, it was clear that our stand to merge FMC with SEBI was well appreciated by the minister, MoAC&P, and he seemed ready for the merger.

As surprising as it may sound, the merger still did not get ahead. I sensed that possibly the bureaucrats, over a regulatory body, would have convinced their bosses to prevent it. The commodity brokers and exchanges certainly did not want the rigorous supervision and control of SEBI over their functioning and must have played their part in the game.

Post my tenure, the commodity derivatives markets continued to operate under FMC and the cash markets through the mandis. In 2006, the first commodity exchange, NCDEX, was established in India. This was followed by Multi Commodity Exchange (MCX), which started its operations a couple of years later, in 2008. Initially, the commodity spot markets did not have a dedicated regulator and functioned directly under MCAFPD. Spot exchanges were specifically exempt from FMC supervision as they did not deal in derivatives transactions.

The NSEL, as the name suggests, was set up as a spot exchange. Ideally, in a spot exchange trades can take place only if backed by physical commodities, meaning a seller actually needs to have the commodities while he is selling and the buyer the entire money that he needs to pay while buying. Delivery has to take place within a pre-defined period of time (T + 10 in NSEL's case). However, NSEL did away with these restrictions and allowed more days than it was mandated for settlement of trades. It appears NSEL introduced products for investors without prescribing and enforcing appropriate margins and robust settlement systems. It is understood that often many trades on the exchange were not backed by underlying physical commodities. The brokers peddled such products to their ignorant clients.

Meanwhile, NSEL's business flourished, with its turnover rising from Rs 2,182 crore in the first year of operations to a whopping Rs 3 lakh crore in its fifth year, which was FY 2013. NSEL apparently became a one-organization show for the commodity spot market, with a market share of about 98 per cent.

In 2011, the scope of FMC was expanded to include spot exchanges too under its regulatory ambit. However, FMC, as already pointed out, continued to be a regulator without teeth; it had no real independence, no control over the intermediaries, including exchanges, no power to investigate and impose significant monetary penalties, and did not demand rigorous MIS from the intermediaries, including brokers. As a result, the unfair practices could not be detected. It was only in mid-2013, two years after NSEL came under FMC's ambit that FMC woke up to the alleged malpractices and sent a notice to NSEL to stop its trades immediately. Trades that were supposed to be settled after thirty days or had no underlying securities were required to be settled immediately. Obviously, the participants panicked and none of the trades could be settled, bringing about the collapse of the exchange.

Finally, in 2015, the government implemented the decision of more than a decade ago to merge FMC with SEBI, creating a unified regulatory regime over the entire derivatives segment. There still remain some gaps in regulatory oversight in this area. RBI regulates the OTC market of both interest rate and currency futures, and the commodities spot market remains largely unregulated. Huge volumes in the OTC market leave a large loophole through which midconducts on the part of irresponsible and self-seeking economic agents can happen. With the digitization of money and securities and democratization of communication technology, risk management of a segment of the market on the strength of firewalls has become a myth. Someone somewhere in a remote corner of planet earth, even without formal regulatory authorization, may be hunting for kinks in the highways of regulation to exploit for profiteering. Thus, unification of the regulatory framework and command, and real-time consolidation of data for a wholistic picture of happenings in the marketplace has become the demand of the time. Regulatory turfs must converge to create comprehensive regulation of the marketplace. I am not necessarily advocating a unified regulator of all or some segments of the market. All I am recommending is consolidation of regulations, howsoever that can be achieved, to prevent (invisible) systemic risk to the financial system of the economy. Financial Sector Laws Reforms Commission (FSLRC), appointed by the government for reforms in all the laws of the financial structure, has recommended unification of markets and regulation by a unique regulator.

The merger happened also because FMC had become a hot potato for the government, and the economic agents were on the back foot. It was one of those rare events where the investors rejoiced on being regulated effectively instead of perceiving the regulator as an arm-twisting, trade-suffocating body. SEBI immediately brought about the much-needed reforms. It created a separate 'commodity cell', new departments for regulation of the commodities market, introduced daily circuit filter limits, brought the commodities market under the integrated surveillance system of SEBI, introduced various stress tests, started online registration of brokers, strengthened the delivery and grievance redressal systems, introduced new commodities like diamond, brass, egg and cocoa, and brought annual audits and disaster recovery plans. These were just some of the changes. SEBI has introduced options in commodities too. All in all, SEBI has started providing the much-needed rigour and discipline to the commodities trading.

23

ENHANCING REGULATORY CAPACITY: CENTRAL LISTING AUTHORITY

When I joined SEBI there were twenty-three exchanges in the country vying for corporate and investor attention. A company could list on any of the exchanges, the preferred ones being BSE and NSE, as they accounted for 90 per cent of the secondary market trading turnover. Preference for BSE and NSE aside, the reality, however, was quite different. The total number of companies listed in India at the time was around 10,000, but only about 1800 (18 per cent) had BSE or NSE as their primary exchange. The rest of the companies, numbering about 8,200, had a regional exchange as their primary exchange. In addition, out of the 165 IPOs made in the years 1999–2000 and 2000–01 (the two consecutive financial years before my joining), as many as 140 (or 85 per cent) had a regional exchange as its primary exchange, and as many as 85 (or 50 per cent) chose to list only on the smaller, regional exchanges.

So while BSE and NSE were the exchanges where the companies 'aspired' to be listed, very few of them actually had BSE or NSE as their primary exchange. Why? Simply because they found it easier to list on regional exchanges than on BSE/ NSE, which had relatively stringent listing criteria when it came to parameters such as scale of operations, years in existence, track record of the promoter, net worth of the company, financial performance, turnover, etc. Out of the 1800 odd companies listed in both BSE/ NSE combined, just six companies had NSE as its primary exchange because NSE's listing criteria were even more stringent than BSE's. Companies rejected by NSE would list on BSE, and those rejected by BSE would list on other RSEs. NSE had a category called 'permitted category', where securities listed on any other exchange were allowed to be traded.

So what was the big deal?

Whereas this difference in listing criteria could have been tolerated, its use by fly-by-night operators to raise money from gullible investors through IPOs on RSEs and disappear after some time was worrying. Most of these 8,200 companies with primary listing on RSEs ran the risk of turning out to be vanishing companies. Further, a good number of the IPO companies of the preceding two years with primary listing on RSEs were not being traded actively even the very next year (symptom of a vanishing company), potentially putting lakhs of crores of investor money at risk.

The differences in listing criteria at different exchanges also created a sort of backdoor entry for smaller, at times shady companies, to get themselves listed on BSE/NSE. Their modus operandi was to initially list only on a smaller exchange, which was malleable in its listing requirements. With most of the shares in the control of the promoters, the companies would then rig their share prices on the RSEs, after which they would graduate to listing on either of the two national exchanges to offload the promoter-held shares to a new set of gullible investors, and sometimes even to funds. Quite a few companies made this backdoor entry from Pune exchange to BSE; expanding their prospects of profiting unscrupulously.

Something had to be done to reduce the disparities in the listing criteria of various exchanges within India. It was important that all exchanges had minimum stringent guidelines for listing so that the interest of investors on all exchanges was protected. A security should either be suitable for listing on all exchanges or not suitable for listing on any. SEBI proceeded to achieve exactly this kind of uniformity, by creating the Central Listing Authority (CLA), covering three broad themes—avoiding conflicts of interest, reduction in reporting, disclosure and compliance costs, and SEBI's acting as a regulator of last resort, leaving frontline regulation to the exchanges.

It is important to note that though the criteria for listing of securities differed across exchanges, the compliance requirements were essentially the same. A prospective issuer informally got feedback from an exchange as to whether the exchange would consider listing of his security favourably. If the issuer did not get an encouraging response, he tried his luck with other lenient exchanges. This created an anomalous situation, in which a security considered not suitable for investors in one locality was suitable for investors in another. Similarly, securities could be delisted on one exchange but not on another. This was another anomalous situation, where one exchange listed, suspended or delisted a security, which the other exchanges did not.

These anomalies came up for consideration before SAT in an appeal (Lunkad Media and Entertainment Limited vs the Stock Exchange, Mumbai). In order to take care of such anomalies, SAT suggested to the government and SEBI to consider the feasibility of providing a centralized mechanism for permitting listing of securities on the stock exchanges. It felt that some sort of uniformity in deciding applications for listing by exchanges would be in the interest of investors. SAT observed,

> It does not stand to reason that a public issue found unacceptable by one exchange for the reason that the issuer company's credibility is doubtful, is acceptable to another exchange, though both the exchanges are supposed to be concerned about the interests of the investors. Investor protection measures

should not be confined to territorial jurisdiction of exchanges. It should be at national level. Decision by a centralised set up may perhaps help to provide transparency and also help to maintain consistency and uniformity in the field of listing.[1]

CLA an Imperative

It was, therefore, desirable that there was only one agency to consider all requests for listing, and granted listing only if it found a security suitable for investors across the country. A security granted listing by the agency would be available for trading on all exchanges. The exchanges then would not have to waste their resources on listing and monitoring compliance. The security would also be centrally monitored, suspended or withdrawn from trading by the listing agency. All decisions of the agency relating to listing, suspension from trading, delisting etc. would be appealable to SAT. Investors and market participants would get all company-related information that is mandatorily required to be filed by companies at one central location, preferably a website maintained by the CLA. The exchanges would concentrate on trading only, while pre-trading activity (listing and compliance of terms of listing) would be managed by CLA, and post-trading activity (clearing and settlement of trades) by the clearing corporations.

Scam 2001 brought out the inherent conflicts of interests in the functioning of an exchange. The exchange was involved in listing, trading and surveillance. Compromises in surveillance led to misuse of information by members of the governing board of the exchanges. The impending corporatization and demutualization of exchanges meant that they would become companies with share capital, and obviously, would themselves go for listing and creating value. A 'for-profit' exchange would then vie with other exchanges to maximize the number of listed companies on it as they are a source of revenue, bringing in listing fees. A larger number of companies listed on an exchange would also potentially help it garner higher trading volumes, giving rise to increased trading revenue. My approach was to mitigate these conflicts, especially when an exchange wants to list on itself. This became a significant issue when, initially, NSE wanted to list on itself rather than on BSE. This was one of the reasons the management of NSE held up the IPO process for a while.

India is the only country where the same stock can list and trade on multiple exchanges. This results in multiple compliances for the company, increasing costs. Further, even an inadvertent error at one exchange results in a penalty, as the listing agreement signed with each exchange acts as a binding contract with that exchange. I saw that there was a need to consolidate reporting and disclosures.

One of the major lessons of Scam 1992 and Scam 2001 for me was that there was no consolidation of information for purposes of monitoring, disclosure, surveillance and effective enforcement. For instance, trading positions in Kanpur, Calcutta, and other exchanges were not consolidated to monitor the trades by and on an entity. This resulted in overexposure, under-monitoring and the shaping of systemic and operational risks. I felt a frontline sub-ordinate regulator was required, which could then effectively take over the integrated surveillance system I had initiated.

Therefore the need was felt for a central authority with powers to approve listing, accept disclosure filings and subsequently act as a monitoring agent of IPO moneys, prior to SEBI stepping in.

Creating Regulatory Capacity

The UK Listing Authority has created significant regulatory capacity. This authority reviews and approves prospectuses. It operates the listing regime of the United Kingdom and also monitors disclosures. In fact, capacity creation is an important challenge for effective regulation of the market, and it is with this underpinning that independent, skilled and focused arms functioning within the overall design of the regulatory framework have been created. Prudential Regulation Authority, Financial Conduct Authority and Payment System Authority are examples of such arms. The reason for the creation of CLA was to build regulatory capacity.

Multiple Benefits of CLA

The most obvious benefits were uniformity of guidelines and standardization of listing criteria, on parameters such as scale of operations, years in existence, track record of the promoter, net worth of the company, financial performance, turnover requirements, and the like, across all exchanges. CLA, besides making sure that companies confirmed to the disclosure guidelines, would also have the power to conduct due diligence on companies wishing to go for an IPO. The CLA had to be convinced that the data provided during application (offer document etc.) by a company for an IPO was factually accurate, that the company did not show any sign of being a vanishing one, that the background of the promoters was clean and that the company's financial health satisfied minimum requirements. Only then would it give the go-ahead for the IPO. The merchant bankers too had to be on their toes, as all the offer document data would now be verified by a SEBI-backed authority directly. So the risk of shady companies finding a place on any exchange in India would be drastically reduced.

There was another reason for creating the CLA. Hitherto, when SEBI viewed an offer document, it vetted it only in the context of the Disclosure and Investor Protection (DIP) guidelines. As mentioned in the chapter on transparency of listed companies, the DIP guidelines of SEBI focused more on disclosures—that is, detailed information provided in the offer document about the companies going in for a public issue. SEBI did not focus on the factual accuracy of the data, which was left to the exchanges and merchant bankers. Hence I wanted to create a separate CLA, an independent authority with sufficient representation from all relevant parties—SEBI, the exchanges and independent experts. This body would specialize as a gatekeeper.

Another advantage of having the CLA was the resulting reduction of duplication of efforts. Until that time, companies wishing to list on five exchanges would have to submit applications to all five. All five exchanges would conduct their own procedure of due diligence, interviews, verification of legal compliance, etc. A body like the CLA would reduce these efforts, as a go-ahead from it to a company would suffice for its listing on any exchange. Even if an exchange wanted to apply its own criteria over and above that of CLA's before listing a company, that would only require incremental efforts on the part of the exchange and the company.

In the long run, CLA was also to closely monitor the post-listing conduct of a company. This would then eliminate the duplication of efforts on monitoring and surveillance too. At the time there were about 10,000 different companies listed in India, but most of them were listed on multiple exchanges. The average was three exchange listings for a company. So there were more than 30,000 company listings on all the exchanges combined. Additionally, in the long run, CLA would also have the powers to recommend changes in the SEBI listing, monitoring and disclosure guidelines to protect investors.

One other aspect that CLA could potentially take care of was the self-listing of stock exchanges. Demutualization and corporatization of exchanges were to happen sooner than later. And exchanges like BSE and Delhi Stock Exchange had every intention to list themselves on their own exchange, which could spell disaster for investors (as it would result in conflict of interest and raise questions about the rigour of due diligence happening at these exchanges). A CLA was the right answer to thwart this conflict of interest, as it would allow a stock exchange to list only after certain strict criteria were met. The exchange would also come under rigorous monitoring by CLA.

When I looked at the global markets, there were no more than two major exchanges in each of the developed countries (in USA, Germany, France, UK, Japan, etc.). Only India was unique, with so many exchanges, each having its own norms for listing, which was putting investor money at risk. A CLA would provide this much needed uniformity.

Criticism against CLA

I was fully convinced of the idea, and within two months of my joining we had announced our intention to create the CLA. There were internal discussions, and a committee was formed. External feedback and media opinions started pouring in. Some supported the idea, some did not. The critics said it would only create one more step of hierarchy and would most likely result in creating distress among companies. From their stand point, the best alternative was to upgrade the existing system—by which they meant making due diligence by exchanges stronger. I thought if it was possible for the existing system to be upgraded, it would have been done by now. Introducing CLA, in fact, was a way to upgrade the system.

The second criticism was that if a majority of RSEs were going to die soon and India would soon have only a few exchanges, why the need for CLA, which was being formed on the argument that there are too many exchanges with too many rules and no standard criteria for listing. This was true, but RSEs still existed and IPOs were still happening. Further, there was no restriction on new exchanges coming up. Eventually, MCX-SX was licensed as the third nation-wide exchange in India. Even today, India has three active exchanges.

The sharpest criticism came from the exchanges, including from BSE and NSE, who felt their core area was being trespassed. They would no longer have autonomy in the matter of selecting the companies that could list on their exchange. I had to assure them time and again that this was not true. CLA would only provide minimum criteria and uniform guidelines for all companies and conduct a basic due diligence to check the fundamentals of a company wishing to raise public money. The final decision to let a company list or not was still with the exchanges.

Making CLA a Reality

So, amidst the criticism, we went ahead and made the SEBI (Central Listing Authority) Regulations, 2003 by February 2003. The regulations allowed a company to approach SEBI in case its application for listing was rejected by CLA. Based on the feedback received and also to avoid complications, we later made CLA the final authority for deciding the listing fate of a company. If CLA rejected a company's application, the company had all the rights to appeal to SAT. Besides public issues, rights issue, bonus issues, and preferential issues, mutual fund schemes and collective investment schemes too would see CLA monitoring. CLA was also given the power to recommend changes in the SEBI listing, monitoring and disclosure guidelines to protect investors. The go-ahead from CLA was to be in the form of a letter of recommendation called, 'Letter Precedent to the Listing'.

CLA was set up with seed capital of Rs 5 lakh from SEBI. It had a senior functionary from SEBI and four staff. The idea, eventually, was to hire people exclusively for CLA and build a dedicated CLA employee base. A committee to decide on public issue applications was formed in CLA under the chairmanship of former Supreme Court Chief Justice M.N. Venkatachaliah.

Among its dozen members was FICCI secretary-general, Amit Mitra, currently finance minister of West Bengal, Prime Database MD, Prithvi Haldea, and former director of Delhi School of Economics, Dr R.S. Nigam. Subsequently, T.V. Rangaswami was appointed as the CEO of CLA. The regulation had specified that each exchange had to have its representative in the CLA committee, so I invited all the exchanges to send their representatives. However, the exchanges weren't exactly supportive of the idea, and their participation in the committee remained low.

During my tenure, the CLA committee met eleven times between its first meeting on 6 May 2003 and its last on 31 January 2005 (just two weeks before I exited SEBI). Most of these meetings were spent on framing the minimum parameters (such as scale of operations, years in existence, track record of the promoter, net worth of the company, financial performance, turnover requirements) and operational rules (on conducting due diligence on companies, promoters, timelines, frequency of meetings, salaries, etc.). The parameters and operational rules for preferential and bonus issues were finalized, while those for public issue and rights issue remained to be finalized.

During these eleven meetings, even though the CLA was still in the process of framing parameters for IPOs, we started referring potential IPOs to the committee for their approval to start training it for the actual work. With each meeting we were making significant progress, and by the eleventh meeting, the CLA stood on firm ground, ready for take-off. But that was when its wings were clipped.

Death of CLA

The eleventh meeting of the CLA turned out to be its last. After I left SEBI, there were no meetings of the CLA at all. The critics of CLA had got the better of the situation. Finally, in January 2007, the CLA was officially disbanded.

Sometime in May 2014, when it was announced that all RSEs had to be officially shut down, many a skeleton came tumbling out of the closets of stock exchanges. Data for only eleven regional exchanges indicated that there were close to 2,000 companies (out of a total of 4,500 companies listed only on RSEs) with market capitalization of Rs 80,000 crore (the total market cap of companies exclusively listed on RSEs was Rs 2 lakh crore) that had the features of a vanishing company. Even BSE and NSE did not emerge uncriticized in this matter. The corporate affairs ministry's coordination and monitoring committee (CMC), which has representatives from the government, SEBI and RBI, estimated that about 1,000 companies listed on either BSE or NSE could be potentially vanishing companies. That meant about 17 per cent of the total number of companies on these exchanges could be vanishing ones. From 2017–18 SEBI clamped down on 300 companies and BSE delisted another 200 for the same reason. The current SEBI chairman is contemplating stricter monitoring of IPO moneys. When one reads about such developments, the death of CLA appears to have been a retrograde step.

24

INTERNATIONALIZING THE MARKET: INDIAN DEPOSITORY RECEIPTS (IDR)

One of the three legislative obligations of SEBI is to develop the markets, which largely means to develop new products for investment and expand the horizons of the Indian capital markets. Internalization of the Indian markets was one of the ways to expand it.

In a way, Indian markets were already international since investors from outside were allowed to invest in India, though only through FIIs and P-notes. However, in my opinion, real internationalization would happen when good enterprises from the rest of the world came and listed in India. This would be something like what happens in the US and European markets, where companies from all over the world seek opportunities to raise money and list on their exchanges through the instrumentality of American Depository Receipts (ADRs) and Global Depository Receipts (GDRs), respectively.

ADRs and GDRs

A depository receipt (DR) is an instrument which allows a company to list its shares in a foreign jurisdiction and even raise capital there (on fulfilling certain conditions, including listing requirements). If the foreign jurisdiction is America, the instrument is called ADR, and if it in other countries (typically London, Luxembourg or Singapore) it is called GDR. ADRs and GDRs are backed by the underlying (domestic) shares of the issuing company. Such underlying shares are held by a custodian bank in the foreign jurisdiction where the company's ADR or GDR is listed, and the bank, in turn, issues the equivalent ADRs or GDRs, which are then traded like any other share in the foreign jurisdiction, in the denominated currency of that country. In most cases, one DR is equal to one underlying equity share. However, in certain cases one DR is equal to more than one equity share, and at times two or more DRs represent one equity share.

For example, in 1999, Infosys made history when it became the first Indian company to issue ADRs on a major US stock exchange—the NASDAQ. In the next two years, there was a surge of Indian companies issuing ADRs on US exchanges. Around ten companies did so. Some of the major ones were Dr Reddy's Laboratories (NYSE), HDFC Bank (NYSE), Satyam Computers (NYSE), Tata Communications (NYSE), Wipro (NYSE) and Rediff.com (NASDAQ). As of June 2017, ADRs of over a dozen Indian companies were being traded on the major US stock exchanges, NYSE and NASDAQ.

As far as GDRs are concerned, Reliance Industries was the first company in India to float GDRs, in 1992. They were listed on Luxembourg Stock Exchange. In 2004, RIL listed its GDRs on London Stock Exchange too. As of December 2016, the total number of Indian GDRs listed on the London, Singapore or Luxembourg stock exchange was more than 100. This number is significantly higher than the number issuing ADRs because of the easier listing, accounting standards, compliance and reporting requirements at the London, and more so in the Luxembourg, stock exchange. Most of the Indian GDRs are listed on these two exchanges.

Companies choose to issue ADRs and GDRs for various reasons, one of them being problems in raising initial or further capital in India (Luxembourg exchange, in particular, has easier listing requirements as compared with Indian markets). Issue of DRs also helps companies to build their brand and gain visibility in a global market, widen their investor base, provide stock schemes to foreign employees etc. From the investor point of view, DRs provide many benefits. They are an easy way to invest in a foreign company without opening a separate trading account in a foreign country (Americans can invest in Infosys ADRs sitting in America), they offer international diversification of one's portfolio, and the stocks of the foreign company are available in the local currency (which means no foreign exchange risks). DRs also follow the same disclosure requirements as any other local stock listed on same exchanges as they are. So there is no additional risk for the investor.

Finally, from the country point of view, DRs have helped the US and UK markets become truly international, with companies from India, Russia, China, Taiwan, Ukraine, Japan, Australia, Brazil and others listing on their exchanges. It expands the range of investment options for investors in developed markets of the US and UK and helps them partake of the exponential growth in developing markets like India, China, Taiwan and Brazil etc.

Arbitrage Opportunity between DRs and Underlying Equity Share Prices

As both shares and DRs are listed in different markets denominated in different currencies (say INR and USD), this often gives rise to arbitrage opportunities, which can be bridged using the concept of fungibility between DRs and shares. Take the example of Infosys shares, which are listed as ADRs too. If ADRs are trading at a discount to domestic share prices, investors can convert their ADRs into domestic shares and sell them at a profit. This facility, to convert ADRs into shares, is called fungibility. During the initial days, ADRs and GDRs were only one-way fungible; they could be converted into underlying equity shares, but the reverse was not allowed.

During my first year in SEBI, in 2002, we facilitated the concept of two-way fungibility; Indian would allow the equity shares underlying DRs to be converted into DRs, to the extent the DRs were earlier converted into equity shares. Thus, now if the domestic shares are traded at a discount to ADR prices, investors can convert their shares into ADRs (to the extent they were earlier converted from ADRs into shares) and sell them at a profit. This two-way fungibility further helped in increasing the liquidity of DRs and allowed investors to reap the benefit of arbitrage between the prices of ADRs/GDRs and the underlying equity shares (in its domestic market).

After having studied DRs and the benefits thereof, I was convinced about introducing Indian Depository Receipts (IDRs) in India on similar lines. It was 2004 by the time we started our struggle to make IDRs a reality.

IDRs

My dream behind introducing IDRs was simple and clear: to allow good quality corporations incorporated outside India to raise resources from the Indian capital markets by issuing IDRs. This would offer Indian investors, sitting in India itself, a chance to participate in the wealth being created internationally by companies from across the globe. At the very least, we expected companies from neighbouring countries like Sri Lanka, Bangladesh and Bhutan, who do not have very developed or deep stock markets of their own, to show interest in issuing IDRs.

The framework governing issue and trading of Indian Depository Receipts (IDRs) in India has its genesis in section 605A, which was inserted into the Companies Act, 1956 by the Companies (Amendment) Act, 2000. To operationalize the framework, the government issued the IDR Rules, 2004, and the SEBI inserted chapter VIA to the SEBI (Disclosure and Investor Protection) Guidelines, 2000, on 3 April 2006. When the SEBI (Disclosure and Investor Protection) Guidelines, 2000 were replaced by the SEBI (Issue of Capital and Disclosure Requirements) Regulations, 2009, on 26 August 2009, this portion was transplanted into chapter X of the latter with suitable modifications. The SEBI (Issue of Capital and Disclosure Requirements) Regulations, 2009, provide for eligibility conditions for the foreign issuer company, minimum subscription, procedure for issue and various other restrictions on the issue of IDRs.

I went through the whole rigmarole of setting up a committee, obtaining public feedback, going to the board and getting the guidelines for IDR listing approved. The DCA notified the Companies (Issue of Indian Depository Receipts) Rules, 2004, pursuant to the Companies Act on my persuasion, for IDR issuance. The guidelines for disclosures with respect to IDRs and the listing agreement to be entered into between the exchange and the issuing company were under SEBI's purview. For this, approvals were obtained, as mentioned above. Some of the key guidelines proposed by SEBI for issue of IDRs were:

– Companies issuing IDRs were required to have a net worth of at least US$ 100 mn, an average turnover of US$ 500 mn for the last three years, a pre-issue debt-to-equity ratio of less than 2:1, and a track record of declaring dividend of not less than 10 per cent in the last five years before the issue
– IDRs were not fungible for at least one year from their date of issue
– In every IDR issue, at least 50 per cent of the issue had to be subscribed by qualified institutional buyers

-   FIIs, NRIs and mutual funds were disallowed from IDR investments (this was later relaxed in 2009); and
-   Quarterly financial disclosure requirements were specified

As we were finalizing the operational guidelines, what acted as a shot in the arm for us was that organizations like Asian Development Bank (ADB) and World Bank were looking at the Indian debt market to raise funds of close to Rs 400 crore and Rs 600 crore, respectively. These proposals were even cleared by the government, acting as an indicator of the growing confidence of the international community in the Indian financial market.

Overcoming Challenges

Surprisingly, the biggest resistance to IDRs came from the ministry of finance, particularly from the secretary, economic affairs. Their concern was that Indian citizens did not have enough savings to invest in Indian companies, so why bring companies from abroad? Second, the foreign companies would be subject to the regulations of the home country.

However, I had a different point of view. First, the companies interested in raising capital in India will have long-term interest in India, and thus will (in the long run) bring capital to India and not just take it away. Mutual funds, with the RBI approval, were already allowed to invest up to US$ 1 billion in overseas stock, which was later enhanced to US$ 2 billion. Then there was the component of fees that could be collected from the companies—an upfront fee of few lakh rupees along with the application and a variable fee of 0.5 per cent of the issue value. (An issue value of Rs 100 crore would fetch a variable fee of Rs 50 lakh).

Also, IDRs would make India a truly international market where companies from across the globe could raise money, boosting India's image as the financial powerhouse. Further, more investment options would bring in more investors to the market and not shoo them away from it. Finally, this was a stepping stone in the creation of our international financial centre.

With persuasion, I was able to make the government see things from my point of view. I got all the necessary approvals and even notified the final regulations. However, by the time this could happen, my tenure came to an end, and we could not actively woo foreign companies to start issuing IDRs. As with several other initiatives, this too was left to my successor to take the dream forward and bring foreign companies on board.

For the next four or five years, foreign companies were not pursued aggressively for IDR issues. As a result there was not a single IDR issue during this period. But during this time some suitable revisions in the IDR rules of both SEBI and the MCA were made to permit retail investors to subscribe to IDRs, etc.

Finally, it was C.B. Bhave who, as chairman of SEBI, took the initiative to bring Standard Chartered PLC on board to issue a US$ 0.5 billion IDR (Rs 2,200 crore) on 25 May 2010. It was the first IDR issuance after eighteen months of intense planning. The IDRs were listed on both BSE and NSE. It was this chairman who further relaxed quite a few norms to make IDR issuance attractive for issuing companies and investors. SEBI removed the one-year lock-in for conversion from IDR to equity shares and allowed FIIs, NRIs and mutual funds to invest in IDRs, enabled electronic holding of IDRs, etc.

Unfortunately, Standard Chartered PLC remains the only IDR to be issued till date, as IDRs are still not adequately promoted. Foreign companies still prefer developed markets like the US and UK for their DRs. A few suggested developments that could help boost IDRs include further easing of norms for allowing smaller or mid-sized foreign companies to issue IDRs, removing restrictions on FII holding in IDRs, achieving seamless fungibility (just like in the mature markets) of IDRs and their underlying equity shares and clarity on taxation.

IDRs, if they had been pursued with the vigour post my tenure, would have demonstrated our ability and seriousness in establishing India as a global financial player. It is worth our efforts to internationalize the Indian capital market.

The ministry of finance in early 2014 constituted a committee under the chairmanship of M.S. Sahoo to review the entire framework of access to domestic and overseas capital markets, and related matters, including Indian Depository Receipts. The important recommendations of the committee are as under:

1. It recommended BhDRs (Bharat Depository Receipts) and not IDRs as available now, which would be a sub-set of BhDRs. The BhDRs would be issued on the back of securities accessible to Indian investors—debt or equity—issued by a company or otherwise, with or without authorization of the issuer. A complete suite of BhDRs would be allowed to be issued and traded in India to make the Indian financial system more competitive, and to provide greater choice to Indian investors.

2. SEBI should be exclusive regulator for the market for securities, including BhDRs, as it is responsible for the protection of investors in securities, and the only market failure associated with BhDRs is consumer protection. This would avoid inconsistency or duplicity of regulations and shifting of responsibilities. The issuance or trading of BhDRs in India needs to be regulated to the extent necessary to protect Indian investors in such instruments and to harmonize DR-related transactions with the extant capital controls regime.

3. There may be multiple levels of BhDRs suiting different classes of investors, and such levels of BhDRs may have different regulatory and compliance requirements. SEBI

should create, at a minimum, two levels of BhDRs: Level-I would be restricted to sophisticated investors and level-II available to all investors, including retail Indian investors. The issuers accessing the Indian market through the level-I framework should have a lower regulatory burden but can access only sophisticated investors by having only million-rupee market lots.

4. The BhDRs may be issued only on those underlying foreign securities which are listed on an international exchange which is accessible to the public for trading and provides pre-trade and post-trade transparency to the public. Such underlying securities must also be in demat form to facilitate gathering of data, particularly about the headroom available for fungibility. The BhDRs must be listed in India. The issuer of the underlying foreign security must be from a 'permissible jurisdiction', which is under legal obligation to share information and cooperate with the Indian authorities in the event of any investigation, that is, it must be FATF and IOSCO compliant.

5. The BhDRs could be issued for both capital raising or non-capital raising purposes. They could be sponsored or unsponsored. Any foreign issuer who is not debarred should be able to issue fresh securities on the back of which BhDRs may be issued in India by a domestic depository. Any person holding listed securities issued by foreign issuers should be able to transfer those securities, which may be deposited with a foreign custodian. And on the back of such securities, BhDRs may be issued in India by a domestic depository.

6. The proceeds from BhDR issues may be repatriated or used within India. No end use restrictions must be imposed on them, as long as they are serving the domestic real economy. The issue size of BhDRs should be restricted to 25 per cent of the class of listed underlying foreign securities. Two-way

fungibility should be allowed to the extent of the aggregate size of the BhDR issues, and to the extent of the size of the original issuance.

7. Both Indian—retail and institutional—and foreign investors should be allowed to invest in BhDRs. The institutional investors must be allowed, enabled and encouraged to move to the prudent investor regime.

Though the government accepted the recommendations of the committee in principle, they are yet to be implemented.

International Financial Centre (IFC)

Through my years as chairman of SEBI, I unleashed a slew of reforms, helping the Indian capital markets to join the league of developed and mature markets of the world in efficacy and size. By end of 2004, BSE and NSE were among the top five exchanges in the world reckoned on the basis of the number of trades annually. India's GDP growth had scaled the range of 8–9 per cent. The IT and telecom sectors were growing exponentially, inflows of FII money were at an all-time high, forex reserves had swelled and India was set to enter the top quartile of global economies. The world was taking notice of India. There was an opportunity to capitalize on India's potential further, and not just in the securities market but in the entire financial domain. I wished India to become an internationally participated-in one-stop destination for the intermediation of the totality of financial services. My assessment suggested the time was ripe to take the next steps towards this end.

There were two major well-developed international financial centres then—London and New York. Hong Kong and Singapore too had financial centres, but they were not so well developed as in New York and London, although Hong Kong was ahead of Singapore to some extent. London's international financial centre was a cash cow for the city. About 60 per cent of the income of the city was generated by the centre. In between London, Hong Kong and Singapore, there were no international centres, and these markets were nearly eight hours apart. I felt there was an opportunity to create an international finance centre (IFC) in India, located conveniently as it is between London and Hong Kong.

Besides, SEBI was also working on IDRs to bring foreign companies to list in India (please see IDR chapter). The IDR regulations and a battery of reforms were all coming together, to cumulatively facilitate India to become an international finance hub.

The Purpose of IFC

The intention of creating an IFC in India was to bring together the best financial minds of our country under one roof and create an international hub for export of financial services from India to the world. The centre was to cater to cross-border services and customers along with domestic economy, companies, individuals and governments. The financial services to be exported included fund raising for individuals, corporations and governments, merger and acquisitions among transnational corporations, wealth management, asset management, global portfolio diversification for foreign funds, global tax management and cross-border tax liability optimization, arbitration, etc. The city in India ideally suited for this seemed to be Mumbai, since it was already the financial capital of the country.

Taking Government into Confidence

I proposed the idea to the government and managed to convince P. Chidambaram, the finance minister, to include the proposal in his budget speech of February 2005. Accordingly, he announced a high-powered expert committee to advise the government on creating an IFC in Mumbai.

The high-powered expert committee was formed, with Percy Mistry as chairman, and included the likes of. O.P. Bhatt, chairman of SBI, Nimesh Kampani of JM Financial, K.V. Kamath of ICICI Bank, C.B. Bhave (future SEBI chairman), Aditya Puri of HDFC bank, Ravi Narain of NSE and Dr P.J. Nayak. I felt happy when someone important in the regime in 2014 asked me for a note on the measures required to make it functional and vibrant. The committee presented its report to the government in February 2007, and some fifty action points were recommended to facilitate the creation of an IFC in Mumbai. These recommendations included action plans in various areas, such as fiscal deficit, monetary policy, taxation, financial system regulations, strengthening of the derivatives and bond markets, and improvement of infrastructure and governance of the city of Mumbai.

However, all this happened after my tenure in SEBI had come to an end. To their credit, the Confederation of Indian Industry (CII) did push the idea with the government even after I had left SEBI. The first session to make public the draft report and to seek public response was held in Mumbai under the chairmanship of the finance minister. The CII invited me to speak in that session. I had pleaded for the formalization of coordination amongst the financial regulators—RBI, SEBI, IRDA and finance secretary. PFRDA did not exist then. The coordination then was more informal than formal, in the shape of the high level committee (HLC) of the regulators, which did meet occasionally and discussed some ragtag agenda. But nothing fruitful came out of those meetings.

The Financial Stability and Development Council (FSDC) under the chairmanship of the FM has since been formed, and the RBI governor was made the vice-chairman. I hope the FSDC is fulfilling the purpose for which it was constituted with legislative authority. Deep coordination amongst the financial regulators is a prerequisite for the creation of the IFC and its vibrancy, as well as for maintaining financial stability and developing the markets and economy as a whole.

The government of Maharashtra, which was to benefit the most, was not seen to be very enthusiastic then. Narendra Modi, then the CM of Gujarat known to seize opportunities of economic development, decided to take the lead but nothing came out of it at that time. The idea for the IFC then seemed to have been altogether lost, until Narendra Modi became the PM and facilitated the functioning of the IFC.

Mumbai's Loss, Gujarat's Gain

This opportunity was grabbed with both hands by Gujarat. In the year 2007 Narendra Modi, then chief minister of Gujarat and a visionary, conceived the IFC near Ahmedabad. It was spread over 900 acres. It was named GIFT—Gujarat International Finance Tec-City. Progress on GIFT got a major boost when Modi started pushing it as the prime minister of India. Various leading financial houses, like Reliance Capital, Kotak Mahindra Bank, BSE Brokers' Forum, etc. have shown interest in setting up financial services centres in GIFT to cater to international needs. India's first international exchange, INX, promoted and sponsored by BSE, has been set up at GIFT City. It recently went live at the hands of the Hon'ble PM. SEBI has since permitted even derivatives trading on it. Separate tax and other laws are being made for companies setting up in GIFT, to facilitate them to provide international services.

Mumbai is also now gearing up for an IFC. The city has allocated the land for it, and has got someone to write a report to help finalize the action plan. Apart from the fact that India cannot have two IFCs, Mumbai, with its deteriorating infrastructure and poor administration, cannot develop as IFC. The government of Maharashtra must reconcile itself to the fact that it has lost the race with its overstay in the green room.

Enriching the Product Basket (REITS):

Helping retail investors get a pie of real estate

The retail investors of the early 2000s had limited (conventional) options for investment. Equity (either directly or via mutual funds), bank FDs and life insurance were the most common investment options. Back then, corporate and government bonds were not available to the common investor. The equity market was perceived to be volatile and comparatively risky, and other markets offered low if not negative real rate of returns. The gullible investors, in the hope of making abnormally high returns without going through the grind of doing due diligence, often fall prey to chit funds and other unregulated schemes. Many of these schemes have, time and again, been discovered to be fraudulent and have sometimes swallowed the entire invested amount. Real estate seemed to be a good alternative option for investment then, with the potential to deliver a significant real rate of return. But investing in real estate has its own set of challenges.

Briefly, the story of Indian real estate goes like this: In a control-and-command economy, where people waited for years to get a telephone, a gas connection or even a scooter, the world of tradable real estate was almost non-existent. It is only after 1991, with the opening up of the Indian economy, the advent of the IT industry and higher economic growth that Indian cities like Bengaluru, Chennai, Hyderabad and Pune catapulted into the big league in the race of rapid urbanization. The decade of 1991–2001 witnessed a real estate price frenzy. The average age of home buyers came down, from the fifties to the thirties, and for the first time the concept of real estate as an investment gained currency. However, very few people were in a position to truly benefit from real estate in this way.

This is because of a couple of things: one, to capitalize on any arbitrage opportunity in real estate prices, the investor had to own excess real estate (in full) to trade, which, unfortunately, only very few had the privilege to indulge in. Second, if one did not already own a property but had some disposable surplus capital, the only way to take advantage of the real estate opportunity was to actually buy an entire property, which was not only cumbersome and risky but also illiquid, entailing huge transaction costs. Thus, a common retail investor was in no position to exploit the investment opportunity in real estate. This did not bode well for the nation, as it lost out on channelizing the huge savings of general public into the infrastructure sector. This money, in search of safe havens or high returns, were eventually landing up in bullion or informal cheat schemes.

The underlying philosophy of the Real Estate Investment Trust (REIT) was to help individual investors benefit from real estate boom, as also provide an alternative to investment in equity and debt. In the case of REIT too, one can hold even a single unit in a real estate property project, like a company share, and it can be traded like equity on the trading platform without one actually having to buy the real estate property. If real estate prices move up, let's say by 20 per cent annually, the capital appreciation in the price of the units is going to be nearabout that. Since real estate prices, in particular in a growing economy, do not go down, the risk of loss of capital is minimal. In fact, there will also be returns, much like dividend from equities and interest on debt securities. The security of investment is underwritten by the real estate underlying the REITs. REIT serves twin purposes: (a) it attracts retail investors, even those with limited surplus, into the real estate market, providing them the underlying features of liquidity and safety of returns. More importantly, as an alternative investment to equities (b) it directs the money to ever needy developers for undertaking a larger number of projects, helping the nation to develop its real estate.

The regulation of the market by SEBI was to provide comfort to the investors as well to the developers as to the safety of transactions and settlement. Eventually, investment in real estate through REITs would have greater multiplier effect than investments in property, which are not traded like REITs.

REITs

Briefly, this is how REITs function as an investment instrument: The legal structure of any REIT would either be a trust or a company, and this varies from country to country. This trust or company would actually own real estate properties and in some cases be financiers for a real estate project. Interested investors are issued units (similar to shares) of this trust or company, the value of a unit being determined by appraisal by the market of the value of the underlying properties and the cash-flow generated by them. By and large, all REITs work on this basic principle, but differed marginally on some parameters, such as tax rules or income distribution intervals.

Real Estate Investment Trusts (REIT) had already been established quite a while ago in countries like the US and Australia. In the US there were nearly 300 REITs with assets in excess of US$ 300 billion. These funds were listed on the US stock exchanges too. In the UK too, real estate investment was done through 'pooled managed vehicles', or REITs. In Asia, this product had arrived in Japan, South Korea and Singapore around a year ago. A couple of Indian real estate companies had already got their projects listed as part of a Singapore-based REIT and had successfully raised funds for their projects through these instruments. This indicated that the Indian real estate developers were open to REITs as a channel to raise capital. I strongly felt it was a pity that this Indian opportunity was being exported and that investors in overseas markets were benefiting from the gains of investing in Indian infrastructure.

Even India was not a complete stranger to this product. While no specific regulations existed regarding REITs, some important

steps had been taken in the past couple of years to make REITs
a reality in India. In December 1999, AMFI had appointed a
committee chaired by Deepak Satwalekar (who was then the MD
of HDFC) to consider the possibility of introducing real estate
investment schemes in India. After a detailed study of REITs in
a number of jurisdictions and a review of the existing structure
in India, the Satwalekar committee submitted a landmark report
to AMFI in October 2000. AMFI then set up a sub-committee
to further investigate how, based on the findings of the report,
REITs might be introduced in India. As it stood then, the sub-
committee had just formulated a detailed working plan, which
was submitted to AMFI in August 2002.

In a nutshell, the following were the key recommendations
of all the reports combined:

- That REITs be introduced in India in the form of a mutual
  fund scheme, that such schemes will be closed for a minimum
  period of three years and redemption/repurchase to the
  investors at the end of three years be given in a staggered
  manner.
- That REITs be eligible for all tax benefits applicable to MFs
  in general, which would enhance their attractiveness for
  investors.
- That such real estate MFs be allowed to invest in: direct
  estate project finance, construction finance, purchase/option
  to purchase of buildings under construction with a view to
  selling them again, debt securities issued by the developer
  and construction companies, and equity of such real estate
  companies.
- There were a few restrictions such as that investments of any
  real estate MFs in any one corporation should be restricted to
  10 per cent of the corpus. There were other restrictions that
  were project-wise, promoter group-wise and geographical
  area-wise.

At SEBI, we studied all the Indian as well as global developments with respect to REITs in minute detail. With everything else in place, ultimately it was the responsibility of SEBI to promulgate the working plan for REITs and convert it into a full-fledged law. As usual, we were more than happy to encourage another path-breaking reform.

From Long-standing to Reality (Almost)

Well aware of the urgency of introducing a product like REIT with its multiple associated benefits, I quickly set the ball rolling to formally launch REITs by kick-starting in November 2002 the unique multi-iterative consultation and feedback process that SEBI followed with the general public before approving any regulation. The aforementioned working plan was displayed on the SEBI website and comments on its merits and demerits were invited. Two rounds of feedback were taken and the implementation of REITs along with the detailed execution plan was finally approved by the SEBI board. SEBI formally notified the REIT regulations. Since a few investor issues, as voiced by investor association representatives, and clarity about pass-through status for tax purposes were still left to be sorted out, the effective date of launch of REITs was left to be announced. We were inches away from making REITs a reality, but destiny, it seems, had other plans.

Everything was going smoothly except that the feedback process took a lot of time. Since this was a new instrument, my team and I took special efforts to personally meet various investor association representatives and real estate developers and made sure their views were considered. REITs were a unique instrument, which had very limited or non-existent history in most parts of the world, so we were cautious about not going very fast in the implementation of REITs.

We also spent a lot of time and energy in tackling the builder lobby. One particular builder was very vociferously against the idea. He felt insecure at the whole concept of REITs and tried every means to negate our efforts. The builders' insecurity emanated from the fact that once REIT was introduced, most of the developers would either have to conform to the dictates of REIT regulations or lose out on attracting investors. REITs would also lead to transparency in pricing, require greater disclosure of real estate developers' activities and increased vigilance and monitoring of their operations, something most developers were certainly not comfortable with. Builders are famous for their political connections and used it generously against us. I personally received quite a few calls from various political quarters pressuring me to drop the process of formalizing REITs.

We accommodated divergent views, and with some gumption even managed to silence the 'well-connected' builder lobby. We finally notified the REIT regulation, as mentioned above. In the bargain, though, precious time was lost (it took almost 2.5 years of incessant efforts!) and by the time of the notification, my tenure had neared its end. Unfortunately, in spite of being a hair's breadth away from introducing REITs into the mainstream, after my departure from the SEBI office, the whole matter was put in cold storage. Almost a decade passed and I heard about no significant development on REITs from where I had left off.

I Had Not Given Up Just Yet

Around mid-2012, a committee was appointed by the department of financial services, ministry of finance, under my chairmanship to recommend restructuring of the investment patterns for the insurance and pension sectors. Through my report, which came out in 2013, I once again strongly recommended creating alternative investment channels in real estate through the establishment of REITs. I also introduced in that report the concept of Infra-REITs. I further emphasized the various advantages of such a product.

Once the report was submitted, I took up the matter of REITs personally with the chairman of SEBI. I requested him to take up the introduction of REITs and informed him that only a few formalities remained in formalizing REITs as the regulations were already notified. Only the effective date of launch remained to be announced. I was taken aback by what he told me next. Before the commencement of his tenure, the regulations had been withdrawn via a notification, rendering our entire efforts null and void. And if REITs were to be established, the entire process had to be followed from scratch again!

The silver lining, however, was that following my 2013 report, the government started pushing for REITs, and SEBI once again went through the entire process, bringing out the draft REIT regulations in 2014. I am told that some tax-related issues were holding up the introduction for more than a year. Finally, in February 2016, I had a chance to discuss this subject with the minister of state for finance, who asked my opinion on the usefulness of the instrument. Even though I convincingly argued for it, it must have been the government's own desire to clear the decks.

While I am happy that REITs seem to be on the road becoming a reality in India, it was for over a decade that this development was still in the making. As the saying goes, 'It is not done, until it is done'—in particular in a vibrant democracy where political and social issues can always overtake economic concerns. Some REITs and Infra-REITs are getting on to the trading platform. One hopes this instrument will get democratized by the time this book sees the light of day. A generation of investors has been deprived of a wholesome, profitable opportunity to get a pie of the historic real estate price growth that India witnessed during the first decade of the millennium. But India's growth story is still to play out fully, and maybe the current generation of investors will profit wholesomely from this new instrument.

AFTERWORD

Wings of Freedom

I had made up my mind during the middle of my three-year tenure that I would not seek an extension at its expiry. This mental resolve was reinforced by the uncharitable statements made about me personally by some of the important politicians.

I used to visit Apollo hospital regularly for my annual health check. In fact, Dr Prathap Reddy, chairman of Apollo Hospital group, who had become a friend after some of the discussions we had when I was chairman, LIC (LIC, Apollo Hospitals Group and ITC were working on a project for full-service old age homes catering to health, housing and hospitality for the elderly) had invited me to get my annual health checks done at Apollo Hospital in Chennai. Somewhere along the way, because of my very involved preoccupations with SEBI and my anxiety to fulfil the chair's obligations, I had not visited Chennai for three years. In any case, a septal ablation procedure to cure the thickening of my heart valve (hypertrophy, as it is called) had been pending.

Since I was not looking forward to the extension and there was a cool comfort in the capital market, in the last fortnight of my tenure I decided to visit Apollo Hospital at Chennai for a health check as well as for the long pending procedure (by which alcohol is introduced in the arteries, which helps in thinning the wall over a period of time). On arrival at the hospital a thorough check-up was done, and the renowned interventionist cardiologist, Dr Subramaniam, suggested that I undergo the procedure immediately. Since he was going to do it himself, I agreed.

Asha, my wife, who had accompanied me for her own health check-up was joined by two of my daughters and sons-in-law in Chennai. After the procedure I was kept in the ICU for 24-hour observation. The next day, I was shifted to the regular private ward. My mobile phone was switched off during the first two days. On the third day, while I was walking (as advised by doctors) along with the hospital attendant assigned to me, my mobile phone started ringing. It was the finance minister, Chidambaram, calling. I took the call. The first question he shot was, 'Where are you, Bajpai? I have been wanting to reach you since yesterday,' I told him I had come to Chennai for a health check. He was courteous and asked me whether the check-up was done and I was fine. I told him, 'Absolutely.' He said, 'Then come to Delhi tomorrow. I have to discuss with you something important.' I told him that since I would be handing over charge as chairman of SEBI in just six days, in all fairness, the matter would have to be discussed with my successor. He said, 'No. I have to discuss with you ideas relating to the capital market to be included in the budget. I want you to come immediately.' If I'm not mistaken, it was a Sunday, and he was telling me to meet him on Monday. Since the doctor had advised me not to travel for next four or five days, I told him, 'Sir, it is very difficult to travel to Delhi so early after my procedure.' After a bit of discussion, we agreed that I would be in Delhi on Wednesday, which was two days before my permitted time to travel.

The time fixed for our meeting was early evening. We started our discussion sharp at 5 p.m. in the office of the finance minister. He ardently discussed quite a few ideas that had been earlier suggested by me, including development of the debt market, waiver of stamp duty on corporatization and demutualization, setting up of NISM and the International Financial Centre at

Mumbai. etc. All those proposals including the last two, were mentioned in the budget speech on 28 February 2005. In fact, the debt market and IFC points were followed up by appointment of the expert committees to speed up the process.

At the end of our conversation, he said, 'Bajpai, we are looking at the appointment of a SEBI chairman.' He added that the search committee chaired by Dr Rangarajan, former governor of RBI and at the time chairman of the economic advisory council of the prime minister, had unanimously recommended that I was the most suitable person and should be given extension of tenure up to sixty-five. I was also told the committee had not recommended any other name. I told him, 'Sir, I am not interested in the extension. I had joined SEBI on an invitation and I am of the firm view that my invitation has expired. I am aware of the political undertones, and even if you make a recommendation, it will not happen.' The FM told me he had appointment with the prime minister at 6.30 p.m. and the chairmanship would be decided at that meeting. I must admit that he indicated he would recommend my name, even though he did also indicate succinctly that there were political issues about my candidature and indirectly hinted that someone else was also under consideration.

While thanking him, I said, 'Kindly tell the prime minister that I am not interested.' In the end, he said he would get back to me with a decision once his meeting with the prime minister was over. This was my last meeting with the finance minister in my official position as SEBI chairman.

I would like to mention here that sometime around the beginning of February that year, a prominent industrialist and an amiable, friendly and helpful person had met me, and during our conversation he had told me that he was going to work for my extension. While thanking him profusely for his gesture, I had told him not try as niether was I interested, and nor would it happen. One day I got a call on my mobile from one of the Rajya Sabha members, whom I knew personally, to say that he was working for my extension, at least for a period of six months. Again I told him very politely to kindly not try; I wanted to retire dignified and happy. I wanted to acquire 'wings of freedom'. For nearly a decade since my elevation to the top ranks at LIC, I had not taken a single break. I had been working twelve to thirteen hours a day. I had to constantly meet people, making statements, deliver speeches. My love of books and golf had taken a serious beating. My socializing with even family members was limited to lunches and dinners.

I have no regrets, though, because it is the nature of the job. The chairman of SEBI is a powerful regulatory position in the financial system of India, and in some quarters it is perceived to be as powerful as that of governor, RBI, because it influences the day-to-day life of the market and the economy. This influence can be gauged from the repercussions of market-wide misconducts—the scams—on the state of the economy and its recovery from the aftermath, the ruin SEBI orders can bring to individuals and business houses or prevent from happening. This influence can also be assessed from the global sentiment about a capital market, more so in a liberalized and globalized economy. It can also be evaluated from the impact the SEBI chairman's opinions and statements have on the market and economy. In the surveys of important people in India, the SEBI chairman usually features among the top ten.

The findings of a survey to discover which Indian structure appeared most on television was interesting. It was not the temple of power like the Rastrapati Bhawan or Parliament House; nor was it the temple of beauty like the Taj Mahal. It was not even the temple of nirvana (emancipation) like Tirupati Devasthanam or the modern temples of learning like the IITs or IIMs. It was the temple of wealth, the Sir Pheroze Jeejeebhoy Towers, which houses the oldest stock exchange in Asia, BSE Ltd. The temple is symbolic. It is a proxy for the securities markets. The survey reflects how intimately the people of India are connected to the securities markets. Rationally speaking, it indicates the significance of the securities markets in their lives and in the Indian economy. Given its role in the life of the people, the securities market is a key institution of the Indian economy.

No wonder, then, that all power centres—political, economic and social—try to influence the appointment of the SEBI chairman. Powerful individuals and groups from each of these arenas sometimes get involved. Every civil servant sees this position along with those of CAG and RBI governor, as the climax of a bureaucrat's career. To be the RBI governor one needs to have at least a doctorate in economics, but the position of SEBI chairman does not require any specific qualification. Hence, aspirations sometimes get pronounced and those who get the post find that the desire to prolong their tenure takes them far. Succession battles reported in the media are an eloquent testimony to what happens in the wake of such struggle.

It is not that I was unaware of the significance of the post I was occupying. In my personal life, the candour and bearing I have cherished practicing grace. All this would apply to my official position too, howsoever significant it may be.

Now I believed my time was up. Hence there was no desire to hold on to the post or desperation to continue. I simply wanted to gracefully vacate the chair. As chairman, I always met people, notwithstanding their standing in their respective professions or vocations, with same grace and receptivity. I might sound immodest writing all this, but this is exactly what propelled me to step back. I had not applied for the post of chairman, SEBI, but had been invited to occupy it.

One's professionalism in the position is what brings one credibility. The craving to continue does compromise the philosophy of professionalism. During my tenure, my stance of professionalism did affect people, organizations and the system. Sometimes it did not meet the expectations of people, especially of opinion makers. It affected even my personal relationships with some of my dear friends. I don't grudge that. They looked at my decision from their perspective based on their information, data, opinions, interests etc. They certainly did not have the same restrictions as the chairman SEBI would have. My oath of secrecy did prevent me from sharing the truth with many people, and that may have turned them against me, as they did not have the full and objective picture. The reality was different from their expectations. The SEBI chairman is only human, and his decisions can go wrong. But so long as these decisions were made in good faith, keeping in mind the oath made in God's name before assumption of the post, one can have no regrets. History will, in any case, condemn or recognize such a person.

After my meeting with the finance minister, I rushed to the airport to catch a flight to be in Mumbai for my last public function, organized by mutual funds, which I had agreed to attend a long time back. Even though I had decided to cancel this engagement after the medical procedure because I was unsure as to whether I would be able to return to Mumbai by that date, since I had to travel to Delhi anyway, I decided not to cancel it and fulfilled my commitment (which I always like to do).

Apparently, while I was on the flight, the finance minister was trying to reach me on my mobile, because around 8.45 p.m., when I had just entered the function *pandal* at the Taj Lands End hotel, I got a call from him. He said, 'Where are you, Bajpai? I have been trying to reach you for the last one hour.' I told him, 'Sir, I was on a flight to Mumbai.' He told me the name of my successor. He also told me to help him settle down at the job, which I promised I would.

In retrospect I am quite satisfied with my tenure as chairman of SEBI. While it is for the historians of the financial market and economy to judge my contribution, the gesture of the government at the conclusion of my tenure was, shall I say, unique.

The only regret that I have is of not having been able to complete a few things that I really wanted to during my tenure. They include the actions initiated on IDRs, IFC, development of the debt market, merger of FMC with SEBI, T+1 and REITs. Except for the merger of FMC, IDR, IFC and now REITs, all these ideas of mine are work-in-progress. It is likely that I was running ahead of the times in pushing those developments, or possibly the political executives then were not ready to back the initiatives at the pace at which I was pushing them, or the policy of gradualism (working in stages) was the order of development in the financial markets.

I, who had broken ranks in my appointment as SEBI chairman, was thinking like a manager and trying to be proactive. It was my belief that markets are dynamic and that no one can successfully hit a moving target from a static gun position; not that I wanted to shoot down anything, all I wanted was to anticipate the possible emergence of risks to the capital market and the financial system and prepare both the market and regulatory apparatus to handle them. Doing this we could avoid disasters in the market. Here I must mention my personal satisfaction at the fact the risk management framework put in place during my tenure as SEBI chairman, which was, of course, periodically strengthened by my successors, has weathered the storms and sustained through the upheavals of the market. There has been no settlement or broker failures ever since; investors have got their money/securities if they have transacted on the trading platform. The confidence of the investors, issuers of securities, intermediaries and the nation at large in the country's capital markets has been resurrected and sustained. The scams which were believed to be happening with decadal periodicity—the Harshad Mehta scam in 1992 and the Ketan Parekh scam in 2001—seem to have kept at bay. Eventually, the expectations of the JPC and other stakeholders from me after the scam to ensure that 'there should be no more scams in the capital market', was actually met, even though we had not committed to do so. SEBI, from being scoffed at for being an inefficient, ineffective and unethical establishment, was now looked upon as a globally respected regulator. The confidence of the SEBI team was restored, and they walked around with confidence, their heads held high.

As my term was to expire on the midnight of 20 February, I would be able to hand over charge only on the morning of Monday, 21 February. I chose to hand over on Friday, 18 February itself, at the close of working hours—of course, with permission of the finance minister and the consent of my successor. Even though I knew I would lose salary for two days, I wanted to reflect on my tenure with grace rather than hang around till the last minute.

I was pleasantly surprised that for the first time, and as far as I know the only time, Government of India has issued a formal press release praising the work of the SEBI chairman. Even though the press release was brief, I still keep it as a certificate of recognition of my work at SEBI by the very same government that did not look very kindly on appointments made by the previous government. Thus closed the chapter of my three years as chairman of SEBI.

I got the 'wings of freedom' that I had always wanted.

Looking Back to Things Done Rightly

While I was about to take the last ride home in the official car, one of the journalists from the assembled media asked, 'Mr Bajpai, what would be your legacy as SEBI Chairman.' I replied, 'I am neither a legend nor has my tenure been legendary,' and added, 'I am a manager by training and made an honest professional attempt to discharge the obligations of the post.'

Liberalization of markets and flowering of free enterprise warrants pragmatic ground rules and effective enforcement. The twin objectives of, 'laying down rules' and 'enforcement' has given birth to regulators and regulatory regimes. The confidence in the efficacy of the regime is central to the creation of an environment for optimal resource utilization, wealth creation and better compliance. The governance of the regime by principles, and not personalities, preferences and prejudices, inspire such confidence. The legacy of a leader resides in the level of confidence in the regime during his stewardship.

I tried as much as possible to pursue the principles of integrity, transparency, accountability, and additionally worked towards, fairness, expediency and risk minimization.

The commencement of my tenure was marked significantly and unjustifiably of berating SEBI as an ineffective, inefficient and subjective organization. Since trust, which stands on the bedrock of integrity, is fundamental to building confidence among the stakeholders, the team was coordinated to ensure that the conduct of the regime reflected both intellectual and financial integrity.

I believe that the greater the transparency, the higher are the chances of the propensity of standards of integrity improving. Transparency also inspires greater acceptability and easier implementation. The use of enforcement powers by the regulatory agencies impact life and liberty. This is one of the important reasons for closer scrutiny and criticism for the use and abuse of powers by the regulators. The principle of transparency has the inherent benefit of alleviating discrimination, building restraint in the exercise of discretion and levelling the approach to crafting policies and imposing penalties.

Every institution, in particular, a public institution, which includes regulatory bodies as also the decision makers must be accountable to the body of stakeholders. An autocratic regime cannot do optimal public good and has the potential to build sentiments of rebellion. The accountability of a public office is reckoned broadly from the following four elements:

1. Giving reasons for decision
2. Exposure to public scrutiny
3. Possibility of independent review and
4. Defining economics of regulatory initiative—cost benefit analysis

The scope of accountability of a regulator includes: (a) ex-ante accountability such as sharing the proposed actions beforehand, (b) ex-post accountability such as reporting actions already taken, (c) explanatory accountability such as disclosure of the rationale of the actions, (d) procedural accountability such as adhering to standards of procedural fairness and transparency, and (e) performance accountability such as achievement in terms of objectives.

The capital market regulator is often challenged to take decisions in a hurry with imperfect information, without back up of research and in the case of India surrounded by the ripples of democracy. Reflection of accountability can become a protective umbrella. Exposing the position papers, draft regulations, enforcement actions with reasoned orders and timelines of response et al. on the website (unique by the standards of those times) for the larger population of stakeholders to comment and react were some of the steps taken to architecting a frame of transparency and accountability. Public comments were welcomed, considered and incorporated.

SEBI encouraged institutions to build capacity for an independent academic review of the regulatory actions, which continues to be deficient even as of today. However, SEBI was deficient in clearly bringing out the cost benefit analysis before making regulatory changes.

I was extremely conscious of regulatory capture. Hence, the experts' committee was broad based, representing all the stakeholders and meetings were democratically conducted. The absence of the chairman (SEBI) and WTM from the committees was intended to ensure free debates, objective recommendations and bridge the democratic deficit, which a regulator often suffers.

Fairness of a regulatory regime is judged from the proportionality of the enforcement action and also the directions. There was always an attempt to take a conscious call on what would be appropriate and proportionate and once that judgement call was taken there was no going back. It would be observed from the various anecdotes in the book that in several instances pressure was brought to alter, modify and/or abandon the judgement call. In such moments the ability of the decision maker to retain composer and exercise judgement without fear or favour comes into play.

The principle of expediency was sought to be pursued with multiple objectives of building credibility, reducing the cost of regulation, enhancing respect in the regime and closing opportunities, if any, for unethical behaviour. The entire functioning was geared to delivering quick responses so that 'regulatory creep', did not seep in.

The initial assessment had revealed that the regulatory framework was inadequate to prevent Scam 2001 and has to be re-engineered comprehensively. The potential threat of unleashing 'regulatory inflation' was looming large. Hence, the principle of 'targeting' was sought to be pursued with a well-crafted approach to 'minimize the risks'. Since the canvas of the regulatory reforms was expansive and the urgency to undertake imminent, a certain amount of 'regulatory inflation' did take place. However, the impact was well contained and counter balanced by the confidence in the regulatory regime. I accept that the intellectual task of defining the underpinnings of the fast paced and varied reforms to opinion makers and in particular, market participants, remained ineffectively addressed. And I share responsibility on that account. A serious attempt was also made to align the regulatory means with the regulatory principles so that the legitimacy of the regime, which was questioned at the beginning of my tenure, shaped up steadily.

Markets, in particular capital markets, are dynamic and continue to undergo an unremitting transformation. The rapidity and profundity of changes are often confounding and regulation of markets remains an evolutionary process. Anticipation, assessment and addressing the current and emerging trends in the conduct and behaviour of the various participants is the call of the leader of a regulatory body. It may be too early to suggest that India's capital market regulation had become fully modern and efficacious, but absence of major market misconduct— scams during those three years or until now—can be considered as a sign of the shaping of a well governed regulatory regime of a capital market. And every time I think of this, it gives me certain confidence in the way I participated in this process.

ACKNOWLEDGEMENTS

The government appointed a serving senior professional (non-IAS) from the financial market to head the voluminously criticized Securities Market Regulatory Body following the infamous Scam 2001. The performance of LIC, especially during the period I was the captain of the behemoth, had inter alia inspired stakeholders to nurture high expectation.

Let me begin by thanking the political executives, who shifted me from LIC to SEBI alongwith the fraternity of stakeholders who nurtured the expectation to deliver a re-engineered regulatory regime. I am deeply grateful to the owners/authors of the material/references, in particular *The Hindu Business Line*, cited in the book.

While expressing gratefulness to all of them who made the publication of this book possible, I would like to mention a few names for their sterling contribution.

The idea of chronicling the transformation initiatives into a book was actually fired in me by my erstwhile colleagues in the chairman office, in particular Mr P.R. Ramesh, who persuaded and assisted me in collecting material and validating the narrations. Thank you, Ramesh.

I would like to profusely thank Mr M.S. Sahoo, chairman of Insolvency and Bankruptcy Board of India (IBBI), an able, trusted and valuable colleague during those years and a friend who played a significant role in some of the important initiatives. He read the entire manuscript from first to the last page, offered extremely useful comments and suggested additions/ modifications and deletions. I am also grateful to Pratip Kar, former executive director, P.K. Nagpal, executive director, Dr Sarat Malik, chief general manager, Mr Seshachalam and Ankit Sharma, colleagues in SEBI who took the pains to go through the manuscript and suggest improvements.

I am grateful to my dear friends Shailesh Haribhakti and Jangoo Dalal for their valuable comments and encouragement. I would also like to thank Alpesh Patel, Ankita Trivedi and Connie Franco for helping me with research, proofreading and finding references for the narrations. Without their help, this book would not have been shaped.

My family, in particular my wife, Asha, daughters Deepti Chaturvedi, Deepali Sharma and Devina Pandey and their respective husbands Ved Prakash Chaturvedi, Mukul Sharma and Ritesh Pandey, who stood by me during those years of trials and tribulations and encouraged me to write deserve a mention here. In fact, Deepti and Ritesh read the manuscript fully and offered valuable comments.

I am grateful to Vaishali Mathur, editor-in-chief, language publishing, Penguin and the editor of my book, and her team for very incisive and diligent work in the editing and other assistance in its publication. I would like to thank Dipti Patel of Word Famous Literary Agent for helping me to reach out and sign up with Penguin for the publication of the book. Lastly, I thank the publishers, Penguin Random House India, for bringing out the book that is before you now.

ABBREVIATIONS

JPC	Joint Parliamentary Committee
SEBI	Securities and Exchange Board of India
IPO	Initial Public Offerings
IFC	International Financial Centre
MD	Managing Director
CEO	Chief Executive Officer
Ken India	Ken India Assurance Company Ltd
EA	Executive Assistant
SEA	Secretary, Economic Affairs
GoI	Government of India
LIC	Life Insurance Corporation of India
GIC	General Insurance Corporation of India
CVC	Central Vigilance Commission
NIA	National Insurance Academy
ACC	Appointments Committee of the Cabinet
CBI	Central Bureau of Investigation
ED	Enforcement Directorate
IB	Investment Banker
RBI	Reserve Bank of India
ICICI	Industrial Credit and Investment Corporation of India
IDBI	Industrial Development Bank of India

IAS	Indian Administrative Service
GDP	Gross Domestic Product
UTI	Unit Trust of India
NHB	National Housing Bank
NSE	National Stock Exchange
HDFC	Housing Development Financial Corporation
IIM	Indian Institute of Management
WTM	Whole Time Members
MIS	Management Information System
DC	Division Chief
SAP	Strategic Action Plan
USAID	United States Agency for International Development
FICCI	Federation of Indian Chambers of Commerce and Industry
BSE	Bombay Stock Exchange
HR	Human Resource
MBA	Master of Business Administration
CFA	Chartered Financial Analyst
MFC	Masters of Finance and Control
CGM	Chief General Manager
GM	General Manager
DGM	Deputy General Manager
HRA	House Rent Allowance
SAT	Securities Appellate Tribunal
IMF	International Monetary Fund
MIT	Massachusetts Institute of Technology
LSE	London School of Economics
SME	Small and Medium Enterprises
DCA	Department of Company Affairs
JS	Joint Secretary

DDT	Dividend Distribution Tax
IOSCO	International Organization of Securities Commission
OECD	Organization for Economic Co-operation and Development
USA	United States of America
US SEC	US Securities and Exchange Commission
MMoU	Multilateral Memorandum of Understanding
FSA	Financial Services Authority
BAFIN	Federal Financial Supervisory Authority (German: Bundesanstalt für Finanzdienstleistungsaufsicht)
CM	Chief Minister
IRDA	Insurance Regulatory and Development Authority of India
BKC	Bandra-Kurla Complex
MDA	Mumbai Metropolitan Region Development Authority
BCA	Building Advisory Committee
RFP	Request for Proposal
L&T	Larsen & Toubro
BAC	Building Advisory Committee
CVC	Central Vigilance Commission
UAM	Urban Affairs Secretary
CPWD	Central Public Works Department
DG	Director General
PSU	Public Sector Undertaking
BoI	Bank of India
HC	High Court
SC	Supreme Court
CIS	Collective Investment Scheme
FII	Foreign Institutional Investor
RTGS	Real Time Gross Settlement

SWIFT	Society for Worldwide Interbank Financial Telecommunication
CC	Clearing Corporation
DP	Depository Participant
NSDL	National Securities Depository Limited
CDSL	Central Depository Services India Limited
EFT	Electronic Funds Transfer
FM	Finance Minister
STP	Straight Through Processing
HO	Head Office
CTCL	Computer-to-computer link software
CCI	Controller of Capital Issues
DD	Demand Draft
KYC	Know Your Customer
QIB	Qualified Institutional Buyer
RHP	Red Hearing Prospectus
SGF	Settlement Guarantee Fund
ONGC	Oil and Natural Gas Corporation Limited
WB	World Bank
ADB	Asian Development Bank
UPA	United Progressive Alliance
OSD	Officer on Special Duty
STT	Securities Transaction Tax
UK	United Kingdom
BJP	Bharatiya Janata Party
F&O	Futures and Options
PFRDA	Pension Fund Regulatory and Development Authority
TRAI	Telecom Regulatory Authority of India
NPA	Non-Performing Asset
EOW	Economic Offences Wing
SIAI	Securities Industry Association of India

MoF	Ministry of Finance
CAG	Comptroller and Auditor General of India
CWG	Commonwealth Games
IBBI	Insolvency and Bankruptcy Board of India
NISM	National Institute of Securities Markets
CPI (M)	Communist Party of India (Marxist)
NDA	National Democratic Alliance
FS	Finance Secretary
CEA	Chief Economic Advisor
ES	Expenditure Secretary
PM	Prime Minister
MP	Members of Parliament
CCD	Cabinet Committee on Disinvestment
GAIL	Gas Authority of India Limited
IOC	Indian Oil Corporation Limited
FPO	Follow-up Public Offering
ADR	American Depositary Receipt
PN	Participatory Notes
HNI	High Net-worth Individual
MAPIN	Market Participant Identification Number
REIT	Real Estate Investment Trust
SRO	Self Regulatory Organization
FMC	Forward Markets Commission
IDR	Indian Depository Receipt
JV	Joint Venture
PCI	Press Council of India
NDTV	New Delhi Television Limited
SME	Small or Medium Enterprise
RTI	Right to Information
HQ	Head quarters
CICA	Capital (Issues) Control Act

OFS	Offer for Sale
DIP	Disclosure and Investor Protection
DIN	Director Identification Number
FV	Face Value
ICAI	Institute of Chartered Accountants of India
FI	Financial Institution
SCB	Standard Chartered Bank
PAN	Permanent Account Number
CFO	Chief Financial Officer
EDIFAR	Electronic Data Information Filing and Retrieval
EDGAR	Electronic Data Gathering, Analysis and Retrieval
CMD	Chairman Managing Director
TCS	Tata Consultancy Services
ROC	Registrar of Companies
EIU	Economist Intelligence Unit
GC	General Counsel
AAR	Authority for Advance Rulings
AGI	Attorney General of India
SGI	Solicitor General of India
RSE	Regional Stock Exchange
FATCA	Foreign Account Tax Compliance Act
FSC	Financial Services Commission
MOBAA	Mauritius Offshore Business Activities Authority
PE	Price Earnings
IT	Information Technology
IMSS	Integrated Market Surveillance System
FIRE	Financial Institutions Reform and Expansion
NASD	National Association of Securities Dealers
IIT	Indian Institute of Technology
HCL	Hindustan Computers Limited

MF	Mutual Fund
NAV	Net Asset Value
AUM	Asset Under Management
AMFI	Association of Mutual Fund Industry
AMC	Asset Management Company
FoF	Fund of Funds
SIP	Systematic Investment Plan
MCA	Ministry of Corporate Affairs
USP	Unique Selling Proposition
SS	Social Security
VC	Venture Capitalist
RTA	Registrars to an Issue and Share Transfer Agents
UIN	Unique Identification Number
TIN	Taxpayer Identification Number
POS	Points of Service
IDFC	Infrastructure Development Finance Company
NTPC	National Thermal Power Corporation
UIDAI	Unique Identification Authority of India
NREGA	National Rural Employment Guarantee Act
RTI	Right to Information
ASE	Ahmedabad Stock Exchange
OTCEI	Over-the-Counter Exchange of India
ICSE	Inter-Connected Stock Exchange
SCRA	Securities Contract (Regulation) Act
CSE	Calcutta Stock Exchange
DVP	Delivery vs Payment
CCP	Central Counter Party
FISE	Federation of Indian Stock Exchanges
AOP	Association of Persons
SE	Stock Exchange

NYSE	New York Stock Exchange
R&D	Research and Development
SUUTI	Specified Undertaking of Unit Trust of India
NCFM	NSE Academy Certification in Financial Markets
AMBI	Association of Merchant Bankers of India
NGO	Non-Governmental Organization
ICSI	Institute of Company Secretaries of India
RAIN	Registrars Association of India
FAQ	Frequently asked questions
IMFI	Indian Mutual Fund Industry
FD	Fixed deposit
NDS	Negotiated Dealing System
WDM	Wholesale Debt Market
SSS	Securities Settlement System
CLA	Central Listing Authority
MNC	Multinational Corporation
NSEL	National Spot Exchange Limited
CDS	Credit Default Swaps
UP	Uttar Pradesh
FCRA	Forward Contracts (Regulation) Act
MCAFPD	Ministry of Consumer Affairs, Food and Public Distribution
CAGR	Compound Annual Growth Rate
MoAC&P	Minister of Agriculture, Consumer Affairs and Public Distribution
NCDEX	National Commodity and Derivatives Exchange Limited
MCX	Multi Commodity Exchange
FT	Financial Technologies
OTC	Over the Counter
FSLRC	Financial Sector Legislative Reforms Commission

MCFS	Modified Carry Forward Scheme
ALBM	Automated Lending and Borrowing Mechanism
BLESS	Borrowing and Lending Securities Scheme
CMC	Coordination and Monitoring Committee
GDR	Global Depository Receipts
DR	Depository Receipt
NRI	Non-Resident Indian
BhDR	Bharat Depository Receipts
FATF	Financial Action Task Force
CII	Confederation of Indian Industry
HLC	High Level Committee
FSDC	Financial Stability and Development Council
GIFT	Gujarat International Finance Tec-City
MOS	Minister of State for Finance
RSS	Rashtriya Seva Sangh
ITC	India Tobacco Company
ICU	Intensive Care Unit
CBDT	Central Board of Direct Taxes
DII	Domestic Institutional Investors

NOTES

Chapter 2: What Will You Do, Gyan?

1. Sucheta Dalal, 'Dear Mr Bajpai', *Indian Express*, 24 February 2002.

Chapter 3: Looking into the Mirror: SEBI's Public Image and Getting the Best Out of People

1. Anupama Katakam, 'After the Horses Bolted', *Frontline*, Volume 18, Issue 09, 28 April–11 May 2001.
2. 'SEBI Now Needs a Change of Leadership', Sucheta Dalal's blog, 18 November 2001 http://www.suchetadalal.com/?id=f3e5fb38-e11c-f5a6-492e83904015&base=sub_sections_content&f&t=SEBI+now+needs+a+change+of+leadership+%2818+November+2001%29 (accessed 5 July 2018)
3. 'Systemic Failure behind Stock Market Turmoil', *The Hindu*, 22 March 2001 https://www.thehindu.com/2001/03/22/stories/0622000d.htm (accessed 5 July 2018)
4. 'Systemic Failure behind Stock Market Turmoil', *The Hindu*, 22 March 2001 https://www.thehindu.com/2001/03/22/stories/0622000d.htm (accessed 5 July 2018)
5. 'Sebi Plans 700 Broker Inspections This Fiscal', *Financial Express*, 19 May 2003 https://www.financialexpress.com/archive/sebi-plans-700-broker-inspections-this-fiscal/83704/ (accessed 8 July 2018)
6. 'Joint Committee on Stock Market Scam and Matters Relating Thereto', Thirteenth Lok Sabha, Volume 1, December 2002 file:///C:/Users/umathva/Desktop/InvestigativeJPC_635612541266248975.pdf (accessed 7 August 2018)

Chapter 5: Re-engineering the Market Microstructure: Approach to Agenda for Action

1. Sucheta Dalal, 'Sebi Needs to Refocus for Improvement', 6 May 2002 http://www.suchetadalal.com/?id=adb6eb0f-68c8-7332-492e8c2886f3&base=sub_sections_content&f&t=Sebi+Needs+To+Refocus+For+Improvement+%286+May+2002%29 (accessed 8 July 2018)

2. 'SEBI Mulls Setting Up Central Listing Authority', *The Hindu Business Line*, 27 April 2002 https://www.thehindubusinessline.com/2002/04/27/stories/2002042701480300.htm (accessed 7 August 2018)

3. https://www.legalcrystal.com/case/69482/joint-secreatary-political-department-govt-meghalaya-main-secretariat-shill-vs-registrar-shillong (accessed 7 August 2018)

Chapter 6: Crunching the Settlement Cycles

1. 'SEBI Scores Yet Another Point with T+2', *The Hindu Business Line*, 7 April 2003 https://www.thehindubusinessline.com/2003/04/07/stories/2003040701700400.htm (accessed on 8 July 2018)

2. 'Googles Googly', *Financial Express*, 24 August 2004 <https://www.financialexpress.com/archive/googles-googly/111770/> (accessed on 12 July 18)

Chapter 7: The STT Saga

1. Sucheta Dalal, 'STT Beats All Odds', *Indian Express*, 4 October 2004 <http://www.suchetadalal.com/?id=e8c80416-6ac3-62c9-492e834be9ff&base=sub_sections_content&f&t=STT+beats+all+odds> (accessed on 12 July 2018)

2. 'Transaction Tax Worry Torpedoes Market', *Financial Express*, 12 July 2004 <https://www.financialexpress.com/archive/transaction-tax-worry-torpedoes-market/106322/> (accessed on 12 July 2018)

3. 'No Impact of STT', *Financial Express*, 1 October 2004 <https://www.financialexpress.com/archive/no-impact-of-stt/90519/> (accessed on 12 July 2018)

4. 'Securities Transaction Tax: Its Proving a Lot Better Than Many Had Expected', *Financial Express*, 5 November 2004 <https://www.financialexpress.com/archive/securities-transaction-tax-its-proving-a-lot-better-than-many-had-expected/118533/> (accessed on 12 July 2018)

Chapter 9: Bloody Monday!

1. 'FM Allays Mkt Fears', *Financial Express*, 30 May 2004 <https://www.financialexpress.com/archive/fm-allays-mkt-fears/62103/> (accessed on 17 July 2018)

Chapter 12: Raising the Bar of Transparency: What Happens in SEBI Should (Not) Stay

1. Rafael La Porta, Florencio Lopez de Silanes and Andrei Shleifer, 'What Works in Securities Laws?' Available via the Internet: www.nber.org/papers/w9882

Chapter 13: The Other 'Dabbawalahs': The Stock Market Black Economy

1. Nilanjan Dey, '"Dabba" trading making splashes', *The Hindu Business Line*, 4 August 2003 https://www.thehindubusinessline.com/2003/08/05/stories/2003080502471300.htm> (accessed on 12 July 2018)

Chapter 18: Eliminating Conflict of Interests: Demutualization and Corporatization of Exchanges (Making Exchanges Independent and Professional)

1. 'Anand Rathi Vs. Securities & Exchange Board of India', Order of Securities Appellate Tribunal, available at: https://www.sebi.gov.in/satorders/anandrathi.html (accessed on 12 July 2018)
2. 'Anand Rathi Vs. Securities & Exchange Board of India', Order of Securities Appellate Tribunal, available at: https://www.sebi.gov.in/satorders/anandrathi.html (accessed on 12 July 2018)

Chapter 21: Segregating Wealth Creators: BSE-IndoNext

1. Prithvi Haldea, 'Time to Let Them Go', *Indian Express*, 22 August 2005 <http://www.primedatabase.com/article/article8.html> (accessed on 12 July 2018)
2. 'Listlessly Waiting for Indonext', *Financial Express*, 14 November 2004 <https://www.financialexpress.com/archive/listlessly-waiting-for-indonext/119086/> (accessed on 11 Jul 2018)
3. Sanjiv Shankaran and Raja Simhan T.E., 'SEBI Sends Positive Signal for Indonext—Common Trading Platform for Regional Exchanges', *The Hindu Business Line*, 30 April 2003, available at: https://www.thehindubusinessline.com/2003/05/01/stories/2003050102471500.htm (accessed on 12 July 2018)
4. 'BSE's IndoNext is a Platform for SMEs', *Economic Times*, 8 January 2005.

Chapter 22: Weaving Dreams: Consolidation of the Derivatives Market

1. Available via the Internet: https://www.moneylife.in/article/nsel-poor-regulation-was-not-by-chance/34294.html
2. 'Forward Markets Commission Has to Be Upgraded', *Financial Times*, 16 February 2004.

Chapter 23: Enhancing Regulatory Capacity: Central Listing Authority

1. M.S. Sahoo, 'A Case for Central Listing Authority', available at: <https://www.nse-india.com/content/press/jun2002a.pdf> (accessed on 12 July 2018)